A CULTURAL HISTORY OF HAIR

VOLUME 5

A Cultural History of Hair
General Editor: Geraldine Biddle-Perry

Volume 1
A Cultural History of Hair in Antiquity
Edited by Mary Harlow

Volume 2
A Cultural History of Hair in the Middle Ages
Edited by Roberta Milliken

Volume 3
A Cultural History of Hair in the Renaissance
Edited by Edith Snook

Volume 4
A Cultural History of Hair in the Age of Enlightenment
Edited by Margaret K. Powell and Joseph Roach

Volume 5
A Cultural History of Hair in the Age of Empire
Edited by Sarah Heaton

Volume 6
A Cultural History of Hair in the Modern Age
Edited by Geraldine Biddle-Perry

A CULTURAL HISTORY OF HAIR

IN THE AGE OF EMPIRE

VOLUME 5

Edited by Sarah Heaton

BLOOMSBURY ACADEMIC
LONDON • NEW YORK • OXFORD • NEW DELHI • SYDNEY

BLOOMSBURY ACADEMIC
Bloomsbury Publishing Plc
50 Bedford Square, London, WC1B 3DP, UK
1385 Broadway, New York, NY 10018, USA
29 Earlsfort Terrace, Dublin 2, Ireland

BLOOMSBURY, BLOOMSBURY ACADEMIC and the Diana logo are trademarks of Bloomsbury Publishing Plc

First published in Great Britain 2021
Paperback edition published 2022

Copyright © Bloomsbury Publishing, 2022

Sarah Heaton has asserted her right under the Copyright,
Designs and Patents Act, 1988, to be identified as Editor of this work.

Series design: Raven Design
Cover image: Bare female figure among lilies, Palermo, Sicily, Italy © Mondadori Portfolio / Getty Images

All rights reserved. No part of this publication may be reproduced or transmitted in any form or by any means, electronic or mechanical, including photocopying, recording, or any information storage or retrieval system, without prior permission in writing from the publishers.

Bloomsbury Publishing Plc does not have any control over, or responsibility for, any third-party websites referred to or in this book. All internet addresses given in this book were correct at the time of going to press. The author and publisher regret any inconvenience caused if addresses have changed or sites have ceased to exist, but can accept no responsibility for any such changes.

A catalogue record for this book is available from the British Library.

A catalog record for this book is available from the Library of Congress.

ISBN:	HB:	978-1-4742-3209-8
	HB set:	978-1-4742-3212-8
	PB:	978-1-3502-8588-0
	PB set:	978-1-3502-8751-8
	ePDF:	978-1-3500-8792-7
	eBook:	978-1-3500-8793-4

Typeset by Integra Software Services Pvt. Ltd.
Printed and bound in Great Britain

To find out more about our authors and books visit www.bloomsbury.com
and sign up for our newsletters.

CONTENTS

LIST OF FIGURES	vi
GENERAL EDITOR'S PREFACE	x
Introduction: Empires of Hair and their Afterlives *Sarah Heaton*	1
1 Religion and Ritualized Belief: Myth, Folklore, and Spiritualism in Victorian and Neo-Victorian Representations of Hair *Richard Leahy*	19
2 Self and Society: Hair Consciousness in the Age of Empire *Jonathon Shears*	35
3 Fashion and Adornment: African American Women in the United States, 1800 to 1920 *Patricia Hunt-Hurst*	53
4 Production and Practice: Hair Harvest, Hairpieces, and Hairwork *Sallie McNamara*	65
5 Health and Hygiene: "Monster top-knots and balloon chignons" *Janice M. Allan*	83
6 Gender and Sexuality: Tresses Adorned and Adored, Locks Coiled and Cut *Sarah Heaton*	101
7 Race and Ethnicity: Strands of the Diaspora *Elizabeth Way*	117
8 Class and Social Status: "The more you have the better" *Elizabeth Carolyn Miller*	139
9 Cultural Representations: Hair as the Abundant Signifier *Sally West*	157
NOTES	169
BIBLIOGRAPHY	197
CONTRIBUTORS	211
INDEX	213

LIST OF FIGURES

INTRODUCTION

I.1	The Seven Sutherland Sisters.	3
I.2	Elizabeth Barrett Browning's hair in the J.H. Leigh Hunt Collection. Courtesy Harry Ransom Center at the University of Texas at Austin.	5
I.3	John Absolon, "General view of the interior," from *Recollections of the Great Exhibition* (1851). Courtesy Metropolitan Museum of Art, New York.	7
I.4	Simon Grennan, *Hair in the Age of Empire*, May 2017.	12
I.5	Advertisement for Parker's Hair Balsam.	14
I.6	Advertisement for Harlene Hair Products. Courtesy Wellcome images.	16
I.7	Mourning brooches containing the hair of a deceased relative.	17

CHAPTER ONE

1.1	Dante Gabriel Rossetti (1828–1882), *Mnemosyne*, 1881. Oil on canvas, 126.4 cm × 61 cm. Delaware Art Museum, Samuel and Mary R. Bancroft Memorial, 1935.	31

CHAPTER TWO

2.1	Dr. Scott's Electric Hair Brush.	38
2.2	Edward's Harlene for the Hair.	41
2.3	"The Beard Movement," *Punch*, March 8, 1856.	46

CHAPTER FOUR

4.1	Hairwork by Linherr & Co., *Gleason's Pictorial Drawing Room Companion*, 1853. Courtesy Trustees of the Boston Public Library.	71
4.2	Advertisement for Edwards' Harlene, 1898. *The Shetland Times*, June 25, 1898.	72

LIST OF FIGURES vii

4.3 Advertisement for the "Kaiser Mustache Trainer," 1904. 74

4.4 One step in palette-working hair. Alexanna Speight, *The Lock of Hair: Its History, Ancient and Modern, Natural and Artistic; With the Art of Working in Hair* (London: A. Goubard, 1871). 77

CHAPTER FIVE

5.1 "The present fashions in hair, 1870." From a Private Collection. 84

5.2 "Human hair sewn onto a braid foundation" (1850s–1880s). © Victoria and Albert Museum, London. 86

5.3 Advertisement for "Postiches, nattes et crêpes." *La mode illustrée: Journal de la famille* 22 (May 31, 1863): 174. 88

5.4 "English plate." *Hairdresser's Journal* 1, no. 4 (June 1863): n.p. 89

5.5 "Fair at Collinée." From chapter 18 of Thomas Adolphus Trollope's *A Summer in Brittany*. Edited by Frances Trollope, 2 vols. (London: Henry Colburn, Publishers, 1840), vol. 1. 91

5.6 "Next Hideous 'Sensation Chignon.'" *Punch* 53 (November 30, 1867): 219. Artist: Edward Linley Sambourne. 95

CHAPTER SIX

6.1 Dante Gabriel Rossetti, *Lady Lilith*, 1866–1868 (altered 1872–1873). Oil on canvas, 97.5 cm × 84.1 cm. Delaware Art Museum, Wilmington, USA/Samuel and Mary R. Bancroft Memorial, 1935. 111

6.2 Dante Gabriel Rossetti, *Lady Lilith*, 1873. Oil on canvas. Rossetti, Dante Gabriel Charles (1828–82) / Universal Images Group North America LLC / Alamy Stock Photo. 111

6.3 William Holman Hunt, *The Lady of Shalott*, 1857. Wood-engraved illustrations from the Moxon edition. Engraver J. Thompson. 113

6.4 William Holman Hunt, *The Lady of Shalott*, 1886–1905. 113

CHAPTER SEVEN

7.1 The Smithsonian Museum of African Art describes the hairstyle of this Yoruba figure as "cone-shaped [...] with cylindrical projections [indicating] stylistic traits from the Oyo and Owo regions." Female figure, Yoruba peoples, Nigeria, mid-nineteenth century. Ivory, black stone, 30.2 cm × 5.3 cm × 8.6 cm. Acquisition grant from the James Smithson Society and museum purchase, 85-9-1. Photo: Franko Khoury, National Museum of African Art, Smithsonian Institution. 119

7.2	This photograph is captioned "The Givers," and it illustrates the social bonds created through hair care on slave plantations. Photograph album: "Rose-mary. A Plantation Home" (ca. 1890–1910), Edward Ward Carmack Papers, 1850–1942. From the Southern Historical Collection, Louis Round Wilson Special Collections Library, University of North Carolina at Chapel Hill. (Original image has been cropped.)	122
7.3	Aquatint cartoon, drawn and etched by E.W. Clay. Philadelphia. Published by S. Hart & Son, 1829. The Library Company of Philadelphia.	125
7.4	Jean-Baptiste Debret, "Esclaves nègres, de différentes nations." Print. One of 153 hand-colored lithographs on 140 sheets for Jean-Baptiste Debret, *Voyage pittoresque et historique au Brésil, ou Séjour d'un artiste français au Brésil, depuis 1816 jusqu'en 1831 inclusivement*, 3 vols. (Paris: Firmin Didot frères, 1834–1839), ii: pl. 22. Hickey and Robertson, Houston/Menil Foundation.	126
7.5	Frederick Douglass, ca. 1865. Photo: J.W. Hurn. Library of Congress, Prints and Photographs Division (LC-USZ62-24165).	129
7.6	Studio portrait of an unidentified African American woman, no date. (The vintage photograph is a carte de visite with the imprint of J.H. Smith, 769 Broad Street, Newark, NJ. A later copy print made by R.H. Beckwith, photographer, Helena, MT, is on a cabinet mount.) Montana Historical Society Research Center Photograph Archives, Helena, Montana.	130
7.7	This man's hairstyle and facial hair are typical of fashionable men's styles at the turn of the twentieth century. Young African American man, 1900. Part of W.E.B. Du Bois's albums of photographs of African Americans in Georgia exhibited at the Paris Exposition Universalle 1900. Library of Congress (LC-USZ62-121113).	132
7.8	This class photograph of college-aged women shows a variety of women's hairstyles worn at the beginning of the twentieth century, some more elaborate and fashionable than others. Junior normal class of Fisk University, Nashville, Tennessee. Images collected by W.E.B. Du Bois and Thomas J. Calloway for the "American Negro Exhibit" at the Paris Exposition of 1900. Library of Congress (LC-USZ62-112357).	133
7.9	Nannie Helen Burroughs, 1909. Photo: Rotograph Co., New York City. Library of Congress, Prints and Photographs Division (LC-USZ62-79903).	134

CHAPTER EIGHT

8.1	Boys at Crumpsall Workhouse, ca. 1895–1897. Source: https://commons.wikimedia.org/wiki/File:Children_at_crumpsall_workhouse_circa_1895.jpg.	141
8.2	*Punch* cartoon with chignon, 1870.	143

8.3	Advertisement for Unwin and Albert, from the opening pages of *The Great Eastern Steam Ship* (London: H.G. Clarke, n.d. [ca. 1857]).	145
8.4	Advertisement for Kosmeo Hair Tonic. *New Age* (January 25, 1908): 258.	148
8.5	Excerpt from Madame Rachel's price list for hair products. *The Extraordinary Life & Trial of Madame Rachel at the Central Criminal Court* (vii).	149
8.6	Cartoon featuring servants from the May 23, 1874 issue of *Punch* magazine.	151
8.7	Advertisement for Pearline soap. *Christian Work and Evangelist* (April 11, 1903): 549.	151

GENERAL EDITOR'S PREFACE

A Cultural History of Hair offers an unparalleled examination of the most malleable part of the human body. This fascinating set explores hair's intrinsic relationship to the construction and organization of diverse social bodies and strategies of identification throughout history. The six illustrated volumes, edited by leading specialists in the field, evidence the significance of human hair on the head and face and its styling, dressing, and management across the following historical periods: Antiquity, the Middle Ages, the Renaissance, the Age of Enlightenment, the Age of Empire, and the Modern Age.

Using an innovative range of historical and theoretical sources, each volume is organized around the same key themes: religion and ritualized belief, self and societal identification, fashion and adornment, production and practice, health and hygiene, gender and sexuality, race and ethnicity, class and social status, representation. The aim is to offer readers a comprehensive account of human hair-related beliefs and practices in any given period and through time. It is not an encyclopedia. *A Cultural History of Hair* is an interdisciplinary collection of complex ideas and debates brought together in the work of an international range of scholars.

Geraldine Biddle-Perry

Introduction: Empires of Hair and their Afterlives

SARAH HEATON

Once one starts thinking about hair in the Age of Empire it appears everywhere. At a friend's house during dinner, when asked what I was currently working on, I mentioned this book. My host went to the family safe and brought an old wooden box to the table which opened to reveal a long thick brown plait of Victorian hair. Perhaps I should have expected this, after all this is a house where tales of Tennyson and Barbara Villiers, mistress of King Charles II, vibrate through the walls.[1] But all these stories which echo through family history become somehow more compelling when the body long gone is somehow manifest. It is the strangest of experiences to sit at dinner among friends and to hold a heavy plait of Victorian hair. Even more remarkable are the stories which unfold around the plait. It is thought to belong to Ellen, an extraordinary woman who followed her brother Sir Roger Palmer, survivor of the Charge of the Light Brigade, out to the Crimea to find herself a husband.[2] This was a girl who had taken over the Palmer Estates at seventeen when her mother died and her father's mental health was in decline. Bored and lonely she wrote diaries and determined to marry for love. Yet she was beautiful and intelligent, and for a family who had fallen out of society's favor she was seen as "capital" and paraded first by her mother, and then her aunts, around debutante balls and society events. Hating it all she took her father out to the Crimea via land. She was not a woman who would sail to Constantinople and keep a safe distance from the action; this was a woman of the empire; she watched battles and met her husband Archibald Peel on Lord Raglan's yacht. While it is thought she died in childbirth aged thirty-four in 1860 her hair has been carefully preserved and has lain quietly in the dark recess of the house. As an object it is unclear what is to be done with it but it certainly cannot be thrown out. Holding the hair of a Victorian woman who ran an estate, wrote, traveled, and married for love is extraordinarily compelling not simply because it takes you to another time and place but because it resonates so powerfully through all the lives which it has touched. Here is not simply the cold dark patina on an object once held, nor the sweat stains on a dress once worn but part of the woman herself: the hair which she touched as she wrote her diaries, which she styled in the Crimea, which was caressed by her husband and held by her children. This piece of hair, along with all those in this volume, continue to have afterlives which resonate through all those who encounter its strands. Perhaps understanding this the Victorians embraced hair in all its forms from long luxurious locks to intricate pieces of jewelry made from human hair and the hair of the dead. This fascination was by no means the preserve of the Victorians but part of a tangle of tresses that reached across the empire and beyond.

This volume concerns the Age of Empire, 1800 to 1920, but cannot help but look further back to the past and forward to the future. In Britain the height of the Age of Empire was the golden age between 1850 and 1870 and the centerpiece was the Great Exhibition of 1851 which showed off an empire. The exotic artifacts, including hair, displayed the global reach of Victoria's empire and the Crystal Palace represented all that could be achieved in the modern world as a statement of confidence and power. Underneath the glitter of the glass and all that was on display was a period of state formation, expansionist policies, war, and conquest in Europe, Asia, Africa, and the Americas. Hair, like many of the objects on display, comes to symbolize the reach of the empire and beyond: the surface of coiffured perfection and the conflict and exchange behind it. The historian Eric Hobsbawm identifies the Age of Empire as 1875 to 1914 and suggests that it is "penetrated and dominated by these contradictions" of peace and ultimately world war.[3] Geographically Hobsbawm notes that in the "new type of empire, the colonial [...] most of the world outside Europe and the Americas was formally partitioned into territories under the formal rule or informal political domination of one or another of a handful of states: mainly Great Britain, France, Germany, Italy, the Netherlands, Belgium, the USA, and Japan."[4] The concept of the West then is less a geographical demarcation than a historical one suggesting capitalist dominance in the new global economy. Although different cultures have their own hair practices there is, during the period, a colonizing impulse which extends to the economies of hair and its fashioning. Whether the empire is seen as a geographical, historical, or cultural construct, arguably it is the Victorian's obsession with hair which fueled the global reach of hair in the Age of Empire and it is the Victorian obsession which the volume returns to again and again.

AFTERLIVES AND THE APOCRYPHAL

In contemporary culture we may not wear our deceased's hair as jewelry but the habit of cutting a baby's lock is common. We are also fascinated by the pieces of Victorian hair jewelry and macabre hair art which turn up on the UK television program *Antiques Roadshow*, and will happily peer at these objects from behind the safety of the glass cabinet in museums such as the Victoria and Albert in London. Fragments of Charles Darwin's beard, apparently collected from his desk, are displayed in the Natural History Museum and a recent exhibition titled "Curious Objects" at Cambridge University included beard and scalp hair sent to Darwin in an attempt to refute his theories in *The Descent of Man*. There is also, perhaps predictably, Victorian hair for sale on eBay. Meanwhile, famous hair often makes the news; recently yet another locket purportedly containing a lock of Napoleon's hair made the headlines. This one was discovered in a terraced house in Surrey, England, and went to auction in July 2015 fetching £7,500.[5] It is not just Napoleon's hair which lives on and fetches a good price. In 1994 a couple, Dr. Alfredo "Che" Guevara, a urological surgeon, and his partner Ira Brilliant, bought a lock of Beethoven's hair apparently cut in 1827. The journey of this lock of hair is meticulously followed in Russell Martin's book *Beethoven's Hair: An Extraordinary Historical Odyssey and a Scientific Mystery Solved*.[6] The book brings to life the journey of a piece of hair across nearly 200 years until it was finally DNA tested by Guevara in 1994.

This sense of living on is apparently literalized even more compellingly in Lizzie Siddal's hair. Married to Dante Gabriel Rossetti she was a model, artist, and poet, painted time and again by the Pre-Raphaelites. Of course her hair lives on in Rossetti's paintings and poetry but it also lives on in the rumors; and of course the rumors suggest that her hair lived on, literally, continuing to grow after she died. Rossetti further added to those rumors in the published lines, "Lies all that golden hair undimmed in death,"[7] lines which according to Galia Ofek "imaginatively endowed his wife's hair with an independent power."[8] Throughout this volume there is a really compelling sense of hair of the Age of Empire having an independent power in all sorts of different ways: from its fetishization, its fashions, its framing of the self, its shear mass, and its afterlives. The Sutherland Sisters and their extraordinary long tresses evince all these aspects of hair (Figure I.1). Often front-page news during the Age of Empire they are still making headlines today. In 2013 the *Daily Mail* exclaimed: "The real-life Rapunzels: How seven sisters with tresses measuring 37 feet between them tantalized their audiences to make their fortune… and patented a 'miracle' hair tonic."[9] The article also notes that a bottle of their tonic was recently for sale on eBay for $249.99 rather than the $9.99 advertised back in 1901.

It is not just head hair which has afterlives. The story of one of the most famous locks of Victorian hair which "lives on" is the lock that Lady Caroline Lamb gave to Lord Byron. Credited with giving Byron the aphorism "mad, bad and dangerous to know" she is said to have sent him a snippet of her pubic hair; apocryphal the tale and the quotation may or may not be, but it lives on in our cultural consumption of Victorian hair.[10] A similar "independent power" appears to be wielded by John Ruskin's wife Effie's luxurious locks. Again these are not tresses of head hair but rather her pubic locks. Numerous books, an opera, and a recent film, *Effie* (2013) by Emma Thompson, have ruminated the reason for the annulment of the Ruskins's marriage. Famously Ruskin is quoted in explanation: "It may be thought strange that I could abstain from a woman who to most people was so attractive. But though her face was beautiful, her person was

FIGURE I.1: The Seven Sutherland Sisters.

not formed to excite passion. On the contrary, there were certain circumstances in her person which completely checked it."[11] Rumors abound as to why Ruskin was unable to consummate the marriage yet it is Effie herself who suggested: "[Ruskin] had imagined women were quite different to what he saw I was, and that the reason he did not make me his Wife was because he was disgusted with my person the first evening."[12] She finally married and had eight children with the Pre-Raphaelite Sir John Everett Millais who, like his contemporaries, was known for his painting of luxurious hair. Perhaps if the Pre-Raphaelites had at an earlier date paid such detailed attention to all of a woman's hair rather than focusing on her head the apparent shock Ruskin felt may not have left him seemingly impotent. A glance through paintings from Walter Crane's *The Laidly Worm* (1881), Sir Edward Burne-Jones's *The Pygmalion Series* to Millais's *The Knight Errant* (1870) finds women's bodies remarkably hairless.

This hairlessness is in marked contrast to the realist painting *L'Origine du monde* of 1866, by Gustave Courbet. His other female nudes, such as *Reclining Woman* and *Woman with a Parrot*, both 1866, tend to be similarly hairless or else their pubis is discreetly covered by hand or gauze which is more typical for the period. While it has been suggested that *L'Origine* was commissioned by the first owner, Turkish-Egyptian diplomat Khalil-Bey, a collector of eclectic representations of the female body, this does not detract from its impact in terms of representing the hirsute female body. Here there is no contextualizing through literary or poetic device; there is no symbolism to imbue a narrative, but rather bold brush strokes which reveal a certain realism of the female body. Yet it manages to step away from being pornographic despite fascinating the gaze. Perhaps this is precisely because of the lack of narrative props which high-end Victorian pornography tended to include. Yet, according to Abigail Solomon-Godeau in her article "The Legs of the Countess," aside from Courbet's painting developments it is nineteenth-century "photography [that] can be credited with the invention of the beaver shot, an image so constructed that its sole purpose is the exposure of female genitalia."[13] She goes on to discuss the fascinating boundary between art, photographic art, and pornography in which, aside from Courbet's hirsute female genitalia, such depictions are restricted to the latter. And of course the painting remained hidden in private collections until it was displayed in the Musée d'Orsay from 1995. Yet whether in Courbet's painting or Victorian pornographic photography these women's pubic hair lives on and seemingly wields a rather different independent power.

AMASSING LOCKS: COLLECTING HAIR

Amassed hair from the Age of Empire lives on perhaps most dramatically in various collections some of which are more recently curated such as Leila's Hair Museum in Missouri and the collection in the Victoria and Albert Museum. One of the most fascinating collections of hair can be viewed at the Harry Ransom Center at the University of Texas at Austin, USA. Until the 1990s the Romantic poet Leigh Hunt's collection could be handled by visitors; now we can gaze at a distance. From Charlotte Brontë, John Keats, Percy Bysshe Shelley, Mary Wollstonecraft Shelley, Samuel Taylor Coleridge, Robert Browning to a black braid of Edgar Allan Poe's, which he had given to Elmira Shelton, the collection is full of nineteenth-century literary hair lovingly described on the website: "They look exactly as one imagines they should: Elizabeth Barrett Browning's curls rather like the coat of her spaniel, Flush; Keats's wavy and luxuriantly brown; the older Wordsworth's hair is blondish, thin, and flecked with gray (Figure I.2)."[14]

INTRODUCTION

FIGURE I.2: Elizabeth Barrett Browning's hair in the J.H. Leigh Hunt Collection. Courtesy Harry Ransom Center at the University of Texas at Austin.

Hunt was seemingly fascinated by the fact that hair lives on and has afterlives. In his essay "Pocketbooks and keepsakes," he says "this is what gives to a lock of hair a value above all other keepsakes: it is a part of the individual's self."[15] This sense of the hair living on and having the potential to connect to the individual at an emotional but also physical level that seemingly defies not only time and space but also death, comes across most clearly in his poem about Milton's hair:

To Robert Batty, M.D., on His Giving Me a Lock of Milton's Hair
By Leigh Hunt

It lies before me there, and my own breath
Stirs its thin outer threads, as though beside
The living head I stood in honoured pride,
Talking of lovely things that conquer death.
Perhaps he pressed it once, or underneath
Ran his fine fingers when he leant, blank-eyed,
And saw in fancy Adam and his bride
With their heaped locks, or his own Delphic wreath.
There seems a love in hair, though it be dead.
It is the gentlest, yet the strongest thread
Of our frail plant,—a blossom from the tree
Surviving the proud trunk; as if it said,
Patience and gentleness in power. In me
Behold affectionate eternity.

The poem beautifully encapsulates the connection hair suggests to the other, that it is somehow living still even when its owner is dead. The poem resonates with the Victorian fascination with the boundary between life and death found in such poems as Christina Rossetti's "After Death"; in Millais's painting *Ophelia* (1851–1852); in the popularity for Gothic novels such as Bram Stoker's *Dracula*; and in paintings such as *The Nightmare* by Henry Fuseli and Gabriel von Max's *Der Anatom* (1869). Further, Hunt links this to a sense of love, so it is not just merely living but it is also alive with sentiment and feeling, even while it is dead. A lock of Milton's hair is included in his collection but seemingly has the weakest provenance as according to the collection's website it is said to have been acquired when Milton's body was interred at the end of the eighteenth century. Yet it is this lock which Hunt appears to have dwelt upon most in his writing perhaps because it was the lock of the long dead poet whom he admired, much as now the rest of the collection resonates with us.

Hunt was not alone in his fascination; in the 1850s John Varden started the collection *Hair of Persons of Distinction*; first displayed in 1853, it is now housed at the Smithsonian National Museum of American History.[16] Working for museums as keeper of collections there appears to be an interesting narrative of ownership surrounding the locks of hair. Varden seems to have explicitly wanted to claim the locks as his own in two senses: first, that once the lock of hair is no longer attached it becomes someone else's, but crucially given his role at the museum as keeper of collections, he wished to keep this collection in private ownership not as one of the museum's. While his collection includes a lock from the sculptor Clark Mills it tends to lean more to the military with Generals Winfield Scott and Sam Houston, and the political with Senators Henry Clay and Jefferson Davis being represented by their hair. Here the impetus appears to be slightly different from that of Hunt's; the collection is all from contemporaries and appears to be more about the science of collecting and cataloguing. There is also the sense that it is about ideas of identity in terms of personal recognition. First, in that it is hair of "distinguished persons" who are invited to submit a lock, but also in his entering the "Hair of Presidents" to compete at the Mechanics Fair of Maryland Institute in 1853 and 1859. On the back of the collection's frame is the inscription: "No1. The Property of John Varden of Washington City September

1855."¹⁷ So while it is therefore about the identity of the individual locks, it is perhaps more importantly about Varden's sense of identity and the kudos conferred as the owner of this prize-winning collection.

SPECTACLES OF HAIR

Important to ideas of national identity were the World Fairs which displayed huge collections of things and objects, and there was hair everywhere. A look through the catalogues for the first Great Exhibition in London in 1851 gives a sense of the breadth of hair in circulation during the Age of Empire. The number of references to hair is exhausting, hinting at the scale of not just the Great Exhibition (Figure I.3) itself but also the sheer presence of hair in culture. In the illustrated catalogue we are instructed that: "We may hereafter find occasion to pay [Messrs. S.H. & D. Gass of London's] stand another visit, as we observe among their productions several objects deserving of notice […] a large vase, most ingeniously composed of human hair, executed by J. Woolley."¹⁸ In the general catalogue almost everything to do with hair can be found. There is a "chatelaine, containing devices formed with human hair," the devices not specified.¹⁹ Similarly unspecific, there are "specimens of working in human hair" and an artist in hair from Clerkenwell with his display of "specimens for lockets, brooches etc."²⁰ B. Lee of 41 Rathbone Place has a display which includes "Bracelets of new design and construction, composed of human hair and gold, mixed

FIGURE I.3: John Absolon, "General view of the interior," from *Recollections of the Great Exhibition* (1851). Courtesy Metropolitan Museum of Art, New York.

throughout; the hair plaited by hand. Brooches of varied designs, composed of several shades of hair. Hair guard-chain, of a new pattern. Albert guards with keys of hair set in gold."[21] The working of hair with the gold suggests the elevated status it had. There is even hairwork framing the Royal family: "Ornamental frame, containing the miniatures of the Queen, H.R.H. Prince Albert, and the Royal Family; mounted in hair and gold."[22] In the "Illustrated Journal" the cataloguer expands on the art of hairwork, pointing to the detail and execution of the artistry to argue for its rank in cultural appreciation:

> These works tend to show the amount of skill, taste, design, and variety that working in hair are susceptible of. It has been a class of manufacture of mediocre perfection hitherto; but from the ready weaving of the material into many forms, and its graceful union with gold, as well as its being peculiarly adapted for souvenirs it may well claim to rank higher in artistic manufactures.[23]

These pieces, their artistry, and the use of gold and elsewhere silver and pearls place them at the luxury end of the market demonstrating hairwork's high-fashion status. The range of hairwork on display at the Great Exhibition suggests an importance which goes beyond demonstrating the skill and the decorative possibilities of the art. Hairwork was made to mark important rituals, betrothals, marriages, and death, rituals which culturally are all about public declarations of the self.

Elsewhere the catalogue is filled with objects concerned with the dressing of hair itself, with "ornamental hair, specimens of dye" and a "headdress of natural hair."[24] A glance at just one page discloses a "double pin for hair," "an arrow for the hair," "flower ornaments" also for the hair, and "hair-pins."[25] There are also "hair powders," "chignon combs," and "brushes of hair, tortoise shell and ivory."[26] Of course, the Great Exhibition was international and so was the hair. From Dresden there are "seven tableaus, embroidered with hair and silk, on silk ground" and from Leipzig there is

> raw German hair, called Brabant hair, of various lengths and colours, including a weft of two and a half. Natural hair, completely purified and prepared for use, applicable for curls, inc. with specimens of the same hair dyed. Hair artificially dressed. The exhibitor states that he employs more than seventy men in the preparation of human hair for sale.[27]

From Berlin there is a "plate with the royal Prussian arms, &c. formed of hair in the manner of brushwork."[28] From Paris, J. Crossat, a hairdresser on the Rue de Richelieu, has "perukes without toupees, and a machine to implant hairs in silk and other kinds of tissues."[29] From Tunis there are "long hair ornaments, with gold [...] head covering with silver. Head covering gaze, embroidered silver."[30] Although the majority of hair-related exhibits are European there are examples of every type of hair adornment imaginable from across the globe. The latter were regarded as exotic objects of fascination rather than engaging women's desire for fashion. The many accounts of visiting the exhibition appear to delineate a separation between the spectacle of fascination and the spectacle of desire, both of which draw the crowds; whereas other exhibits demonstrating new technologies and inventions found less appeal in their lack of wonder.[31] Reference is also made to the production practices behind the maintenance of hair with examples such as "Tangeer bark used in making a lye for washing the hair."[32] Precisely because of the ambition and scientific scrutiny that impelled the Great Exhibition there is a breadth of hair exhibits which encompasses all aspects of the trajectory from production, exchange, through to display in all sorts of cultural contexts, which offers a fascinating insight into the hair of empire.

Although in the displays there is a sense of the production and practice which goes in to Victorian hair, as well as the global trade, it is still a display of spectacle and achievement thus eliding narratives of poverty and need which underpins much of the economies of hair. There was a huge market in hair and it was the poorest who would sell their locks, locks which if they appeared at the Great Exhibition would be "hidden" in the artwork. Interestingly, there are no exhibits at the Grand Exhibition from Sweden which now houses what is claimed to be the largest collection of nineteenth-century hair in Europe at the Bangsbo Museum in Denmark. During hard times Swedish women revived the archaic Scandinavian art of *bijouterie* (trinkets) to support their families. These women were called *hårkullor* (hair ladies) and they traveled Europe to sell their hairwork and send the money back home. The museum exhibit includes "hair watch chains, usually made for men out of their wives' hair, and bracelets, necklaces and rings worn by women and made from their husband's clipped locks. Wreaths and plaques made from the hair of dead relatives, amongst other oddities like human hair mittens."[33] Here are women who out of poverty traveled far from home to serve the consumer fetish for hair of the rich.

FASHIONING HAIR: FASHIONING IDENTITIES

Much of the fascination for hairwork in the nineteenth century derives from Victorian sensibilities surrounding death and concerns with ideas of identity. In death the hair becomes a stand-in for the person, just as it arguably does in the locket given in love. But it is, as attested by the revival of the craft in Sweden and the predominance in Europe during the nineteenth century, also a fashion. A fashion which waned according to Anne Louise Luthi after the 1880s when, in 1887, Queen Victoria agreed to wear silver jewelry on state occasions, signifying the end of the mourning period. After this time "hair jewellery was now regarded as being in the worst possible taste."[34] Perhaps one of the most significant pieces of hairwork display which had ensured its fashionable status prior to this was the full-length, full-sized portrait of Queen Victoria at the Paris Exhibition of 1855.

For a period during the Age of Empire, hairwork was the height of fashion but perhaps inevitably the fashions in hair changed throughout the period. Fashion theorist Joanne Entwistle points out that clothing and the relationship to the body is important in the constructing of identity; she suggests that fashion is a "situated bodily practice [...] our experience of the body is not as an inert object but the envelope of our being, the site for our articulation of our self."[35] Hair is fascinating as a site of identity construction in that it appears to exist at a boundary, in Warwick and Cavallaro's terms, in an even more compelling way than is generally understood. They argue that "dress foregrounds the difficulty of establishing the body's boundaries. Though both literally and figuratively attached to the body, dress is simultaneously part of the material being and independent of it."[36] This interrelationship between the body and adornment becomes even more pressing with hair: hair is part of the body yet can be fashioned; it can be covered or intertwined into its adornments; and it too, as has been seen, can work independently from the body. Further, as the literary critic Deborah Lutz suggests, hair is "part of the body yet easy to separate from it, hair retained its luster long after the rest of the person decayed. Portable, with a shine like certain gems or metals, hair moved easily from being an ornamental feature of the body to being an ornament worn by others."[37] During the

Age of Empire, when bodies were relatively covered, hair was often at least partly on display in many cultures. It can also be as easily refashioned during the day as changing an outfit. The mobility of meaning in hair complicates the fashioning of the self when "the language of clothes and bodily adornment generally experiments relentlessly with ways of defining and redefining the boundaries between the self and the Other, subject and object, inside and outside."[38] If both clothes and the body suggest ideas of the self then the hair, which can be styled like clothing but is also corporeal like the body, suggests both the public and the private simultaneously.

Across Victorian culture there was a fascination with the boundary between the public and the private. This can be seen in the architectural changes taking place, the changes in mobility and spatial practices for both men and women in terms of public and private spaces, the rise of key-hole humor, the emerging police force as well as the fascination with crime stories, and the pornography industry. During this period, when the body and physiognomy were scrutinized to reveal character, the revealing of the body was restricted yet hair was on display in all sorts of ways from the Great Exhibition through to the intricate dressing of fashionable hair. As Geraldine Biddle-Perry and Sarah Cheung suggest: "Just as the human body is dressed and adorned in order to participate in society, so human hair is combed, cut, coloured, curled, straightened, plaited, swept up, tied back, decorated, plucked and shaved."[39] While according to the literary critic Royce Mahawatte: "As a bodily practice, women's hair does not simply connote abstract timeless values, but connects with the economic and social world around it."[40] Throughout the Age of Empire there were continual shifts in hair fashion reflecting the economic, social, and cultural consciousness of the time.

HAIR FASHIONS: WOMEN WORE IT UP

During the Age of Empire hair fashions were on the move. Since 1815 an international style was prevalent in clothing and extended to hairstyles and adornment.[41] This can be demonstrated by even a brief overview of the key changes in hair fashion in England. During the Regency period hair reflected the neoclassical styles which were fashionable for dress. Inspired by ancient Greece, hair was worn up with curls either side above the ears and adorned with ribbons. From the 1820s this was worn with a clear center parting. By the 1840s to 1860s it had turned into a chignon on top with locks either side worn with combs and flowers. Ears were revealed and the chignon at the back of the head was often twisted or more intricate in design. After the 1860s curls and waves were often put into the hair prior to it being dressed. In 1872 Marcel Grateau's curling tongs helped women to achieve the desired effect. By the early 1870s hair was lifted higher with hair and curls bought forward over the forehead. This pompadour effect was often added to with great twists of hair or braids falling down over the shoulder, often false to ensure the required mass.[42] This luxuriant mass of hair went out of fashion in the mid-1870s as did the wearing of false additions, and a far neater, slim-line head silhouette was created with hair worn very close and high up on the head. A few curls might escape for the evening and curled fringes that lay close to the forehead became *de rigueur*, again following the fashion of royalty—this time the Princess of Wales. Despite the decline in fashion for false hair adornment, false fringes, attached with silver clips, meant that one could follow fashion without compromising one's luxuriant tresses. Toward the end of the century, and before hair was cut short in the flapper style, hair was worn in a much softer fuller bun on top. For the fashion-forward, the hair weighted to the front of the head Gibson

Girl-style. When looked across the century the changes in hair style, perhaps as would be expected, reflect the changes in dress style, the silhouette of one complementing the silhouette of the other. In much the same way that dress designs modify the presentation of the shape of the body they also modify the shaping of the hairstyle.

The styling of hair also works in close relation to the styling of headwear, particularly for daywear. Until the end of the century women covered their hair in public, with only part of their hair on view. Until the 1870s indoor caps were also worn ubiquitously, becoming the preserve of the elderly and the lower classes into the twentieth century. Therefore, head coverings varied according to the hairstyle but were also integral to it. This symbiotic relationship between hair and headwear is even more compelling in other cultures; from the Tunisian coverings on display at the Great Exhibition to the African American hair wear discussed in chapters in this volume, the extent of hairstyles and head wear is endless. In Britain the typical Regency bonnet has either a soft or a structured back which neatly covers the hair, with an open peak allowing the curls over the ears to be on display and huge ribbons securing it in place. During the early period there were also more elaborate hats which were all replaced by the more modest poke bonnet firmly tied under the chin with ribbons in the 1840s.[43] By the mid-century this style was adapted to become the spoon bonnet, worn further back, with a narrower brim and the ribbons were left untied. Another style during the period was the leghorn that had a wide brim which dipped at both the front and the back. This style was trimmed, often elegantly, with flowers, lace, and ribbons. When the hairstyle shifted so that hair was styled decoratively at the back of the head then the hat moved high and forward on the head to display the beautiful, often expensively bought, chignons.[44] Toward the end of the century when hair was elaborate at both the front and the back of the style hats were worn even higher; they were elaborately trimmed with not only flowers and fruit but also insects, feathers, and even small birds. Hair styling for women was all about adorning it whereas for men it was about cutting.

SHADES OF FASHION

Fashion in hair was not restricted to styling but also concerned a woman's hair color (see Figure I.4). The Victorian period is stereotypically known for its fetishizing of golden hair from the golden child through to the abundant tresses of the Pre-Raphaelites. It was also a way in which to characterize women both in literature and in art but also in life in a culture that was seemingly compelled to discover not merely someone's identity but their nature through their physiognomy. This fed into the new policing practices and the anxieties about the growth of the urban population where one was surrounded by strangers who needed to be "read," which also meant that women's hair in particular was there to be read. Just as a few strands of hair stood in for the absent individual in both the love-token locks and those of mourning, so a women's hair came to stand for the self. In an era rife with anxiety about a woman's nature her hair became an easy-to-read open book. In literature and art, hair color was very clearly aligned to symbolism; the golden angel in the house, the innocent child or young woman, was inevitably blonde. Inevitably, though, these golden tresses became contaminated and were no longer so easy to read. As Galia Ofek suggests of Margaret Oliphant's Lucilla's tawny hair:

> Precisely because of its evasive quality, Lucilla's hair is out of representational bounds; it is so uncontainable that the normative conventions and hair etiquette would be

inapplicable, and therefore irrelevant, to the reader. Her hair defies Charlotte Yonge's, or indeed any other woman's, beauty regimes and rules. Similarly, systems of male signification are intercepted and resisted: Lucilla's hair colour, which is so unclear, would have confused contemporary physiognomists, slipping between the different categories.[45]

The anxiety about the hues of golden hair resides most significantly in the Pre-Raphaelites' work when their depictions explore the boundaries of female sexual desire and passion verging on madness.

The anxiety of vacillating hair color appears in *Dracula* when Lucy changes from her former locks of "sunny ripples" (146) to a "dark-haired woman" once she is a vampire.[46] But this easy symbolism between the pre-vampire innocent blonde to post-vampire dark hair is complicated by the dream sequence when two of the female vampires are dark and one is blonde:

> Two were dark, and had high aquiline noses, like the Count, and great dark, piercing eyes that seemed to be almost red when contrasted with the pale yellow moon. The other was fair, as fair as can be, with great wavy masses of golden hair and eyes like pale sapphires. I seemed somehow to know her face, and to know it in connection with some dreamy fear, but I could not recollect at the moment how or where. All three had brilliant white teeth that shone like pearls against the ruby of their voluptuous lips.[47]

Stoker seemingly thwarts symbolic convention only to restore it, questioning the ability to read "nature" via physiognomy. Not only may the body be unreliable when read; it may also be itself unreliable.

FIGURE I.4: Simon Grennan, *Hair in the Age of Empire*, May 2017.

Such shifts in symbolic meaning can similarly be found in the golden locks of Lady Audley in *Lady Audley's Secret*. Sir Michael is seduced by the childlike golden locks, not seeing the secrets hidden in the strands. Elsewhere the symbolic shifting of gray hair has more to do with fashion. Miss Havisham's gray hair mid-century attests to her withering body yet toward the end of the century gray hair was in fashion: "Many women were using hair powders (used to absorb grease and create a soft look), which likely contributed to the trend of fashionable grey hair."[48] It is her right to fashion which has Kate Clephane assert at the end of the period that "I like a gray fur with gray hair."[49]

HAIR FASHIONS: WHISKERS AND BEARDS

Men's hair was equally subject to the vagaries of fashion. Both their head and their facial hair followed trends which aligned them to different expressions of masculinity. At the turn of the century the fashion for men's hair moved away from the wigs they had been wearing. These now became the preserve of those such as lawyers, judges, and footmen, and either a wig or powdered hair remained the requirement at court. The legacy from the previous century was thus retained for the dressing of ritual. For most men there was a move to more natural and shorter hair. Similarly to women, men were influenced by neoclassical styles. The society fashion icon Beau Brummell wore his hair flowing but natural and he was meticulously clean-shaven, as was the fashion for most men.[50] He is reputed to have used his tweezers carefully every morning. Similarly these other more natural styles were an art. Men used pomade and wax to carefully nurture these natural styles. They are variously referred to according to the classical style: for example, the Caesar was short at the back and the front but longer over the ears; the Brutus was closely cropped all over and very disheveled and a style which Brummell himself wore. Facially, while some side-whiskers may grow there was rarely a beard in sight.

From the mid-century onward fashionable men wore their hair fairly short, simply parted, and brushed according to personal preference. They were, however, far more hirsute and styled on the face. According to the fashion historian Joan Nunn:

> Sideburns, allowed to grow further down the face, developed a variety of side-whiskers—broad and bushy "mutton-chop" whiskers,—or long and combed out, known as Piccadilly weepers or Dundrearys (from the character of Lord Dundreary in Tom Taylor's play *Our American Cousin*) during the 1870s. Side whiskers might be worn with or without a moustache, as might the fringe beard [...] Full beards covering the chin, combined with a moustache, were cut in many different ways—very full and very bushy, rounded and neat like General Grant's in America, or slightly more pointed like that of the Prince of Wales in England. A narrow pointed beard from just under the lower lip to an inch or so below the chin, known as a goatee, was worn by Napoleon III with a long moustache waxed out straight to the sides. A waxed moustache turned up at the ends was associated with Kaiser Wilhelm II of Germany and might be referred to as a "Kaiser" moustache.[51]

Huge and often quite subtle variations were available to style facial hair according to the fashion and masculine expression. At the end of the century there was a return in men's hair styling to the clean-shaven natural appearance seen at the beginning of the century—this style from the dandy Beau Brummell now returned via Oscar Wilde. The styling of men's hair appears to be a self-identifying practice clearly aligning to particular expressions of masculinity during a period when different masculinities were emerging (See figure I.5).

FIGURE I.5: Advertisement for Parker's Hair Balsam.

The styling of men's hair was a more public and social practice than society women's hair which tended to be dressed in private in the boudoir until the beginning of the nineteenth century. At this point barbers diversified both in terms of luxury offerings but also extending to women's hairdressing. Men's barbers had always been homosocial spaces of male ritual and part of the performance of masculinity. They were a semi-public social space where men drank, bet, and conversed in a space which offered a level of intimacy and "resembled a gentleman's club" where "patrons caught up on local news, debated the latest political developments, or placed bets on the day's races."[52]

ECONOMIES OF HAIR

Women's hair was until the end of the century dressed at home in the domestic space. The first exclusively female hairdressing salons appeared toward the end of the century. The Canadian woman Martha Mathilda Harper is credited with opening the first women's hair salon in Rochester, New York, in 1888. She developed her own hair tonic and hair brushes which were eventually sold in department stores, she invented the reclining shampoo chair, and perhaps most importantly she franchised her business internationally. The franchising was underpinned by a desire to help other poor women like herself.[53] Taking a ritual of feminine practice, which in its perceived vanity is oft read as women's collusion in patriarchal restraint to liberate women, Harper created an empire of hair which was philanthropic.

In contrast the barber shop has a long history which at the beginning of the nineteenth century was primarily a homosocial space that cut across classes and focused on the practice of shaving. According to Jessica Clark:

From the late 1860s, however, expanding opportunities for luxury consumption and a new emphasis on consumer pleasure contributed to the delineation of distinct categories of male grooming establishment: utilitarian penny barber shops concentrated in the East End, efficient middle-class shops located throughout the metropolis, and elite West End hairdressing saloons developed in conjunction with those catering to new female shoppers.[54]

These diverse social spaces afforded different cultural practices. For the poor these barber shops were often places to drink and gamble staying open late at night while the high end devoted the space to complicated grooming rituals, branded through their advertising; even to visit one of these new elite barber shops suggests a sense of identity construction even before the hair is touched. Toward the end of the century these high-end saloons divided their shops up to allow female customers. The introduction of separate entrances, the position of female suites upstairs, and the introduction of booths allowed for a sense of privacy in these public spaces which accorded to the requirements of female bodily practices. Of course the sector is not just about cultural practices but has an important economic driver. This can be seen even more clearly in America where the barbershop was a very important sector for the African American, offering postbellum economic stability.

There were also industrial developments that changed the face of hairdressing for both men and women. Alexandre-Ferdinand Godefroy invented the first hair dryer in 1888 in his salon:

> The contraption was to be hooked up "to any suitable form of heater," which would send hot air through a pipe to a dome surrounding the woman's head. The device was impressively multipurpose: to use it for shampooing, Godefroy suggested removing all pieces except one resembling the brim of a sombrero, which fastened around a woman's head to redirect suds into the sink. ("Still another use to which the device may be applied," Godefroy wrote, "is that of shaping wig-holders.")[55]

Meanwhile, in 1872 Marcel Grateau, a Parisian, invented curling tongs to create the Marcel wave, and Erica Feldmen is attested to—or perhaps is said to—have created flat irons to straighten hair. There was also an international economy in the exchange of cut hair to be used for false hairpieces and hairwork. In addition there are the many dyes, hair potions, and adornments to be made and circulated which the numerous adverts in Victorian magazines and newspapers attest to.

A browse through a nineteenth-century magazine will find adverts for "Burnett's Cocoaine for the hair—the Absolute Cure for Dandruff"; Dr. Watson's hair restorer; Edwards' Harlene (Figure I.6); Koko for the hair; Buckingham's dye for the Whiskers; Peerless Dyes; Rowland's Macassar Oil; Moustache Wax; and one of my favorites, Dr. Scott's Electric Hairbrush. One 1885 advert for the latter shows a small girl in a nightgown in front of the fire writing a letter: "Dear Santa, Please send three of Dr. Scott's Electric Hair Brushes, one for Papa, who is bald; one for Mamma for her headaches; and one for sister to brush her hair, for Aunty says that is what makes her hair so long and glossy. Yours, faithfully, Flossie." There is a lovely narrative to the advert which is forward-looking rather than the more usual listing of the miracle cures a product will perform—although underneath the small tableau there are the requisite claims stating it "is the best brush in the world and cures Headache, Neuralgia, Dandruff, Baldness, Falling Hair and Diseases of the scalp." Who wouldn't want one?

 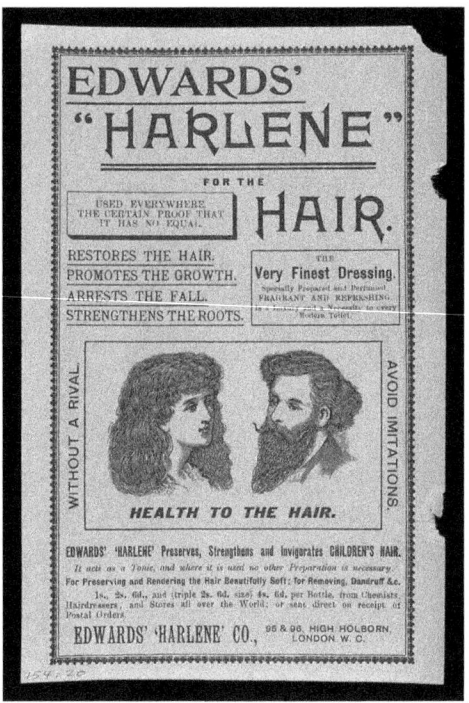

FIGURE I.6: Advertisements for Harlene Hair Products. Courtesy Wellcome images.

The rise of the advertising industry is encapsulated here along with the body anxiety which is still at the heart of the personal grooming economy. Dr. Scott also had an electric toothbrush and flesh brush in his range to ensure that he had the whole body covered, disappointingly all of them actually contained magnetic rods rather than any electricity. But this invention has led to one of the more interesting afterlives of Victorian hair in the American folk and blues band named Dr. Scott's Electric Brush.

MOURNING HAIR

Our contemporary cultural fascination with the Age of Empire and its things suggests our complex relationship with the period. In some ways this fascination can be understood by the Victorian's own fascination with hair as a stand-in for the dead. Hair and other relics used in mourning have a long history across cultures. But perhaps because of the fashion for elaborate hairwork and hair jewelry during the Age of Empire it is unsurprising that the sometimes simpler forms of hair-mourning jewelry were popular and equally fashionable (see Figure I.7).

These simpler forms were made in "settings of black and white enamel, jet and gold, often with the words 'In Memoriam' and a panel of simply twisted hair. The differences between these two types of jewellery were sometimes confusingly blurred, especially when brilliant-cut diamonds, turquoises, corals and garnets were used in the settings. Presumably these were not worn in deepest mourning."[56] It could be suggested that all the hairwork and locks of Victorian hair circulating in our contemporary culture stand in for

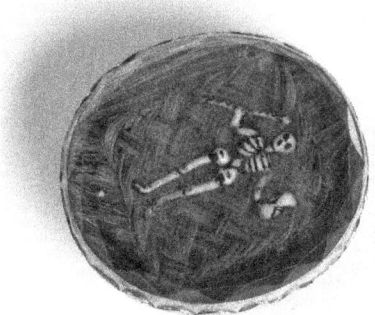 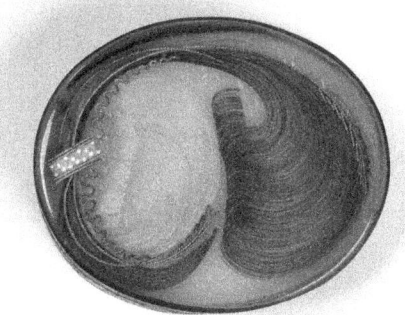

FIGURE I.7: Mourning brooches containing the hair of a deceased relative.

the Age of Empire; perhaps this blurring occurs because the locks of the living all become the locks of the dead. The graphic artist Simon Grennan evokes this in his illustration shown in Figure I.4, the amassed colored hair suggesting the residue of the living, the once alive, the once touched. Deborah Lutz in what can be read as an extension of Daniel Miller's understanding of the resonance in things suggests the afterlives of hair: "This belief that an afterlife shimmered through objects […] was another holdover from ancient folk customs […] Enlivened by the spirit world too, the hair of others worn on the body strengthened the connection between the living and the dead."[57] Hair then has its own stories, histories, and symbolic resonances which the chapters of this volume explore. This interdisciplinary work is written primarily with a literary and fashion context from which the authors present a collection of essays that talk to each other from their researched based practices as well as through their object orientation: hair. The chapters intersect to provide a plurality of meanings in the study of hair from a variety of disciplines and perspectives. Thus the meanings in and of hair in the volume emerge to show that hair can be understood to have a biography. Indeed the period being one of formation and expansion is one which gave meaning and expression to the enormous changes through cultural expression so that inevitably icons of the period such as Rossetti come under particular scrutiny in different chapters in the volume. This influence of the bourgeoisie and its "conquest of the globe by the capitalist economy,"[58] returns the volume time and again to Great Britain and the United States. But as suggested at the outset behind the dominant cultural practices and fashioning of hair is a global industry and colonizing impulse. Nowhere is this more starkly demarcated than in slavery which the chapters on Fashion and Adornment, and Race and Ethnicity. This is further examined in the broader context of the artificial hair trade in the chapter on Production and Practice. The economic trade behind hair cultures is considered from different perspectives in the chapters on Health and Hygiene, and Class and Social Status. The tools of the hair trade and how they are wielded appear throughout the volume from adverts and hair products through to the effect scissors can have on hair. These are tangled tresses which trail across all the chapters showing how entangled the hair of the Age of Empire was and how it insists on our continued remembrance and resonates, lives on, in afterlives with an "independent power" insisting on our resurrecting of the dead.

CHAPTER ONE

Religion and Ritualized Belief: Myth, Folklore, and Spiritualism in Victorian and Neo-Victorian Representations of Hair

Unweaving the Tangled Tresses of Influence and Obsession

RICHARD LEAHY

INTRODUCTION: THE UNTAMED HAIR OF SPIRITUALISM AND THE SUPERNATURAL

The use and fashioning of hair in association with spiritualist practices is broad and far-reaching through history. In 1654, Emma Wilby writes, a "cunning-woman" claimed to have cured a headache by "boiling a lock of the client's hair in wine and throwing it in the fire."[1] Cunning folk, those who practiced traditional magic and pagan witchcraft, were officially outlawed by the Vagrancy Act of 1824, yet the influence of their practices and rituals continued to be felt in the developing mythic and spiritualist beliefs of the period. Cunning folk continued to use hair both in the creation of their own appearance and in spells and magic. Ronald Hutton details how cunning folk fashioned their hair in order to heighten their mystique, and mark themselves as distinctly other. He notes Victorian cunning man Billy Brewer "promenaded Taunton in a long Inverness cape and sombrero hat, his hair falling in long dishevelled grey locks," and another magic-practitioner nicknamed "Pigtail" Bridger, "who wore his hair as his nickname suggested."[2] Hair was a vital component in the performance of the spiritualist's identity; it embellished their mystery and helped cultivate the detached position they occupied on the periphery of society.

The nineteenth-century fascination with the supernatural and spiritual has been widely discussed, with Richard Noakes establishing the "dilemma" of "the Victorian association of spiritualism with the supernatural" and the problematizing of that idea by "the Victorian quest for order behind phenomena purporting to come from the other world."[3] The instability of faith and belief during the early to mid-century created a social psyche that wanted to believe in something, yet wanted that something to be severely rational and physically tangible. Janet Oppenheim suggests British spiritualists valued its rituals and practices for the religious comfort that this belief offered, and how it "tended to emphasise the purportedly scientific foundations of their beliefs when they urged the claims of spiritualism to public attention and respect."[4] Hair was often presented as bridging this gap; it was ethereal in its materiality, and was taken as a representation of the whole individual. In this need for the rationalization of a supernatural other, we may witness the consolidating of the mythic and folkloric origins of the spiritual with the emergence of psychological understanding. Thomas Carlyle reflected on the blurring of these concepts in *Sartor Resartus*:

> Notable enough too, here as elsewhere, wilt thou find the potency of Names, which indeed are but one kind of custom-woven, wonder-hiding Garments. Witchcraft and all manner of Spectre-work, and Demonology, we have now named Madness and Diseases of the Nerves.[5]

Classical notions of folkloric magic and spiritualism intertwined with rational scientific investigations. Hair occupied a unique space within these concepts. Representations of hair in art and literature often suggested the ongoing influence of pagan and mythological beliefs, while also reflecting the developing rationality and scientific faith of the nineteenth century.

The association of hair with the construction and performance of identity aligned to the suggestion that it can somehow represent or indicate the deviant or degenerate personality is apparent in Cesare Lombroso's work on criminal type. Lombroso, in *Criminal Man*, acknowledges hair many times, often associating "thick hair," or an "abundance" of hair as being an indicator of criminality.[6] Interestingly, Lombroso embraced the supernatural later in his life, reappropriating his scientific rationality to spiritualist beliefs: hair remained an important means of conveying the image of the "other," albeit now in a spiritual rather than criminal sense. In *After Death—What?*, he describes a photograph taken in the séance of a psychic named Randone, which he alleges shows "the form of a girl wrapped in a veil, with abundant hair falling to her knees."[7]

The emphasis put on the unkemptness and abundance of hair by Lombroso, in both a criminal and a supernatural sense, suggest that it functions as a means of delineating non-socio-normative identities, or a sense of cultural unorthodoxy. This opposition between the untamed and restrained hair extended to hair length when, as Carolyn C. White notes, there was a "transition from large, extravagant hairstyles of the 18th century to the short, more restrained styles of the 19th century."[8] This shift in styles established a direct opposition between the popular, more restrained hairstyles and those that were wilder and less refined; hair, in both its styling and its use in ritual practices, became a symbol of the variable cultural dichotomy between what was deemed normal and other.

Hair's heritage as an important facet in the representation of an individual in archaic spiritualist practices continued into the nineteenth century. As well as representing spiritualist identity, hair was also used in the mesmeric rituals of its practitioners. A series of séances that became known as the Cross-Correspondences focused on former

British prime minister Arthur Balfour's attempts to communicate with his deceased wife, Mary Lyttleton. Lyttleton was alleged to have attempted to contact her husband through a number of sessions of automatic writing conducted by various mediums over a thirty-year period following her death in 1875. Subsequent studies of the collection of correspondences have emphasized the importance of the fetishization of a lock of Mary's hair, which Balfour originally cut from her head on her deathbed and kept in a silver casket, in his interpretation of the automatic writings as apparent recreations of her hair, the last bodily reminder of her life. Jill Galvan notes that Jean Balfour, a descendant of Arthur who became the lead archivist of the correspondences, dedicated a large section to the topic, "The 'Lock of Hair' References": "These references in the scripts reportedly included a number of little drawings, along with those allusions to maidens' hair and repetitions of the sigma, which because of its curved or bent-line shape, was interpreted as a pictorial rendering of the tress."[9] The need to interpret the curved lines as an image of Mary Lyttleton's hair indicated Balfour's desire for some kind of afterlife for his lover. The lock of hair as the physical signifier of her was, for him, witnessed in the automatic drawings of spirit mediums. Galvan elaborates on this idea when she writes:

> The sustained attention to the scribblings—the wide, loose variety of drawings that got called a sigma—the strange equivalence of the sigma with the hair in the first place—all of this begins to seem like a desperate, endlessly frustrated, attempt to capture the hair itself. Lyttleton's physical body, through the material form of the mediums' handwriting—an attempt to lay claim to the body in the at best very limited way automatic handwriting will allow. In other words, in the quasi-virtual realm of the cross-correspondences, there arose a powerful, reactive craving for the material vestige of the self. Removed during Lyttleton's last illness, the hair was desired as a sign of her vulnerable, mortal being and the true emotions this had experienced.

The highly material nature of the late Victorian era, following improvements in mass production, consumerism, and commodity capitalism, appears to have influenced the yearning for material signifiers of the body post-death. Hair provides a unique materiality that is in some senses evanescent even after death; its physicality and its psychical link to the deceased are reminiscent of pagan and folkloric visions of hair. David Pickering, in *Cassell's Dictionary of Witchcraft*, summarizes this use: "Because the hair, like other body parts, is reputed to retain a mystic link with the body after it has been cut off, it has always been much valued by practitioners of witchcraft (particularly as the head is the seat of a person's psychic power)."[10] Pickering also highlights how strands of hair were used in "image magic" and "witches bottles" in order to represent the intended subject of a spell or concoction. As well as being able to convey a sense of identity to a living person, hair acted as a residual symbol of that identity in death. Representations of this phenomena in both Victorian and neo-Victorian art and literature extrapolate the notion of hair as being representative of personality, subjectivity, and the individual's body, while also closely acknowledging the pervasive mythic, folkloric, and supernatural influences on representations of hair.

THE HAIR OF LITERARY SUPERNATURALISM

A number of prominent nineteenth-century writers were interested in some form of spiritualism or another. Sir Arthur Conan Doyle's interest in supernatural beings, Charles Dickens's belief in mesmerism, and even the influence of William James's psychical research over his brother Henry's ghost stories all indicate the ongoing influence of archaic supernatural beliefs in representations of hair in their common predilection to use it symbolically as a means of conveying or establishing this often inhuman "other." Doyle's portrayals of atavistic beastliness are often marked by lank hair, especially in the Holmes stories; Dickens circumscribed to what Galia Ofek terms the "Victorian Medusa-Rapunzel dichotomous paradigm" in his representations of female hair, again suggesting the ongoing influence of mythic and folkloric ideas; and Henry and William James's involvement in the testing of hair in Psychical Research,[11] as well as Peter Quint's red-haired menace in *The Turn of the Screw*, are just some examples of the supernatural connotations of literary hair in the period. Thomas Hardy, in *Return of the Native*, also subscribes to this supernatural, pagan treatment of hair in his descriptions of Eustacia Vye:

> To see her hair was to fancy that a whole winter did not contain darkness enough to form its shadow—it closed over her head like nightfall extinguishing the western glow.
>
> Her nerves extended into those tresses, and her temper could always be softened by stroking them down. When her hair was brushed she would instantly sink into stillness and look like the Sphinx. If, in passing under one of the Egdon banks, any of its thick skeins were caught, as they sometimes were, by a prickly tuft of the large Ulex Europaeus—which will act as a sort of hairbrush—she would go back a few steps, and pass against it a second time.
>
> She had pagan eyes, full of nocturnal mysteries, and their light, as it came and went, and came again, was partially hampered by their oppressive lids and lashes; and of these the under lid was much fuller than it usually is with English women.[12]

The description of Vye encapsulates a number of the dominant themes conveyed through representations of hair; she is othered in this depiction—her hair is described as being in tandem with her nerves, extending the metonymic connection between hair, the body, and self. The image of her nerves reaching into her hair is Medusan in its semiotics, as is the dark description of her "pagan eyes, full of nocturnal mysteries." Representations of hair, particularly when influenced by spiritual or mythological ideas, suggest the division between body and identity, and how elements of the differentiated body, such as Vye's hair, may be an indicator of interior spiritual characteristics. The Medusan connotations of Vye's hair engage with ideas of entrancement through vision, and the sealing off of perceptions to solely focus on Gorgon-esque hair. As Deborah Lutz argues, "a dash of paganism, persisting into the nineteenth century, also added magic to hair's religious aura."[13]

In 1830, Scottish writer Walter Scott published his *Letters on Demonology and Witchcraft*, where he reflected on the nature of pagan, wiccan, and other classifications of spiritual belief. His recanting of anecdotes suggests the ongoing supernatural fascination with hair in the nineteenth century. He tells the alleged story of an encounter a "poor visionary" had with the "Restless People"—a crowd of men and women whom he had believed dead for years. Scott writes that after speaking in an unknown language, and roughly pushing him to and fro "all vanished but a female sprite, who, seizing him by the shoulder, obliged him to promise an assignation, at that very hour that day sevennight; that he then found his hair was all tied in double knots (well known by the name of elf-locks), and that he had almost lost his speech."[14] Elf-locks, an early western form of dreadlocked hair, were apocryphally viewed as being made by elves while children slept. However, they were later fashioned into an icon of otherness, as Abigail Bardi points out in her analysis of the disguised Rochester in *Jane Eyre*. Charlotte Brontë uses gypsy-based iconography, and depictions of these elf-locks to emphasize anxieties regarding both spiritual and social otherness. "The uses of the uncommon word 'elf-locks'," Bardi writes, "and of the homonym-like 'grizzled' and 'bristled', plus the red cloak, hint that Brontë's Gypsy draws directly from the trope established by Scott [in his Waverley novels]."[15] Scott's awareness of the elf-lock hairstyle and its subsequent pervasiveness in his own tropic depictions of gypsies, as well as Brontë's, again portray the supernatural levels of otherness that hair embodied within the nineteenth century.

FETISHIZATION AND TRANSACTION: CONTENDING SPIRITUALISM IN THE ROSSETTIS' NARRATIVES OF HAIR

Dante Gabriel Rossetti was possessed by a fetishistic interest in hair. Many of his paintings—*Lady Lilith, The Blessed Damozel, Beata Beatrix*, and others—all depict golden-haired women, and he is alleged to have become obsessed with the hair of his sitters. Interestingly, William Rossetti acknowledged the importance of hair in the creation of the Rossetti name. In his biography of his brother, William wrote of how the "Rossetti race" were so called in Italy due to their "florid complexion and reddish hair."[16] Hair was fundamental in creating the Rossetti identity, and the origin of the family name establishes the discourse of patriarchal aestheticism that Dante Gabriel colluded with and Christina criticized.

Dante Gabriel Rossetti is recorded as having attended up to twenty séances, with William Bell Scott stating in a letter: "One thing I must remember to tell you. Our old friend Gabriel has gone into spiritualism, and fancies he can call up bogies, and make them knock on a table."[17] He believed that he could communicate with his deceased wife, Elizabeth Siddal—a former sitter of his whose golden hair fascinated him. After her death, he hid a collection of poems within her hair upon burial, only to have her exhumed seven years later to retrieve the poetry. Upon her exhumation, it was found that her hair had "grown profusely post-mortem."[18] He detailed the power that this experience had over him in his poem "Life-in-Love," writing "Mid change the changeless night environeth, / Lies all that golden hair undimmed in death"—an image that Joanna Pitman argues conveyed a "terrifying supernatural radiance" to him.[19] Pitman writes of Dante Gabriel Rossetti "panting through the streets of London in pursuit of a head of irresistible hair, or breaking off in mid-conversation at parties, as if hypnotised, on seeing a mass of gorgeous hair enter the room."[20] Hair became the focal point for his desires, and often proved to be metonymic of its owner's body and identity.

Christina, on the other hand, gravely denounced her brother's interest in spiritualism and distanced herself from his beliefs:

> PLEASE GOD. I will have nothing to do with spiritualism, whether it is an imposture or a black art, or with mesmerism, lest I clog my free will; or with hypnotism, lest wilful self-surrender become my road to evil choice, imagination, conduct voluntary or involuntary.[21]

Christina's condemnation of spiritualism and the supernatural, as well as her brother's obsession with golden hair, frames "Goblin Market" within a new context. When taking these details into account, the poem may be read as a criticism of spiritualism, the supernatural, and her brother's fetishization of hair. "Goblin Market" is a poem widely appreciated to function on the symbolically transactional account of hair exchange. Kathy Psomiades writes: "In 'Goblin Market', gold and white, simultaneously the colours of hair and precious metal, of flesh and ivory, turn femininity into a value form."[22] This gendered interpretation of Rossetti's poem is elaborated on, and given more value, when considering it as a potential satire of the spiritualism that surrounded Christina Rossetti, and that which her brother Dante Gabriel Rossetti practiced. Christina had a precedent for criticizing the objectification of women in her brother's art; "In an Artist's Studio" is the most commonly acknowledged poem dealing with such an issue, and when considering Dante Gabriel's documented fascination with golden hair, it is easy to see the Goblin Men as avatars for his obsession. Early critics acknowledged the magic and enchanted nature of Christina's poem, claiming that it was "as wild as if some vision by Grimm, or Tieck, or Andersen had found its way to the author's eyes and verse; it is a perfect little fairy gem."[23] Modern critics, such as Serena Trowbridge, have also identified the Gothic supernatural elements of the poem, particularly in the Goblin Men and enchanted fruit; however, a closer attentiveness to hair in the poem can unravel a covert spirituality, as well as filial discourses of hair and its representations.

The golden locks of Laura and Lizzie are held up as a symbol of goodness and purity at first. Rossetti describes Laura's "glossy head" (l. 52),[24] and her "gleaming neck" (l. 81), which is compared to a "moonlit poplar branch" (l. 84). These images of Laura's hair emphasize the influence of spiritualism and the ongoing influence of ritualistic belief through traditional pagan language. The comparison between the hair falling down Laura's neck and the "moonlit poplar branch" is particularly significant, as the poplar tree had an important symbolic meaning in pagan spiritualist belief. It is alleged to have been associated with "moon magic due to the connection with Persephone," as well as being connected with the Celtic tradition of the "Faery Queen who grants the seeker a 'tongue that cannot lie'."[25] This directly relates to the fear of temptation and sin that pervades Rossetti's poem, while also emphasizing the value of the sisters' golden hair as an emblem of corruptible purity.

This metaphor is further emboldened by the transactionary nature of the subsequent treatment of hair. After Laura proclaims that she has no coin to spend on the Goblin Men's fruits, they respond:

> You have so much gold upon your head.
> They answered all together:
> "Buy from us with a golden curl." (lines 123–125)

Critics have widely explored the notion of the hair in this section as commodifying the body within a patriarchal system of exchange. Psomiades argues that the poem conveys how "women's hair is the sign of their translatability into a system of economic values."[26] This is certainly the case, to some extent, yet our understanding of how this commodification others the sisters can be aided through an acknowledgment of the supernatural and spiritual influences acting upon it. David Pickering notes how lovers traditionally exchanged shorn locks of hair "as a sign of their complete trust in one another, a token of faith that the other would not use it for purposes of witchcraft."[27] Galia Ofek further corroborates Pickering's statement, as she writes of the "binding ritual which signalled romantic attachment and even possession."[28] As the transaction is decidedly one-sided in "Goblin Market"—the eternality of hair held in contrast to the passing joy of consuming the forbidden fruits—the implications of hair exchange are tinged with ritual connotations of ownership. The Goblin Men exchange a lifetime of bodily possession over Laura for a brief sampling of their fruits. Lizzie warns Laura of the possession the Goblin Men take over their subjects by reminding her of Jeanie, who, after eating the Goblin Men's fruit and being subsequently abandoned, "Found them no more but dwindled and grew grey" (l. 156). Hair is used as an indicator of the vitality of the young women the Goblin Men consume; the progression from golden hair to gray hair is also later acknowledged as Laura pines after the Goblin Men, Rossetti stating:

> But when the noon waxed bright
> Her hair grew thin and grey;
> She dwindled, as the fair full moon doth turn
> To swift decay and burn
> Her fire away. (lines 276–280)

The possession of Laura by the Goblin Men is exemplified through her graying hair. She no longer has the luster of youth, and is consumed to the point where her golden hair becomes valueless and she is entirely possessed. Rossetti's lexical choices of "dwindled," "decay," and "burn" indicate an invasive corruption that takes place in Laura, as her hair becomes a metonym for her body and mind.

RITUALS OF THE MUSE: ENCHANTED HAIR AND MEDUSA'S SNARE

It is possible to consider Christina Rossetti's treatment of hair in this poem as a subversion of her brother Dante Gabriel's obsessive fetishization of hair. His fascination with the semi-religious, semi-mythical figure of Lilith offers an insight into Christina's treatment of hair in "Goblin Market." In Dante Gabriel Rossetti's companion poem to "Lady Lilith," "Body's Beauty" (1868), he writes: "Of Adam's first wife, Lilith, it is told / (The witch he loved before the gift of Eve,) / That, ere the snake's, her sweet tongue could deceive / And her enchanted hair was the first gold."[29] Dante Gabriel's treatment of hair shares semantic similarities to that of his sister; he makes reference to Eve and the Snake, connoting biblical levels of temptation, but adds an air of the supernatural by calling Lilith the "witch," and making focus of her Medusan "enchanted hair." Rossetti's *Lady Lilith* was originally painted using Fanny Cornforth as the model, but it was later repainted in 1872 to 1873 to portray Alexa Wilding instead (see Figures 6.1 and 6.2). An 1867 replica of the painting, created by Rossetti himself in watercolor, features a translation from Goethe's *Faust* personally attached to the frame by Rossetti:

> Beware of her fair hair, for she excels
> All women in the magic of her locks,
> And when she twines them round a young man's neck
> She will not ever set him free again.[30]

The quotation inscribed on the reproduction of *Lady Lilith* provides an image of the enchantment he felt when confronted with golden hair. Medusan imagery is yet again evoked by the restrictive nature of the hair that "twines […] round a young man's neck," as well as a deliberate engagement with the "magic of her locks." The accompanying quotation elaborates yet again on the image of hair as carrying spiritual connotations. Similar to the "enchanted" hair of his own companion poem, the selected quote from

Goethe emphasizes the magical, overwhelming effect that hair had on Dante Gabriel Rossetti. The interchangeable nature of his models, replacing Fanny Cornforth with Alexa Wilding in this painting, indicates the objectification of the red-gold hair; as Christina writes in "In an Artist's Studio": "One face looks out from all his canvasses."[31]

In a letter to his sister written in 1852, Dante Gabriel admonished his sister for sitting for portraiture, proclaiming that: "You must take care however not to rival the Sid, but keep within respectful limits. Since you went away, I have had sent me, among my things from Highgate, a lock of hair shorn from the beloved head of that dear, and radiant as the tresses of Aurora, a sight of which may dazzle you on your return."[32] The rapidity of his changing of the subject, from Christina to the hair of Elizabeth Siddal, offers an insight into the powerful effect his sitters' hair had on him, and of Christina's criticism of the anonymization of his muses. The vampiric imagery of Dante Gabriel Rossetti as he "feeds upon her face by day and night" from Christina's "In an Artist's Studio" offers a criticism of Dante's obsession, and helps to establish her poetry as in some part being influenced by a rejection of his preternatural fetishization of hair. Suzanne Waldman suggests that in the mid- to late 1850s, "[Dante Gabriel] Rossetti suffered an unfavourable loss of ordinary, happy sexual passion [and] entered into circumstances favourable to the fetish, as his sexual life became aestheticized into the admiration and painting of women whose features could be substituted for the genital goal."[33] This aestheticization and objectification of women through their hair was charged with latent mythological influence in Dante Gabriel's art and poetry; his women become Lilith, Aurora, Medusa, and Rapunzel figures, objectified and anonymized through the attention placed on their hair.

INTERTWINED INTERTEXTUALITY

Christina Rossetti criticizes both her brother's obsession with hair and his interest in spirituality through an engagement with the fantastical and ritualistic. In "Goblin Market," she describes Lizzie and Laura, after the latter's partaking in Goblin Fruit, as nestling "Golden head by golden head" (l. 184), further envisioning them as:

> Like two blossoms on one stem,
> Like two flakes of new-fall'n snow,
> Like two wands of ivory
> Tipped with gold for awful kings. (lines 188–191)

Christina's imagery in this passage combines elements of the spiritual, fantastical symbolic associations of hair, with the patriarchal objectification found in her brother's art. The two sisters' purity is emphasized in their likening to the whiteness of "snow" and "ivory," continuing the theme established by the "moonlit poplar branch." Their depiction as "two" intimately connected beings suggests a cooperative rather than individual autonomy. The reference to "wands" suggests a certain level of ritualistic influence, and may be considered to be a reflection of her brother's conflation of hair and mythic imagery. This line also carries associations of power, particularly phallogocentric power, especially when considered in combination with the next line: "tipped with gold for awful kings." Again, the phrasing of this hair-based image belies a sense of absolute possession; the gold hair, and by extension the sisters, are "*for*" awful kings. There is a sense of ownership within Rossetti's words, something that reflects the one-sided, transactionary nature of hair within the narrative of the poem.

The frontispiece used for the first collection of Christina Rossetti's poems that included "Goblin Market" was illustrated by Dante Gabriel Rossetti, and shows the two sisters nestling their "golden head by golden head" together. Serena Trowbridge suggests "Dante Gabriel Rossetti's illustrations play down the grotesquerie of the poem, producing a bland fairy-tale scene which normalises the content of his sister's poem, portraying the goblins as small furry creatures rather than as a genuine threat to their safety."[34] This further establishes Christina's poem as being at least in part an admonishment of her brother's objectification of women through hair. In "The World," another poem from the same collection as "Goblin Market," Christina uses a very similar depiction of hair to many of her brother's:

> By day she wooes me, soft, exceeding fair;
> But all night as the moon so changeth she;
> Loathsome and foul with hideous leprosy
> And subtle serpents gliding in her hair.[35]

The "subtle serpents" in the woman's tresses indicate the influence of the mythic Medusa in the representation of hair, the similarity of this to Dante Gabriel Rossetti's "Lady Lilith" and its accompanying poems' Medusan hair, indicating a potential filial intertextuality. Anne De Long dissects the Medusa myth in a way reminiscent of the Rossettis's hair-based discourse:

> These Medusan features dramatise and heighten inspirational anxieties about evanescence and passivity, for when one's muse is Medusa, one must look quickly or risk paralysis. Self-possession, or the traditional Romantic tendency to "other" the muse, forbids braving the Medusa's stare, preferring to decapitate and objectify or fetishise her, freezing or killing her into art.[36]

In both Rossettis's poetry, we are presented with this type of Medusan muse, who possesses via her inspiration and is othered in the objective fetishization of hair. The wand-like Lizzie and Laura and their magic golden tresses, Dante Gabriel's obsession with the magic of Lilith's hair, as well as his devoutness to many of his sitters', relate to De Long's notions of Medusan qualities—"flashing eyes and floating hair"—that can other the muse through freezing them as artistic object. It was in this dichotomy that the Rossettis discovered an ideal means of expressing their differing ideals on the treatment of women as art; Christina took issue with the commodification of women as an artistic object, and the objectification of hair; Dante Gabriel, on the other hand, found Medusa-based imagery provided him with a way of portraying the obsession he had with hair, and the possession of his muses upon him.

THE RELICS OF HAIR IN THE NEO-VICTORIAN

The depiction of themes such as otherness, possession, and the supernatural through hair-based imagery has its afterlife in neo-Victorian literature where it remains an important metonymic and metaphoric device within modern imaginings of the Victorian period. Here ideas of spirituality and the supernatural are transmuted into much more modern ideas of possession, desire, and sexuality. A.S. Byatt's *Possession* and Sarah Waters's *Affinity* both deal with what Silvana Coella calls "the quest for 'possession' of the material and symbolic traces of the past";[37] hair becomes important in this regard not only as a signifier of its owner but as a symbol of intergenerational desire and obsession. Mark Llewellyn suggests that "what we see(k) in this version of neo-Victorian fiction is satisfaction for our interest in the Victorians and their hidden sexuality."[38] The acknowledgments to the folkloric and supernatural otherness of desire in the Rossettis's poetry and other nineteenth-century examples of hair evolve into a more direct commentary on the possession of sexuality in neo-Victorian texts, yet one that still engages with the symbolic value of mythic roots and possessed tresses.

The pervasive interest in hair relics in the twentieth and twenty-first centuries solidified the intergenerational and intertextual presence of hair in neo-Victorian literature and symbology. Materially, hair provides us with a physical link to literary figures from the past. Museums and libraries around the world have collected locks of hair from authors such as Mary Shelley, Elizabeth Barrett Browning, Charlotte Brontë, Edgar Allan Poe, and Percy Shelley. Koudounaris states that by the nineteenth century, "the idea of having a relic—this personal keepsake—with quasi-magical power had spilled over into the secular world, with the desire to just keep a piece of the person around, as a touching reminder, devoid of the sacred connotations of what a relic originally was."[39] Within its materiality is an indicator of the body and by extension the social associations of that individual. Hair represents individual identity as well as inheritance; alongside the ongoing supernatural influence and use of hair in neo-Victorian literature, we may also observe a strengthening value of the physical materiality of hair. This is potentially due to the improved understanding of the genetic makeup of hair, and how it shares DNA and aspects of its physical presence with past ancestors.

A.S. Byatt's *Possession* contains an intriguing hair-based intertextuality woven through the novel, which replicates the Rossettis's relationship with, and symbolic use of, hair. Critics have suggested that Byatt found a "model for Christabel LaMotte in the poet Christina Rossetti,"[40] further evidenced by the fact Byatt wrote of how her "mind has been full since childhood of the rhythms of Tennyson and Browning, Rossetti and Keats."[41] As well as these textual resonances, there is also an acknowledgment of spiritual and supernatural practices in Byatt's text which further solidify the mirroring of Rossetti in LaMotte. Byatt makes direct reference to this similarity when she writes of Roland Michell's attempts to divine who Randolph Henry Ash's mystery love letter is addressed to: "He had no idea who she might be. Christina Rossetti? He thought not. He was not sure that Miss Rossetti would have approved of Ash's theology, or of his sexual psychology."[42] In this supposition, we may assume the inference of LaMotte as a Rossetti surrogate—particularly because LaMotte is later detailed to have a similarly conservative attitude to that of Rossetti.

In Byatt's textual recreations of Victorian poetry, penned under the fictitious LaMotte and Ash, we may detect the intertextual resonance of the Medusa/Rapunzel dynamic of the Rossettis's work. In one of the first LaMotte poems that the text presents us with, Byatt engages directly with this dichotomy:

He hears the foul Old One
Call quavering there
Rapunzel Rapunzel
Let down your hair
Filaments Glosses
Run trembling down
Gold torrent loosed
From a gold Crown. (p. 35, lines 9–16)

There is a clear lexical similarity in Byatt/LaMotte's use of the image of the golden crown to Rossetti's depiction of Lizzie and Laura in "Goblin Market." Alongside this, we may also interpret De Long's notion of how Medusan features raise "anxieties about evanescence and passivity."[43] When representations of hair sway from the Medusa-figure to Rapunzel, or when the Medusa figure becomes objectified, this results in the passivity that may be read through the "quavering" and "trembling" of the Rapunzel surrogate.

UNRAVELING "OTHERED" HAIR

Another piece of the fictional LaMotte's writing features a similar depiction of hair. In LaMotte's "The Threshold"—a title that carries significantly liminal connotations—Byatt again describes hair in a Rossetti-esque manner: "First came the gold lady, stepping proudly, and on her head a queenly crown of gold, a filigree turret of lambent sunny gleams and glistering wires above, crisping gold curls as heavy with riches as the golden fleece itself."[44] This extract presents hair as having a similarly transactionary value to the sisters' in "Goblin Market"—the "crisping gold curls [...] heavy with riches" suggesting both objectification and commodification of hair. Potential connotations drawn from the word "turret" also suggest the passivity and confinement of the folkloric Rapunzel. The mythic suggestions are not limited to this image however; Byatt also references the "Golden Fleece," a further indication of the influence of Greek myth and legend on nineteenth-century poetry and, by extension, the neo-Victorian.

Randolph Henry Ash, LaMotte's secret lover, also textually discusses hair in his work, where it eventually becomes representative of their hidden affair. In a short story entitled "The Glass Coffin," Byatt/Ash creates a quasi-supernatural, and highly folkloric, image of a woman lying in the coffin: "So under the surface of the thick glass lay a mass of long gold threads, filling in the whole cavity of the box with their turns and tumbles, so that at first the little tailor thought he had come upon a box full of spun gold, to make cloth of gold."[45] Eerily reminiscent of the accounts of Dante Gabriel Rossetti's exhumation of Elizabeth Siddal, Byatt uses the distinctly Victorian notion of hair as a transactionary object of exchange in a way that emphasizes the necessary passivity of the muse. The woman in the coffin is seen mainly for her hair; the golden nature and implied wealth of which swallows up her identity through objectification. There is also a reflection on the relationship between muse and artist in this extract, as the first thought the tailor has upon seeing the masses of golden tresses in the coffin is that it may have been a "box full of spun gold, to make cloth of gold." The tailor, or the artist, immediately envisions the woman in the glass box—which itself carries connotations of visibility, voyeurism, and passivity—as a material, as something from which to draw artistic creativity, thus creating a commodity and objectifying the muse. This parallels Roland's feelings for Maud, Ash's feelings for LaMotte, and Dante Gabriel Rossetti's for his various golden-haired sitters. Perhaps it is this that makes hair such a compelling device for presenting the obsession and possession of the artistic muse; hair, particularly in the nineteenth century, was both an indicator of individual subjectivity and a material object that could be fashioned into artistic objects. Byatt acknowledges this idea herself in a conversation between Roland, Maud, and the shopkeeper of a Whitby Jet shop:

This is pretty. Jet pearls and silk.

Oh, not *silk*, sir. That's hair. That's another form of mourning brooch, with the hair. Look, these ones have "IN MEMORIAM" round the frame. They

cut it off at the death-bed. You could say they kept it alive.
Roland peered through the glass at the interwoven strands of fine pale hair.

> They made all sorts of it, very ingenious. Look—here's a plaited watch chain out of someone's long locks. And a bracelet with a pretty heart-shaped clasp, ever such delicate work, in dark hair.[46]

Semantically, hair may be read as a material that bridges the phenomenological divide between muse, or inspiration, artist, and art. This notion helps to exemplify the different types of obsession and possession at work in the text. The shopkeeper describes using hair in mourning brooches as a means of keeping the individual alive. This process occurs in the creation of art, as the sitter, inspiration, muse, or influence is in some way kept alive by the process of turning influence into art. Hair physicalizes this idea, and exposes the way in which ownership can be thought of in regard to artistic creation. Byatt's representation of her antagonistic literary critic, Mortimer Cropper, also engages with this idea in depictions of his own research. Byatt describes his personalized slippers as he covertly researches letters in another academic's bathroom:

> His slippers, mole-black velvet, were embroidered in gold thread with a female head surrounded by shooting rays or shaken hair. These had been made in London, to his specification. The figure was sculpted on the portico of the oldest part of Robert Dale Owen University, the Harmonia Museum, named after the ancient Alexandrian academy, that "bird-coop of the muses." She represented Mnemosyne, Mother of the Muses, though few now recognised her without prompting, and she was most often taken, by those with a smattering of education, as the Medusa.[47]

The misappropriation of Mnemosyne for Medusa centers largely on hair, or what emanates from the head. This brings to mind mental creativity and influence, as well as highlighting the different levels of *possession* of both muse and artist in the figures of Mnemosyne, mother of muses, and Medusa, the restrictor of the artistic gaze. This comparison and confusion is made yet more fluid when acknowledging Dante Gabriel Rossetti's painting of Mnemosyne which features Jane Morris as his muse, and the distinctive golden hair that characterized his depictions of women in his art (Figure 1.1).

The layered references to mythical and folkloric figures who are partly defined by their hair continue in LaMotte's poem "The Fairy Melusine." Melusine, a European folkloric figure, is described, again, in reference to her golden hair:

> Her living hair was brighter than chill gold
> With shoots of brightness running down its mass
> And straying out to lighten the dun air
> Like phosphorescent sparks of a pale sea,
> And while she sang, she combed it with a comb
> Wrought curiously of gold and ebony,
> Seeming to plait each celandine-bright tress.

Melusine is presented similarly to Mnemosyne, in both the phonetic similarity of their names and the representations of their golden hair. There are connotations of inspiration in the "phosphorescent sparks" of hair, the figure of the muse in the combing of the hair—a very Dante Gabriel Rossetti-like image—and a combination of Rapunzel and Medusa-based imagery in LaMotte's poem. These connotations are further deepened by Roland and Maud's interpretation of this myth, as they make another link to a different

FIGURE 1.1: Dante Gabriel Rossetti (1828–1882), *Mnemosyne*, 1881. Oil on canvas, 126.4 cm × 61 cm. Delaware Art Museum, Samuel and Mary R. Bancroft Memorial, 1935.

mythical woman, related muses, hair, and the spiritual: Lilith. Maud suggests that the quasi-biblical mythology of Lilith makes her an "avatar of Melusina."[48] The representation of these similar folkloric women—Lilith, Medusa, Melusina, and Mnemosyne—suggests the supernatural and uncanny sense of possession that the novel, and indeed many Victorian depictions of hair, functions by. The concept of the muse as something that liberates artistically yet captivates entirely finds semantic resonance in the materiality and "thingness" of hair.

The intergenerational *possession*, which gives Byatt's novel its title, revolves around hair. Maud, who is eventually proven to be a descendant of Ash and LaMotte, shares the same gold hair, which entrances Roland as much as LaMotte's did to Ash. We may witness this in the overtly sexual depiction of Maud unfastening her pinned-up hair in front of Roland for the first time:

> She began slowly to undo, with unweaving fingers, the long, thick braids. Roland watched, intently. There was a final moment when six thick strands, twice three, lay still and formed over her shoulders. And then she put down her head and shook it from side to side, and the heavy hair flew up, and the air got into it. Her long neck bowed, she shook her head faster and faster, and Roland saw the light rush towards it and glimmer on it, the whirling mass, and Maud inside it saw a moving sea of gold lines, waving, and closed her eyes and saw scarlet blood.[49]

Roland watches with the candor of a voyeur as Maud unweaves her hair. The methodical, in-depth description of such a simple act makes the unraveling appear as if in slow motion; and the minutiae of description—such as the division of strands as they fall, and the glimmer of light upon the golden tresses—suggest a near fetishization of hair. There is something oddly hypnotic in Byatt's depiction of this scene, as Roland watches "intently" as the "thick strands" of hair separate and multiply. The fetishistic experience depicted in Roland's obsession over Maud's hair is an example of the literary echoes of prior mythic obsession with hair in the works of fictional Randolph Henry Ash and the very real Dante Gabriel Rossetti.

THE SEDUCTIVE SPIRIT

Similar themes of ownership and possession, which often reach uncanny levels due to an association with spiritualism and the supernatural, may also be found in Sarah Waters's neo-Victorian novel *Affinity*. Hair again takes a prominent role as a symbol of control and subjectivity, and is closely associated with the practices of nineteenth-century spiritualists. Hair is vital in the portrayal of the affinity between Margaret and Selina, and becomes part of the mechanisms of passivity and control that occur in their relationship.

The novel details how upon entrance to Millbank Prison each prisoner must have their hair shorn, something corroborated in reality by the 1825 Rules and Regulations Handbook for the prison: "The Prisoner shall have his or her hair cut short, and shall be bathed or washed and cleansed, as the Surgeon will direct (if a Female, in the presence of Females only)."[50] Hair is used as a surrogate for the body, and the ownership of the hair by the prison reflects the possession of the prisoners' bodies. In the shearing of the women on their entrance to the prison, presumably due in part to the health issues of having potentially lice-filled heads in close proximity, there is also a clear sense of the penal subservience that they are subjected to. The shearing of hair imbues a sense of authority on behalf of the institution and of passivity from the individual; the cutting of hair acting synecdochically for the incarceration of their body. Unlike the actual Millbank, however, Waters's version does not permit sending locks of hair away as the real prison did.[51] This makes the exchange of locks within this novel particularly scandalous, and overtly symbolic due to the taboo surrounding it. The act of exchanging hair carries connotations of authority and ownership, as well as potential supernatural connotations of hair-based magic and ritual.

Hair's associations with the sexual and spiritual may be witnessed in the scene where Margaret secretly explores Selina's box of possessions that were taken upon her entry to prison. When she sees Selina's lock of hair in the box, Margaret describes how it "coiled in its shadows like a slumbering serpent."[52] The latent sexuality of this image helps to support the masculine position of ownership through its phallocentrism. Subsequent images of Selina's woven locks reinforce the serpent-like qualities of the rope of hair, again reminiscent of the Medusa figure:

> *Her hair.* Her hair, bound tight and plaited into one thick rope, and fastened, where it had been cut from her, with coarse prison twine. I put my fingers to it. It felt heavy, and dry—as snakes are, I believe, for all their glossiness, said to feel dry to the touch. Where the light caught it it gleamed a dull gold; but the gold was shot through with other colours—with some that were silver, some that were almost green.[53]

Selina's golden hair possesses Margaret as much as Lizzie's does to the Goblin Men, or as the intertextual and intergenerational presence of hair in *Possession* does to its characters. The depiction of hair in this extract suggests a sense of awe on Margaret's behalf when she is confronted by the preserved hair; she does not hold it, instead she "puts her fingers to it," a gesture of reverie and intimacy. Fastened with "coarse prison twine," the lock of hair symbolizes both the bond between the two women and the insurmountable divide created between them by Millbank. The hair is forbidden, yet again metonymically suggests the body and identity of Selina Dawes. It provides Margaret with a symbolic and physical link to the alleged spirit medium, its incarceration within the prison suggestive of the taboo of the interclass, same-sex relationship that the two women appear to be interested in. When threatened with the possibility of the other matrons in Millbank discovering her reveries over Selina's lock of hair, Margaret describes how "The plait of hair might really have been a snake, then: I flung it from me as if it had suddenly woken and shown me its fangs."[54] The hair, similarly to how it does in its Victorian textual predecessors and in Byatt's *Possession*, acts as an avatar of the individual. Through its materiality, it becomes an icon of the bond between the two women and how such a bond would have been socially and culturally difficult.

The magic, transcendental, nature of hair in this text is further exemplified in the rope of hair's narrative journey. Margaret is sent Selina's woven tresses, by means she at first deems to be supernatural, and her reaction furthers the understanding of the plaited hair as symbolizing the interweaving of their desires. At first believing the rope of hair to be a disembodied head on her pillow, Margaret soon realizes:

> It was not a head. It was a curling rope of yellow hair, as thick as my two fists. It was the hair that I had tried to steal from Millbank Prison—it was Selina's hair. She had sent it to me, from her dark place, across the city, across the night. I put my face to it. It smelt of sulphur.[55]

The rope of hair functions as proof to Margaret, evidence both of Selina's dedication to her and of her supernatural powers. Margaret later describes how she has "taken her rope of hair, and combed it, and plaited it; and this I keep about me and sometimes kiss."[56] The hair's metonymic representation of Margaret's desire for Selina is obvious here. It is an avatar of her, and through its physical materiality, an indicator of the bond between the two women. Margaret tells Selina that her "spirit does not love [hers] it is *entwined* with it."[57] Like the plaited hair, the two women's souls are similarly interwoven. The lock of hair's physical materiality provides an ideal vehicle for the portrayal of their intimate emotional links.

When it is revealed to Margaret that she has been duped by Selina and Mrs. Vigers, she dwells on the implicit trust involved in allowing another person to possess someone else's hair. "She had sent me her collar," Margaret states, "She had sent me *her hair*. We were joined in the spirit and joined in the flesh—I was her own affinity. We had been cut, two halves together, from a single piece of shining matter."[58] The imagery of the plaited rope of hair resonates in the imagery of Margaret's profession of unity with Selina; the importance of sending her hair is marked with disbelief by Margaret, and the interweaving of their souls finds an ideal image in the semantically similar plaited tresses.

CONCLUSION: ONGOING MYTHIC AND SPIRITUAL NATURE OF HAIR

Unconventional hair in the Age of Empire repeatedly acts as a sign of deviancy in its portrayal of "othered" entities, in both the criminal and the supernatural sense. In art and literature this relates closely to the concept of the muse and the associated possession and obsession. The artist must take parts of their muse, or inspiration, and convert them into a form of art; these inspirations can consume and obsess, as they did for Dante Gabriel Rossetti. The processes of making hair relics physicalize this, as the creator takes a part of the subject and refashions it into an artistic object. This, along with the supernatural and spiritual connotations of hair, contribute to the othering of the subject, sitter, or muse, which may be witnessed in the presence of hair in séances, the Rossettis's hair-based conflicts, and in the afterlives of hair in neo-Victorian representations of nineteenth-century otherness.

CHAPTER TWO

Self and Society: Hair Consciousness in the Age of Empire

JONATHON SHEARS

INTRODUCTION: NINETEENTH-CENTURY HAIR CONSCIOUSNESS

Let us begin with two images, seemingly diametrically opposed, of nineteenth-century womanhood which, taken together, make hair central to navigating the relationship between self and society.

Isabella; Or, the Pot of Basil (1820) is a Gothic narrative poem by Keats, adapted from Boccaccio's *Decameron*, in which the titular figure disinters the corpse of her murdered lover, Lorenzo, and buries his head in a pot containing a basil plant which she tends obsessively while pining away for her lost love. Keats gives full macabre rein to his imagination in reworking the exhumation of Lorenzo's body and the decapitation, in which a series of disconcertingly intimate actions converge on the image of Isabella's long, dark hair:

> Soon she turn'd up a soiled glove, whereon
> Her silk had play'd in purple phantasies,
> She kiss'd it with a lip more chill than stone,
> And put it in her bosom, where it dries
> And freezes utterly unto the bone
> Those dainties made to still an infant's cries:
> Then 'gan she work again; nor stay'd her care,
> But to throw back at times her veiling hair. (stanza 47)[1]

Keats appalls through his use of contrast: glove and soil; the touch of glove on once tender lip; a bosom meant to nurture children rather than function as shrine to a relic of murder and dismemberment. But arguably it is Isabella's hair that amplifies the horror to its greatest degree, demonstrating, as it falls about the face and into the dirt, a young woman's utter absorption in her grisly task. If the lip and bosom are chilled frozen—chiming with the reader's feelings—the hair moves freely and uncontrollably. The mundane action of semi-consciously sweeping it back from her face—"at times" or periodically—encapsulates the combination of concentration and mental abstraction that

Keats aims to embody. At roughly the same period Mary Shelley has Victor Frankenstein explain that his inability to make a second monster was due to the fact "I went to it in cold blood, and my heart often sickened at the work of my hands."[2] Here, Isabella's brushing away the veil of hair that obscures her vision seems to demonstrate the opposite, as her heart does not register any such disgust. It may well be an example of a "boundary ambiguity," as Galia Ofek phrases it, "between the living and the dead, the human and the inhuman," but most of all it demonstrates the loss of the mind's capacity to edit behavior or comprehend right and wrong.[3] Hair focalizes the madwoman's loss of agency, despite her apparently exaggerated exertion of it; and if the image troubles, then this is one of the reasons why.

The second image of female hair also involves its disarrangement and occurs at the opening of *David Copperfield* (1849–1850) when David's recently widowed, heavily pregnant mother is confronted by Betsey Trotwood:

> "Take off your cap, child," said Miss Betsey, "and let me see you."
>
> My mother was too much afraid of her to refuse compliance with this odd request, if she had any disposition to do so. Therefore she did as she was told, and did it with such nervous hands that her hair (which was luxuriant and beautiful) fell about her face.
>
> "Why, bless my heart!" exclaimed Miss Betsey. "You are a very Baby!"
>
> My mother was, no doubt, unusually youthful in appearance even for her years; she hung her head, as if it were her fault, poor thing, and said, sobbing, that indeed she was afraid she was but a childish widow, and would be but a childish mother if she lived. In a short pause which ensued, she had a fancy that she felt Miss Betsey touch her hair, and that with no ungentle hand; but, looking at her, in her timid hope, she found that lady sitting with the skirt of her dress tucked up, her hands folded on one knee, and her feet upon the fender, frowning at the fire.[4]

It was proper, as Susan P. Casteras tells us, for young Victorian women to wear their hair up or concealed under a bonnet or cap.[5] Any contrary behavior, such as that of the maid Sarah in *Shirley* (1849) who "resolutely refused to imprison in linen or muslin the plentiful tresses of her yellow hair," usually led to accusations of pertness and impropriety.[6] This scene of unveiling allows Betsey to "read" Clara Copperfield shorn of these social proprieties, the luxuriance of her hair signaled not so much by color or sheen as by the way it falls about her face, indicating her youthful vulnerability, the "emblem of her femininity."[7] The disarrangement of Clara's hair is code for her state of mind—made more legible by the fumbling of hands which on this occasion are as nervous as the heart—but unlike Keats's Isabella it is a sign of keen self-consciousness or shame (which seems to be for some combination of falling pregnant, widowhood, and the exposure of the hair itself). Sobbing is a form of breakdown, but an appropriate one in this case, because, unlike that of Isabella, it upholds the semiotics of power on which the relationship of the two women, and the social codes of which they are mindful, depends. Clara Copperfield shows herself to be acutely hair-conscious. So much so that she anticipates the reassuring touch of Betsey's hand on her hair—once again the relationship between hair and the hands that could impress the will upon it is central to establishing its social function—which would indicate consolation and intimacy, but which doesn't actually come. Isabella's hair, in contrast, reveals her complete mental collapse.

It would be reasonable to argue that in the difference between these two characters' actions inheres a larger distinction in capillary symbolism in nineteenth-century conceptualizations of womanhood of the sort that Ofek separates into examples of the recurring Medusa and Rapunzel figures (the former indicative of male fears of castration by powerful women and the latter, at least in folklore, of the weakness of women requiring protection).[8] Indeed, Holman Hunt's famous painting of Isabella, with black hair flowing over the golden pot that she cradles protectively in her arms, is one of Ofek's archetypal Medusa images.[9]

But it is not purely my concern in this chapter to establish the content of such binary divisions—that is, to categorize male or female characters through their hair—even while we can see this occurring in all manner of texts—including the literary, advertising, medical, and religious—in the nineteenth century, and even while these are useful starting points.[10] What I really want to explore in what follows is the ways in which hair begins to "take on" social and cultural meanings. In other words, this chapter focuses on how hair comes to bear meaning in examples of hair consciousness, and how these partake in nineteenth-century, but particularly Victorian, formations and expressions of the self. This will involve attending to individual acts of self-fashioning, but also to the failures to fashion an identity through the hair, its tendency to prove intractable or resist the individual and collective will, from whence, the evidence suggests, much of the anxiety that characterizes hair consciousness emerges.

CONTRADICTORY CLAIMS: TECHNOLOGY AND ADVERTISING

To reiterate, one of these women is hair-conscious—indicating attention to the interrelationship between self and a larger social order—while the other is not. That fact is revealed as much by the actions of Isabella and Clara in relation to their hair and its unanticipated movement as by the facticity of the hair itself. From where did hair consciousness derive and where might we find examples in nineteenth-century literature and culture?

There is no doubt that nineteenth-century hair needed continual attention and that readers were frequently reminded of that fact in all sorts of ways. The demise of the fashion for the elaborate wigs worn in the eighteenth century meant that hair was much more publicly visible than it had been for some time. Writing in 1814, Alexander Rowland, purveyor of the male grooming product Rowland's Macassar Oil (a sticky preparation derived from palm oil used to slick back the hair), took advantage of hair's increased exposure by giving advice for a good grooming regimen to both men and women. Exercise, he alleged, was notorious for drying the hair and destroying its natural elasticity: "to prevent its taking effect on the Hair, first rub the head dry with a cloth, then apply the Macassar Oil to the roots of the Hair, so that the skin on the head may be quite moist, and continue it, after each time of perspiration."[11] Use of the oleaginous Macassar became so widespread that cloth covers called antimacassars were placed on the backs of chairs to prevent staining. Rowland had more advice about hair care: "Ladies whose Hair is long" were advised to "use the Hair-brush frequently, especially if it is inclined to be damp, which is the cause of Dandriff [sic] arising in the Hair."[12] Pomade, or pomatum, and powder had been used to manage unruly hair since the seventeenth century, but were cautioned against by Rowland: "Gentlemen wearing powder, should have the Hair thoroughly combed with a fine tooth-comb every week, in order to remove the powder and pomatum, which, if suffered to remain, make such an impression on the pores, as to cause the head-ach, and also has a tendency to turn the hair grey."[13] Neuralgia—nervous headache—was commonly attributed to the overuse of hair products and the makers of St. Jacobs Oil advertised its ability to conquer recurrent pain.[14]

The range of combs and brushes available for purchase by the mid-Victorian period was extensive, but deciphering their various merits required understanding the latest technological advances. Dr. Scott's Electric Hair Brush (Figure 2.1), for example, was guaranteed to cure neuralgia or bilious headache in five minutes through a complicated electromagnetic procedure.

FIGURE 2.1: Dr. Scott's Electric Hair Brush.

It had the other boons of preventing hair loss, curing dandruff and other "diseases of the scalp," and arresting premature grayness. A good brushing could also "soothe the weary brain." Such advertising frequently deployed the tactic of using testimonials from satisfied customers—Rowland used this technique too—to buttress the claims of science with anecdotal evidence. In the case of the Electric Brush, a Miss A.J.A. Stanley writes of suffering such pain from neuralgia that she "was blind for upwards of a week," since when she relates "I have been using [Dr. Scott's Electric Brush] constantly, and have been free from headache," while E.P. Guest, a chemist of Brentwood, recounts "one of my customers, whose head was 'as bald as a bladder of lard,' has quite a thick CROWN OF HAIR GROWING from the use of your DR. SCOTT'S BRUSH." Scott attacked his competitors, warning against the use of a brush with wires instead of bristles, as the latter tended to promote baldness. If the large, full wigs of the eighteenth century had largely fallen out of fashion—although antiquated figures such as Solomon Gills, the maker of navigational instruments in *Dombey and Son* (1846–1848), can be found sporting one—male pattern baldness and alopecia could now be rectified by "imperceptible" hair coverings such as those pioneered by Florian Sobocinski of Leicester Square, who specialized in natural waved bandeaux, which claimed to be "perfectly indistinguishable from the Natural Hair."[15] Scalpettes and frizettes were other popular forms of partial wigs.

Late Victorian women were actually encouraged to save their own hair after brushing in a "ceramic, bronze, or crystal container called a hair receiver" to produce their own additions and extensions, although most hairpieces were made from the human and animal—particularly horse—hair, circulating on the open—and black—market.[16] Hair was a commodity as much as the products used to manage it,[17] and two memorable examples from literature of the period demonstrate the economic realities of feeding nineteenth-century hair consciousness. In *Little Women* (1868–1869), Josephine March is compelled to sell her long, dark hair to acquire the money that will allow her mother to travel to Washington, DC, where her father lies gravely ill in a military hospital. Her "chestnut mane" is a sign of a defiant spirit and a healthful independence early in the novel, but also of Jo's developing womanhood (hairstyle was one of the most important factors in distinguishing young men and women from immature boys and girls). Meg's reminder of her responsibilities is noticeably focalized by the hair:

> "Really, girls, you are both to be blamed," said Meg, beginning to lecture in her elder-sisterly fashion. "You are old enough to leave off boyish tricks, and to behave better, Josephine. It didn't matter so much when you were a little girl, but now you are so tall, and turn up your hair, you should remember that you are a young lady."
>
> "I'm not! And if turning up my hair makes me one, I'll wear it in two tails till I'm twenty," cried Jo, pulling off her net, and shaking down a chestnut mane.[18]

Jo's subsequent shearing is an act of self-assertion but also a recognition of her social and moral standing: "I felt wicked, at being unable to acquire money," she remarks, "and was bound to have some money, if I sold the nose off my face to get it."[19] The family's shock at her haircut suggests a type of symbolic violation—a rape of the lock perhaps—but one that was self-authorized by the consciousness of impoverishment: "'Didn't you feel dreadfully when the first cut came?' asked Meg, with a shiver." Jo hits out at her social status through her hair. But the lost locks also visit a figurative death on the family (inadvertently reinforcing the instability of Mr. March's condition): "Mrs. March folded the wavy chestnut lock," remarks the narrator, "and laid it away with a short grey one in her desk," a common nineteenth-century custom of memorialization.[20] In both senses the sudden severance of Jo's tresses makes apparent to other members of the March family their state of desperation: hair is used by Alcott as a metonym for the moral concomitants that seem to undeservedly attend financial degradation.

Florence Dombey's encounter with a hair dealer underlines a different type of social consciousness: the abrupt realization of the porousness of social boundaries in Victorian London. Florence's luxuriant hair is evidently in no need of the likes of Edwards's "Harlene" or William Lasson's "Hair Elixir"[21]—whose advertising included images of the toilettes of women with such preposterously luxuriant, dark manes, often cascading to the floor, that they made a mockery of the notion that the hair of these women could ever be "worn up," controlled by caps, or by the decorative combs favored by polite society—but it marks her out as vulnerable. Not unlike the scene of Clara Copperfield's unveiling, in this case Florence is kidnapped by the rag dealer, Good Mrs. Brown, and forced to remove her clothes, replacing them with a set of grimy substitutes. In the action of pinning on a tattered bonnet, her tresses spill out, to the excitement of the rag woman who immediately scents a more valuable prize than the one she's already acquired:

> In hurriedly putting on the bonnet, if that may be called a bonnet which was more like a pad to carry loads on, she caught it in her hair which grew luxuriantly, and could not immediately disentangle it. Good Mrs Brown whipped out a large pair of scissors, and fell into an unaccountable state of excitement.
>
> "Why couldn't you let me be!" said Mrs Brown, "when I was contented? You little fool!"
>
> "I beg your pardon. I don't know what I have done," panted Florence. "I couldn't help it."
>
> "Couldn't help it!" cried Mrs Brown. "How do you expect I can help it? Why, Lord!" said the old woman, ruffling her curls with a furious pleasure, "anybody but me would have had 'em off, first of all." Florence was so relieved to find that it was only her hair and not her head which Mrs Brown coveted, that she offered no resistance or entreaty, and merely raised her mild eyes towards the face of that good soul.[22]

Unlike Alcott, Dickens allows Florence to avoid the ignominy of having her hair cut off, but the threat to which her hair exposes her is unmistakably encapsulated by the unknown woman, menacingly brandishing her scissors. For Ofek, "Dickens chose to play the part of the valiant knight [...] and rescued Florence before she lost her hair and her freedom,"[23] although the catalyst for Mrs. Brown's change of heart is the sympathy of motherhood as Florence's hair brings to mind her own lost daughter, stopping her in her tracks.

The two episodes have different outcomes but are linked by the commodification of the hair, which is an economic concomitant of the kind of nineteenth-century hair consciousness I have begun to set out. Sifting the advice of the advertising, and both the genuine and the pseudo-medical, literature, evidently, however, involved balancing some contradictory claims. These texts are also implicated in discourses, to paraphrase the argument of Judith Butler, that compel individuals to conform to a historical idea of the category of man or woman (although that is actually what ensures, as much as jeopardizes, the safety of Florence Dombey).[24] These categories, as we have seen in the advertising of the likes of Lasson, could involve stretching signification to extremes. Edwards's advertisement for "Harlene" for the hair is another good example, wherein a young mother is depicted brushing out her floor-length hair while her daughter looks on in rapt admiration, clearly codifying well-kept hair as the sign of good motherhood (Figure 2.2).

"Mamma, shall I have beautiful long hair like you when I grow up?"
"Certainly, my dear, if you use **'Edward's Harlene'**."

FIGURE 2.2: Edward's Harlene for the Hair.

Living up to such universal ideals was no doubt a problem, and it was a problem that was exacerbated by the Victorian drive to improve upon nature, or rather to achieve the results that nature ought to have supplied, through the requisition of unnatural means. The contradictory claims—wash hair regularly but not too often, apply product but be careful not to overdo it, brush regularly but only with the right brush—clearly led to casualties, a phenomenon which is never more evident than in Thackeray's satirical novel *Vanity Fair* (1847–1848) where hair contributes more than its fair share to the *vanitas vanitatum* motif.

VANITY AND FASHION VICTIMS

For Thackeray, hair is firstly a marker of the transience of fashion, as his narrator explains in accommodating readers who may have been puzzled by references to the styles of the Napoleonic era: "At the time whereof we are writing, [...] the Great George was on the throne and ladies wore *gigots* and large combs like tortoise-shell shovels in their hair, instead of the simple sleeves and lovely wreaths which are actually in fashion."[25] That simplicity, in Thackeray's world of irony, is no guarantor, however, of genuineness or indeed loveliness, as is made apparent in the cases of the aging socialites, Lord and Lady Bareacres (the name implying the demise of the landed gentry but also perhaps their follicle shortfall?), and the equally mature Lieutenant-General Tufto. In the case of the former we find Thackeray poking fun not at age per se but at the futility, and vanity, of attempting to hold back the years through the use of hair dye: "Lady Bareacres' hair, which was then dark, was now a beautiful golden auburn, whereas Lord Bareacres' whiskers, formerly red, were at present of a rich black with purple and green reflections in the light."[26] Read in this way, Lord and Lady are alike victims of hair consciousness and the fine line between fashioning a "natural" and unnatural look. The hazards of the overapplication of dye, or the use of a homemade preparation, often led to discoloration, and the color purple was a particular danger for those who wanted to darken their gray. In 1817, Atkinson's vegetable dye was sold with the guarantee that it would successfully color gray, giving "so permanent a colour, that neither Washing, Perspiration, nor any other cause, can possibly remove it." However, in 1857 the satirical journal *Punch* ran an article titled "The Fool's Head of Hair," in which they extracted from the "advertising columns [...] the following rather comic appeal to the vanity of simpletons":

> NO MORE GREEN. RED, OR PURPLE-DYED HAIR.—NOTICE—
> Any Lady or Gentleman who has been so unfortunate as to have their hair dyed any of the above-named colours now common, by the use of spurious imitations of ——'s TYRIAN LIQUID HAIR DYE, can have restored, free of charge, to a native brown or black to defy detection, by applying at his Subscription Hair-Cutting and Hair-Dyeing Rooms, —— — Hair and whiskers dyed on the most reasonable terms by an annual subscription. Price, per case, 5s. 6d., 8s., 12s., and 1 guinea.[27]

Punch mocked: "If [the proprietor] had known with what colour Tyrian is synonymous, he would have called a dye intended to transmute that colour Anti-Tyrian."[28] Tyrian was associated with the color purple. Lady Bareacres's transition to auburn is less obviously comic than her husband's to purple and green, though even here hair implies the pretensions of the aging *beau monde*, bringing to mind Twain's comment in *A Connecticut Yankee in King Arthur's Court* (1889): "When red-headed people are above a certain social grade, their hair is auburn."[29]

In the case of Tufto, Thackeray really goes to town. A wig, which has "nothing to do with our story," causing the narrator to digress from his plot, becomes a quintessential example of the vanity of age (as opposed to the vanity of youth characterized by George Osborne, Jos Sedley, and the other bewhiskered crew of would-be dandies):

> Those who know the present Lieutenant-General Sir George Tufto, K.C.B., and have seen him, as they may on most days in the season, padded and in stays, strutting down Pall Mall with a rickety swagger on his high-heeled lacquered boots, leering under the bonnets of passers-by, or riding a showy chestnut, and ogling broughams in the

Parks—those who know the present Sir George Tufto would hardly recognise the daring Peninsular and Waterloo officer. He has thick curling brown hair and black eyebrows now, and his whiskers are of the deepest purple. He was light-haired and bald in 1815, and stouter in the person and in the limbs, which especially have shrunk very much of late. When he was about seventy years of age (he is now nearly eighty), his hair, which was very scarce and quite white, suddenly grew thick, and brown, and curly, and his whiskers and eyebrows took their present colour. Ill-natured people say that his chest is all wool, and that his hair, because it never grows, is a wig. Tom Tufto, with whose father he quarrelled ever so many years ago, declares that Mademoiselle de Jaisey, of the French theatre, pulled his grandpapa's hair off in the green-room; but Tom is notoriously spiteful and jealous; and the General's wig has nothing to do with our story.[30]

Tufto is the image of pomposity with his boots, leer, and strut, but his head really sets him apart as a man who has failed to fashion an acceptable identity through his hair. Indeed, his actions suggest he is a victim of the twin foes of acute hair consciousness and the intransigence of nature. Tufto's appearance bespeaks the inability to edit the self through the hair and the anxieties of being mocked accordingly. Damned if he does and damned if he doesn't, Tufto is a martyr of the grammar of hair dyes and grooming products, which make him the butt of hearsay and gossip—"Ill-natured people say that his chest is all wool, and that his hair, because it never grows is a wig"—a figure to be scorned, but also strangely pitied for his efforts. Tufto—his name also a joke on his thinning follicles—is the criniculturist's jargon come menacingly and uncannily to life, a grotesque dupe parading around the fashionable routes of Hyde Park. It doesn't take much to imagine him as one of Scott or Lasson's complacently "satisfied" customers, and his character should be read in dialogue with the claims of those advertisers. He makes boundaries ambiguous—particularly those between the animate and inanimate—just as obviously as the disturbed Isabella. The narrator is quite happy to be the medium for further gossip, repeating with *faux* regret Tom Tufto's speculation about how his grandfather came to lose his hair.

Tufto and the Bareacres are not alone in Victorian fiction. We could add Mrs. Merdle from *Little Dorrit* (1855–1857)—"The lady was not young and fresh from the hand of Nature: but was young and fresh from the hand of her maid"—whose hair, unnaturally long and luxuriant for her time of life, is forbiddingly "dark" and "unfeeling," to those for whom hair consciousness has exposed their vanity.[31] The opposite is also true of course, and many characters in Dickens are marked out for being financially excluded from such misadventures. In *David Copperfield*, the penury of the schoolmasters in Murdstone's Salem House is exposed by their inability to afford hair oil, hairpieces, and wax for the mustache: "He was a gaunt, sallow young man, with hollow cheeks, and a chin almost as black as Mr. Murdstone's; but there the likeness ended, for his whiskers were shaved off, and his hair, instead of being glossy, was rusty and dry."[32] It is important to recognize that the decision of the Master to shave off his mustache is not due to fashion or for the sake of his health, but because he cannot afford to keep it—just as he cannot afford to oil his hair. As John Strachan has explored in detail, the nineteenth-century mustache needed regular waxing by products such as bear grease.[33] In Gaskell's *Cranford* (1851–1853), the absence of such hair products actually becomes a synecdoche of the differences between social groups and the awkwardness experienced in making transitions across social boundaries. While Mrs. Forrester, "the delusive lady," gossips about "Rowland's Kalydor, and the merits of cosmetics and hair oils in general,"[34] the actions of the farmers and laborers of the neighborhood when in civilized company underline their lower status: repeatedly "sleeking" back undressed hair becomes a sign of the consciousness of class just as much as the more spectacular actions of a figure like Jo March:

> By this time the shop was pretty well filled, for it was Cranford market-day, and many of the farmers and country people from the neighbourhood round came in, sleeking down their hair.
> "Come in—come to my sister at once,—Miss Jenkyns, the rector's daughter. Oh, man, man! say it is not true," she cried, as she brought the affrighted carter, sleeking down his hair, into the drawing-room.[35]

The market is straightforwardly a site of culture clash, and so hair consciousness; but in the second example, Gaskell makes a juxtaposition between two types of fear—that of the women of Cranford following the news of the death of Captain Brown and that of the carter at his awareness of his incongruity in the drawing-room. Noticeably it is his hair to which he first attends in the forlorn attempt to blend in.

BLENDING IN AND STANDING OUT: MALE GROOMING

The derogatory attitude to the vanity of male grooming in the Regency is famously evidenced in Austen's *Emma* (1815) when Frank Churchill leaves Highbury on the pretense of getting his hair cut in town, to the disgust of Mr. Knightley. It is an indicator of Churchill's frivolous nature (his real motive is famously to acquire a piano for Jane Fairfax). But as we have already seen, male hair consciousness throughout the nineteenth century was more frequently focused on the face than the head. Facial hair was important as it was the most reliable way of distinguishing between man and boy, as Dickens's young confidence trickster, Fascination Fledgeby, discovers to his disadvantage in *Our Mutual Friend* (1864–1865). Fledgeby's insecurity is wonderfully captured by his self-consciousness surrounding the reluctance of his whiskers to sprout forth: "Fledgeby, as he sat facing Georgiana," avoids eye contact and betrays "the discomposure of his mind in feeling for his whiskers with his spoon, his wine glass, and his bread."[36] His underhand courtship of the vulnerable Georgiana Podsnap—and his role as inexperienced masculine seducer—is manifested by his overattentiveness to the vestigial mustache. When we are reintroduced to Fledgeby in Chapter 16 of Book Two, the effect is even more pronounced as he fantasizes about its growth:

> Fledgeby has devoted the interval to taking an observation of Boots's whiskers, Brewer's whiskers, and Lammle's whiskers, and considering which pattern of whisker he would prefer to produce out of himself by friction, if the Genie of the cheek would only answer to his rubbing.[37]

No amount of the magic promised by the hair trade can assist Fledgeby's self-fashioning it would seem, and his situation is not helped by the flourishing state of the mustache of his coconspirator, Alfred Lammle, which is one of the wildest and most preposterous in all of nineteenth-century fiction, pendulous and ginger, regularly stroked by its owner as a sign of mature consideration: Mr. Lammle frequently "plunged into his whiskers for reflection," Dickens informs us.[38] The rising suspicion between the two men as their plans begin to unravel emerges amusingly in Fledgeby's loss of composure when he launches a personal attack on Lammle's facial hair: "'You have a pair of whiskers, Lammle, which I never liked,' murmured Fledgeby, 'and which money can't produce […] I'll bowl you down. I will, though I have no whiskers,' here he rubbed the places where they were due, 'and no manners, and no conversation!'."[39]

Other male characters of the period find the mustache to be variously a site of personal pride and an awkward reminder of social inadequacy. In *Nicholas Nickleby* (1838–1839), the fortunes of the dandyish milliner, Alfred Muntle, going under the name of Mr. Matalini for business purposes, can be tracked by the state of his mustachios: "he had married on his whiskers; upon which property he had previously subsisted, in a genteel manner, for some years; and which he had recently improved, after patient cultivation by the addition of a moustache, which promised to secure him an easy independence."[40] Dickens leaves us in no doubt that the fate of that mustache makes clear the moral and financial descent of the profligate Matalini, as he is revisited, now divorced and following the collapse of his business, toward the end of the novel, discovered in penury "amidst clothes-baskets and clothes, stripped up to his shirt-sleeves, but wearing still an old patched pair of pantaloons of superlative make, a once brilliant waistcoat, and moustache and whiskers as of yore, but lacking their lustrous dye."[41] The wilting and dull mustache does an economical job of filling in the gaps in Matalini's biography. In Thackeray's *The Newcomes* (1853–1855), the cultivation of a mustache is also the sign of sophistication, and more particularly of Clive's independence through his choice of career as an artist. It indicates his growing distance from his father's wishes. The cavalryman and artist are alike discerned by their facial hair: "he has quitted the law for the Muses, and it would appear that the Nine are never wooed except by gentlemen with mustachios," observes the gregarious Charles Honeyman of the latest fashions.[42] Returning from his apprenticeship as a painter in Rome, Clive enters a barber's shop to have his flowing blond locks removed but "with his mustachios he could not be induced to part; painters and cavalry officers having a right to those decorations. And why should not this young fellow wear smart clothes, and a smart moustache, and look handsome, and take his pleasure, and bask in his sun when it shone?"[43] The association of the mustache with the military was a long one, and indeed the rank of servicemen could be distinguished by the length of mustache worn.

Beards were popularized by soldiers returning from the Crimea in the 1850s, where they had encountered the long ones sported by the Ottomans.[44] And from the mid-1850s until the 1860s *Punch* ran a regular series of cartoons titled either "The Beard Movement" or "The Moustache Movement" (invoking the title of a farce by Barnabas Brough of 1854). In one example a self-conscious, but physically slight, beau walks past two bonneted young women, the legend reading "*Young Snobley (a regular Lady-killer)*. 'HOW THE GALS DO STARE AT ONE'S BEARD! I SUPPOSE THEY THINK I'M A HORFICER JUST COME FROM THE CRIMEAR!'" (Figure 2.3).

In another satirical journal of the mid-century, *The Favorite* (1854), an imagined conversation between "The Razor" and "The Scissors" sees the former predict he will "be left to rust in sheaths, while you and your fraternity will be polished with trimming and making fantastical dirty beards and moustaches."[45] The incursion of French habits—made more visible by the recent presence of foreign visitors to the Great Exhibition in 1851 where their poor hygiene and facial hair were routinely remarked[46]—is invoked as an argument for shaving. The tide was evidently against such protest, however, as witnessed by the extensive arguments advanced in favor of facial hair by Thomas S. Gowing in his series of light lectures collected as *The Philosophy of Beards*, also published

FIGURE 2.3: "The Beard Movement," *Punch*, March 8, 1856.

in 1854. Gowing argued that the beard was a natural, rather than social, artifact; the codes surrounding facial hair were, for Gowing, historically specific, but not as signs of culturally contingent masculinity so much as outward evidence of his universal claims: "Though there are *individual* exceptions, the absence of Beard is usually a sign of physical and moral weakness," he initially proposes, before arguing that the vogue for shaving is not based in scientific facts about hygiene—which are spurious—but due to the "forgetfulness of the true standard of masculine beauty of expression, which is naturally as antipodal as the magnetic north and south poles, to that of female loveliness."[47] It is natural for the male youth to be barefaced, as the features are delicate, but as they coarsen with age and the lines about the mouth become harsher a beard softens the expression and lends luster to the eyes.[48] The beard also has the physical function of protecting the face and neck: barefaced men are more susceptible to colds, moisture, and scrofula in Gowing's lecture.[49] Once again, hair is used to regulate the distinctions between genders and the generations, but also illness and health, in the popular consciousness.

Many ex-servicemen returning from the Crimea found work on the flourishing railways, but, even earlier than this, porters had been advised to wear beards due to working in cold and smoky conditions. In one cartoon from the "Beard and Moustache Movement" sequence of 1853, *Punch* depicts a middle-aged lady and her small daughter at a station being assisted by a bearded railway guard and a group of equally hirsute porters, ringing bells and carrying luggage, whose status is immediately confused due to the abundance of facial hair:

> *Railway Guard.* "Now, ma'am, Is this your luggage?"
> *Old Lady (who concludes she is attacked by Brigands).* "Oh yes! Gentlemen, it's mine. Take it—take all I have; but spare, Oh spare our lives!!"[50]

Thick facial hair was associated with courage and resilience—Gowing likens it to the mane of a lion, which he claims would look much less ferocious without one[51]—as we see in the example of Horace Holly in Rider Haggard's *She* (1886–1887), where his hardiness is signified—with a nod towards Darwin and evolution theory—by his hair which "grew right down on his forehead," and his whiskers which "grew right up to his hair, so that there was uncommonly little of his countenance to be seen."[52] The overall impression is of a "gorilla," but Holly's pronounced "ugliness" has its compensation on the long journey to Africa, where "I had come off much the best, probably owing to the toughness of my dark skin, and to the fact that a good deal of it was covered by hair, for since we had started from England I had allowed my naturally luxuriant beard to grow at its own sweet will."[53] Gowing would have approved.

The "Beard and Moustache Movement" *Punch* cartoon of 1853 demonstrates that in the wrong context—like the carter from *Cranford* in the drawing-room—facial hair led to, and signified, danger. Misreading the signs was easily done, and is mercilessly mocked by Thackeray in the figure of Jos Sedley, the effeminate, corpulent dandy, who self-consciously cultivates whiskers to establish his association with the cavalrymen on the eve of the Battle of Waterloo. Having no official capacity in Brussels, and having been left behind with the women when the men go off to fight, on receiving an inaccurate report that the French are victorious and descending on the city, Jos's panic at being mistaken for an officer leads him to drastic measures that demonstrate the full extent of his cowardice:

> He looked amazed at the pale face in the glass before him, and especially at his mustachios, which had attained a rich growth in the course of near seven weeks, since they had come into the world. They *will* mistake me for a military man, thought he, remembering Isidor's warning as to the massacre with which all the defeated British army was threatened; and staggering back to his bedchamber, he began wildly pulling the bell which summoned his valet.
>
> [...]
>
> "*Coupez-moi*, Isidor," shouted he; "*vite! Coupez-moi!*"
> Isidor thought for a moment he had gone mad, and that he wished his valet to cut his throat.

"*Les moustaches,*" gasped Joe; "*les moustaches—coupy, rasy, vite!*"—his French was of this sort—voluble, as we have said, but not remarkable for grammar.

Isidor swept off the mustachios in no time with the razor, and heard with inexpressible delight his master's orders that he should fetch a hat and a plain coat. "*Ne porty ploo—habit militair—bonn—bonny a voo, prenny dehors*"—were Jos's words—the coat and cap were at last his property.[54]

The irony is that no enemy would take Jos Sedley's addition of a mustache to his accoutrements as a sign of valor. It is entirely appropriate that his vanity comes back to haunt him in the form of his hair, the sense of self-image "conditioned by the discursive environment in which [...] hair was constructed as a signifier,"[55] in this instance of masculine gallantry and boldness, has been violently disrupted by the perceived threat to his person. If Horace Holly cannot impose his will upon his facial and body hair, the opposite is true of Sedley, but there is no doubt as to who is the more shamed for acting upon his hair consciousness. The potential for the owner of the mustache to lose control of its signifying function, symbolically alienating him from his own self-image, comically indicates the perils of fashioning the person through nineteenth-century hair semantics. Jos's willingness to invest an overabundance of meaning in his hair makes him vulnerable. For Andrew H. Miller, the scene encapsulates the more quotidian fears of the gentleman with "the implicit violence of the servant's vision [...] firmly suggested by the presence of Isidor's razor along his master's neck."[56] Miller focuses on the fact that throughout the novel the French-speaking Isidor plainly covets the clothes and jewelry of Jos—for the same reasons that Good Mrs. Brown wanted those of Florence Dombey—but it is Jos's incapacity to look after his hair for himself that brings Isidor—as the potential lower-class insurgent—into closest, and potentially deadliest, proximity with his master.

SOCIAL ANXIETY AND FOLLICULAR DETERMINISM

Many of these examples demonstrate that the attempt to impose the will upon the hair can be undermined both by its materiality—owing to nature or genetics—and by the play of mendacious signifiers through which hair was socially construed and interpreted, neither of which the nineteenth-century subjects that we have focused on so far could be said to be firmly in control. Quite simply, follicular fashioning was a strange type of self-assertion because it required relinquishing control to others, whether that be to the barber or hairdresser and his razors and scissors (bringing to mind the macabre Sweeney Todd from the Victorian penny dreadful *The String of Pearls* [1846–1847]), to the inventor of the latest lotions, tonics, combs, and brushes, or simply to the sister, mother, or servant who tended to the hair on behalf of its owner. This perhaps explains why the image of the servant dressing the hair of master or mistress is another common one in nineteenth-century fiction: it bespeaks social and personal anxieties because it so often implicates the shrinking gap between the social classes. The common view that genteel women should have their hair dressed twice a day for the sake of hygiene and aesthetics meant frequent time spent before the mirror at the dressing table.[57] It is an issue that Mary Elizabeth Braddon dwells on at some length in *Lady Audley's Secret* (1862) where Lucy Audley is presented as at risk from her open relationships with her waiting women such as Phoebe Marks and, in this case, the lady's-maid, Martin:

Among all privileged spies, a lady's-maid has the highest privileges; it is she who bathes Lady Theresa's eyes with eau-de-cologne after her ladyship's quarrel with the colonel; it is she who administers sal-volatile to Miss Fanny when Count Beaudesert, of the Blues, has jilted her. She has a hundred methods for the finding out of her mistress' secrets. She knows by the manner in which her victim jerks her head from under the hair-brush, or chafes at the gentlest administration of the comb, what hidden tortures are racking her breast—what secret perplexities are bewildering her brain. That well-bred attendant knows how to interpret the most obscure diagnosis of all mental diseases that can afflict her mistress.[58]

Recalling Isidor shaving off Sedley's mustaches, but also Clara Copperfield's error in believing Betsey Trotwood has laid a comforting palm upon her head, Braddon gives the impression that the foreign hand might, overtly or surreptitiously, impress its own will on the owner of the hair. As it transpires, it *is* Lady Audley's openness with Phoebe about her past life in those intimate moments of dressing the hair—and the latter's revelations to her husband, Luke Marks—that prompts her to take rash action in burning down the Castle Inn with Luke asleep upstairs. Strikingly blonde, Lucy had earlier ironically attested to the precariousness of her illicitly attained social position, and the vulnerability to which her bigamy and hereditary "madness" could expose her, when she explains to Phoebe what constitutes their difference: "My hair is pale yellow shot with gold, and yours is drab […] Why with a bottle of hair dye, such as we see advertised in the papers, and a pot of rouge, you'd be as good-looking as I any day, Phoebe."[59] This is no inconsequential complement, given the ease with which Braddon implies Lucy has climbed the ladder of Victorian society to wed a baronet. All that separates the two women is the right bottle of hair dye.

The thought that the hair—or an unguarded moment whilst dressing it—might allow another to read the secret thoughts and desires of its owner is an extreme version of the many smaller anxieties to which hair consciousness tends in the nineteenth century; a particularly tactile—or perhaps "hands-on"—demonstration of the belief common to phrenologists, such as the American Orson Squire Fowler, that hair could indicate the character.[60] In the first example from *Lady Audley*, it is less the categories into which hair might fall—dark or light, fine or coarse—that discloses the inner life—what we might call the follicular determinism of nineteenth-century phrenology—and more, as with the examples with which I began, the movement of the hair—anticipated or unanticipated— or the owner's reaction to that movement, which makes their inner world transparent. It is what reveals the hidden anxieties of a Fascination Fledgeby just as much as it allows a youthful Jo March to consciously flaunt her impudence.

The failure to assert control over the hair—that is the loss of personal control—in both physical and social terms is perhaps best encapsulated in the case of Margaret Hale in Elizabeth Gaskell's *North and South* (1855). The otherwise relatively plain Hale's dark hair is what first attracts the romantic interests of mill-owner Mr. Thornton, but it is unruly and intractable and worked on by herself and her mother to ensure the required respectability:

Margaret's black hair was too thick to be plaited; it needed rather to be twisted round and round, and have its fine silkiness compressed into massive coils, that encircled her head like a crown, and then were gathered into a large spiral knot behind. She kept its weight together by two large coral pins, like small arrows for length. Her white silk sleeves were looped up with strings of the same material, and on her neck, just below the base of her curved and milk-white throat, there lay heavy coral beads.[61]

Margaret, as was true of many young Victorian women, must fight the destiny to which fate, or biology, has assigned her by applying the control of multiple pins. But her hair truly becomes an index of her personality in her relationship with her servant, Dixon, and her ability to exert her own control over that relationship. While early in the novel Dixon takes out her impatience on her mistress "by brushing away viciously at Margaret's hair, under pretence of being in a great hurry to go to Mrs. Hale," in the next chapter Margaret takes back control in dismissing Dixon when she asks "Mayn't I unfasten your gown, miss, and do your hair?," reminding her of her position of privilege.[62] The relationship between mistress and servant is kept in check via the attention permitted to the former's hair.

But hair consciousness in *North and South*, and more generally the complicated relationship between one's hair and its perception by others, is again viewed by Gaskell as not merely a matter of the physical attempts to dress it and impose the will upon it. Margaret Hale is another character who loses control of the signifying function of her hair, this time to a lower-class character. Hair figures prominently in Margaret's relationship with Bessy, the daughter of the factory-worker Nicholas Higgins, who contracts a fatal illness from exposure to the harsh conditions of the mill. In a sentimental section of the novel, Bessy informs Margaret that she has been dreaming of her, and the fact that Margaret's hair isn't conventionally beautiful doesn't prevent Bessy's conscious mind from reworking its semantics through the content of her dream:

> Yo'r very face,—looking wi' yo'r clear steadfast eyes out o' th' darkness, wi' yo'r hair blown off from yo'r brow, and going out like rays round yo'r forehead, which was just as smooth and as straight as it is now,—and yo' always came to give me strength, which I seemed to gather out o' yo'r deep comforting eyes,—and yo' were drest in shining raiment.
>
> Why, even my father thinks a deal o' dreams! I tell yo' again, I saw yo' as plainly, coming swiftly towards me, wi' yo'r hair blown back wi' the very swiftness o' the motion, just like the way it grows, a little standing off like; and the white shining dress on yo've getten to wear.[63]

Bessy's simple reverence of the lady of higher status is expressed through her hair, as, although failing in reality to match up to Bessy's dreams, Margaret finds the role of Radcliffean heroine inscribed upon her person through the way her locks move. Even so, the image works on a number of levels, firstly demonstrating the pervasiveness of hair consciousness through the ease with which Bessy encodes Margaret as a woman of independence and desirability through her hair, despite the contrary evidence up until this point in the novel, and secondly revealing the fact that even her illusion has to accommodate the slightly odd "way it grows, a little standing off like." Rather like Peter Quint in James's *The Turn of the Screw* (1898), whose red hair makes him an aggressive sexual predator in the fantasies of the governess, largely because he fits an already well-established model of villainous men with red hair, Margaret Hale is prescribed a role to which her hair is perceived to assign her. But there is also the sentimental reading, which Gaskell plays up, in which Bessy, through her vision, is seen not to be deluded but actually to have read Margaret—who later rises to the status of independent heroine—more accurately than she could herself. The vision of her hair discloses some latent truth that the action of the novel will ultimately expose.

CONCLUSION

The relationship of Bessy and Margaret is just one of many in the nineteenth century noticeable for being fashioned through the hair. As we have seen, readers of this period were overloaded with information about hair, while the chances to cheat nature and to "fashion and act out" an identity, or even an ideal notion of manhood and womanhood, appeared to be within grasp as never before.[64] Yet, while science could explain the biology of follicles and pigment, it was still wedded to older understandings of temperament and the widely accepted premises of phrenology and craniology as a way of reading character. The cant of criniculture no doubt exacerbated anxieties and self-consciousness. Technological advances also carried as many hazards as benefits: for every successful Lucy Audley—and the implication is that she is a bottle blonde—there was a Lady Bareacres. For every Clive Newcome there is a Fascination Fledgeby. The premises of follicular determinism meant that the hair became a site of the individual and collective will but also of its failure, but this wasn't just another way of expressing the difference between Keats's Isabella and Dickens's Clara Copperfield. One is hair-conscious—as were so many others—and the other is not, but as we have seen the absence of attention to the hair *and* an overattentiveness to it could likewise mark out physical and mental difference and make individuals socially unacceptable. Undoubtedly hair was used in the nineteenth century to distinguish between man and woman, youth and age, gentility and coarseness, cleanliness and dirtiness, illness and health. The worry was that the slippage between these categories did not always seem to come under the purview of the self-assertive individual—as in the case of Jo March—and was more commonly an index of the inability to exercise control on the part of the body that was read more frequently and imbued with more significance than any other. For all these reasons, nineteenth-century hair gives us one of the most reliable ways to plot the relationship between the self and its larger social context.

CHAPTER THREE

Fashion and Adornment: African American Women in the United States, 1800 to 1920

PATRICIA HUNT-HURST

Fashion means the prevailing style of a product at any time. For this chapter, fashion applies to hairstyles, headwear, women's clothing, accessories, and other modes of adornment.[1] Adornment is the practice of enhancing one's appearance. It can be (1) a permanent alteration to the body, such as piercing, tattooing, and scarring, or (2) external, which means it is temporary and "can be put on or taken off at will."[2] The adornment discussed in this chapter is external rather than permanent. Hairstyles, headwear, clothing, and accessories are all elements of fashion and adornment, and in the 120-year period covered by the Age of Empire a vast amount of change occurred. Further, the fashion and adornment of hair has a wide breadth of difference and meanings across cultures and ethnicities. This chapter examines hair, headwear, and other forms of fashion and adornment as worn by African American women in the United States between 1800 and 1920, to look beyond what was fashionable in "Society" for hair but also to explore how fashion and adornment of hair is pervasive.

The majority of African American women living in the United States between 1800 and 1865 were enslaved on plantations and farms in the Southern states where the opportunities to partake in fashionable styles of dressing the hair or wearing fashionable headwear or clothing were rare or nonexistent. In the period under discussion, after the American Civil War, that is, 1865 to 1920, women of color enjoyed not only freedom but also some of the rewards of working for themselves and making their own money, as well as wearing fashionable hairstyles, headwear, and clothing.[3] The period ends with the birth of the Harlem Renaissance and the contributions of gifted African American musicians, authors, painters, and others who marked their place in history through their artistic and literary gifts.[4] By 1920, fashion participation was a norm for many African American women rather than a rarity.

ENSLAVED WOMEN, THEIR FASHION AND ADORNMENT, 1800 TO 1865

When reflecting on fashion and adornment for African American women how the hair is worn is closely linked to what is worn. It is necessary, therefore, to explore hair in terms of clothing and headwear because of the close symbiotic link. "By all accounts, there was a great difference between slave clothing and slave owners' clothing, one that was intentional."[5] This would also be true for hairstyles and headwear as well. For the most part, enslaved women did not have access to fashion. Treatment was brutal, work was long and hard, and the necessities for living were meager. Although enslaved men, women, and children on Southern plantations were allotted hats, clothing, shoes, and fabric by the plantation owner or overseer at least once a year, there was not a lot of time to give to dress and adornment.[6] However, just as hair, headwear, and clothing define men and women in the twenty-first century as individuals there is no doubt that enslaved men and women arranged or wore their hair, headwear, and clothing in such a manner as to reflect some individuality and personal taste and style. A fugitive slave notice in an 1834 edition of the Macon, Georgia, *Weekly Telegraph* indicated that one runaway woman "usually wore on her head and neck yellow cotton handkerchiefs."[7] In another example, a runaway woman was noted for her hairstyle, "nearly straight, done up in a twist and fastened with a comb."[8]

"The dressing of the hair was a fashion element shared by all classes, as it could be accomplished without any expenditure at all."[9] Like other aspects of dress and adornment, hairstyles were also a reflection of fashion and changed as often as dress styles did between 1800 and 1865. Hair and its arrangement were an important element of adornment for enslaved women. Wrapping or threading sections of hair with cloth or twine was a hair method in place in the nineteenth century: "it kept hair from knotting and also to cause it, when released, to curl."[10] For special occasions, such as weddings, Christmas, or Sunday dressing in the slave community, women wrapped or threaded their hair at night, kept it covered with a headwrap, and then unwound the hair and arranged it.[11] Enslaved women working in the plantation house also gave attention to their hair. Photographs from the 1840s onward reveal that women not wearing a day cap or headwrap wore fashionable hairstyles, such as puffs of hair above the ears in the 1840s, ringlets on the sides with a center part in the 1850s, and in the 1860s the hair pulled back from the face and covered by a net or snood.[12] The value placed on hair thus made a shaved head a form of punishment inflicted on enslaved women for tasks left incomplete or poorly done, or due to pure meanness by the overseer, plantation mistress, or planter.[13]

During the nineteenth century it was "improper" for women "to venture out of the house bareheaded."[14] Thus hats and bonnets were fashionable as well as necessary headwear for women, and headwear would affect the hair styling. The changing shape and ornamentation of bonnets and hats was a topic in the fashion columns of women's magazines throughout the period. For example, evening hats were "composed of black tulle, spotted with gold, and edged or bordered with a gold fringe."[15] In another example, "spring bonnets are generally very plain, of either silk or satin, with a very full ruche or quilling of tulle, around the front."[16]

Headwear and "the style and quality of clothing given to slaves depended upon their occupation, as well as their perceived importance and visibility to the white community."[17] Headwear for enslaved women included hats, bonnets, day caps, and headwraps. Hats were generally of straw with wide round brims; straw or cloth bonnets had large brims to protect the face and head from the sun; and a curtain of fabric at the back of the bonnet kept the back of the neck covered. Dress historian Gerilyn Tandberg described the slat bonnet as a style worn by "middle- and lower-class women in rural areas."[18] The crown of the cloth bonnet had wooden slats encased in the fabric that were vertically positioned the length of the head from forehead to back. The fabric at the back and sides of the bonnet below the chin were long to cover the neck.

Day caps were worn indoors, particularly by older and married women. Some plantations required enslaved women working in the house to wear a day cap, which was also recognized as a cap worn by working women. The day cap worn by fashionable women would have been made of fine cotton and trimmed with lace, whereas a working woman, whether enslaved or not, would wear a day cap of white sturdy cotton or linen without lace trimming.

Headwraps (also known as a turban, head-handkerchief, tignon, or head-rag) were made from fabric. This was the headwear generally associated with enslaved women prior to the American Civil War. However, wrapping a piece of silk or other type of fabric around the head was a style in and out of women's fashions throughout the nineteenth century, usually a style worn for evening dress. In March 1846 a fashion column in the *Lady's Magazine* indicated that fashionable women would be wearing "turbans in muslin, embroidered with silver."[19] Whereas, the headwrap worn by an enslaved woman was an item worn daily to protect the head and hair from the sun and the grit of working in the fields. It could be a headdress of preference rather than a fashion item on the plantation, particularly if the women had a choice between hat or headwrap.

The headwrap became a symbol of slavery as well as an item of African American material culture. It marked the "black woman's social status as different from that of white women."[20] As early as 1786, free black women in New Orleans were required to wear headwraps or turbans known as tignons. The decree was issued by the acting governor of Louisiana, a colony of Spain at the time, to prohibit the free women from showing their hair: "the hair of these women was to be covered with a head kerchief when it was combed high."[21] The restriction "was instituted [...] to render these women less beautiful," and "covering the head thus neutralized the outward expression of sexuality."[22] The tignon also prevented "a light-complexioned woman from 'passing for white.'"[23] The free women of color took advantage of the order and wore brightly colored madras and plaid fabric to adorn their head in turbans that were arranged to reveal the forehead and wrapped high like a crown on the head.[24] Rather than defy the decree by not covering their hair, the women instead used stunning fabric to add beauty to the concealment. Even though the women complied with the decree, the imposition of the headwrap as a mark of inferiority was not a factor; however, the turban remained a headdress associated with slavery throughout most of the nineteenth century and evolved into a negative stereotype associated with an "Aunt Jemima" or "Black Mammy" servant in the twentieth century.[25]

Men and women living or traveling in the South recorded their observations of life in the South in their journals and diaries. Their writings confirmed the headwrap's use by enslaved women on plantations. English actress Frances Kemble, married to a planter and living on a plantation in Georgia in the late 1830s, described a group of enslaved women dressed in their Sunday best. Kemble noted that their "head handkerchiefs, [...] put one's very eyes out from a mile off; chintzes with sprawling patterns."[26] In his book *A South-Side View of Slavery; or, Three Months at the South in 1854*, Nehemiah Adams wrote that women were in "very plain, humble clothing and turbans."[27] Annie Harper lived on a plantation in Mississippi during the American Civil War. She wrote about the red and yellow turbans worn by women picking cotton on the plantation. Observations made by Kemble, Harper, and other white people in the South inform us that many enslaved women wore headwraps made of bright-colored fabrics. Headwraps were also made of printed patterned fabric, spotted, or woven of plaids or other patterns in a variety of colors. The fabric for headwraps was given to many of the women in the yearly allotment, while others received the fabric as Christmas gifts, as a reward for a job well done, or from other sources.[28] Other visitors observed white turbans of cloth, rather than brightly colored ones. For example, James Roberts Gilmore, a New Yorker, visited the South on many occasions prior to the American Civil War. He described an elderly slave wearing a turban that "was evidently a contribution from the family stock of worn-out pillowcases."[29] Rarely do the comments from observers reflect anything more about the headwraps other than the color or pattern of the fabric, though the height of the headwrap, rather than how it was wrapped, was noted by some. Phoebe, for example, enslaved on a plantation in South Carolina, worked in the infirmary and in the children's nursery. She wore a "handkerchief turban of unusual height."[30] Like the enslaved women assigned to field work, house servants wore the headwrap for function and as a symbol of personal expression, wrapping the cloth around their head in a way that best suited them.

It is difficult not to think about headwraps as a source of creative outlet and personal expression on the plantation. Enslaved women had little control over what they were given to wear; however, having a piece of fabric to wrap around the head, was left to the individual's aesthetic style and skill at wrapping and knotting the fabric around the head. It is most likely that it is this individual expression seen during slavery that gave this method of adornment a resurgence in the late twentieth century as young African American women adopted headwraps, turbans, and tignons as a way to connect to the past, and take a symbol of servility and make it a cultural statement of pride.

Besides headwear, enslaved women were typically given a dress, some undergarments, and other items depending on whether they worked in the house or in the fields. Shoes, if provided, were made of rough leather; and shawls or blankets were given for the colder months, as well as some type of cotton or wool stocking. Field hands worked at hoeing, planting, raking, and digging, as well as carrying out other agricultural tasks required on the plantation. Days were long and hard. Fashion was not a factor for the women assigned to work in the fields; dresses had to be "loose enough to fit anybody and only generally reflected the clothing styles of the period."[31] Enslaved women who worked in the plantation house as cooks, housemaids, ladies' maids, nursemaids, or child-nurses carried more status on the plantation and were usually given better fabric for headwear and better clothing due to their close proximity to the plantation owner and his family.[32]

Many planters purchased clothing ready-made while others had all of the clothing for the slaves made on the plantation by enslaved women, most of whom worked long hours in the house or field during the day, and then were required to sew or mend clothing for their own families and others' at night after the day's work was done.[33] House servants typically received their clothing in one of two ways: clothing that was made or purchased just for them in relatively fashionable styles but of serviceable fabrics that were easy to clean; or hand-me-down clothes from the plantation mistress. This latter method was an English tradition that "grew stronger in the United States during the nineteenth century."[34] Visitors to the plantation ascertained an enslaved woman's rank by the clothing she wore, rather than by how new it was.

Between 1800 and 1865 fashionable dresses changed from loose-fitting dresses with high waistlines to dresses with fitted bodices and long, full skirts. Necklines, sleeves, and ornamentation changed along with the fit and silhouette of skirts. Dresses for enslaved women working in the fields rarely followed fashion but instead came in two general styles: (1) a dress with a v-shaped, collarless neckline, no sleeves, and large armholes, and with full skirts shorter in length than what was considered fashionable, or (2) had a semi-fitted, front-buttoning bodice with a high round neckline with or without a collar, long sleeves, and a full skirt that varied in length from mid-calf to the floor. The v-shape, collarless neckline and large armholes of the first style "allowed the women to work more comfortably in the heat."[35] Full and long skirts were appropriate styles in fashion for women to wear during this period yet hindered movement; working women could shorten the skirt by tying rope or string around the hips and then pulling up the skirt to shorten it which made the skirt blouse over the rope or string. Shortening the skirt kept it out of the wet or muddy fields and allowed a woman to return it to its proper length at the end of the day.[36] Dresses worn by women working in the fields were constructed out of inexpensive and plain blue or brown cloth. Coarse homespun, of cotton or wool woven on the plantation, was a typical fabric used. Another fabric used for dresses was cotton calico with a figured pattern of stripes, geometric shapes, flowers, or spotted with dots. A fugitive slave notice published in the *Winyaw Intelligencer* in 1819 indicated that Rachel "carried with her a considerable quantity of fine cloathing [sic], such as homespun, calico, cambric."[37]

Dresses for house servants were usually of a more stylish silhouette, of better construction, and included more fashionable trim than those given to field hands. Dress historian Joan Severa pointed out that a dress could look new but be out of date. She stated: "this was not unusual for a dress of any woman over fifty, let alone a servant woman, since 'keeping up with fashion' was considered a vanity reserved for the young."[38] In this same way, a stylish dress might be less in fashion for reasons of comfort. For example, a dress might be more short-waisted than fashion dictated and sleeves "slightly relaxed to allow full use of the arms for active work."[39] In addition, sleeve fullness would make "lifting and caring for a baby easier."[40] Severa in the examination of the dress of an unknown black woman as shown in a photograph noted that the dress worn must have been made for someone else, since it was "not well fitted, apparently having been altered and taken in through the body; it was probably made [...] for a larger woman and then handed down to the sitter."[41] Severa also pointed out that the woman's hairstyle was more fashionable than the dress, "yet this garment has more importance as a hand-me-down; it emphasizes not only 'making do' but also the universal interest in fashion."[42] Dark colored cotton and spotted chintz were common fabrics used for dresses, due to the fact that dirt did not show and could be wiped off easily.[43] Black alpaca was used for "common day dresses" and was an appropriate dress fabric for child-nurses and ladies' maids.[44]

Women's undergarments during this period included chemises, petticoats, and drawers. Since clothing, at this time, was not washed on a regular basis, the cotton chemise worn next to the skin protected a dress from body oils and perspiration. The chemise was generally knee length with a wide neckline and short sleeves. It served as a nightshirt for sleeping and as a slip worn under the dress during the day. During the summer enslaved women who worked in the fields wore the chemise as a dress; its short sleeves and wide neckline made it a "practical garment to wear in hot summer."[45] Corsets, although fashionable and appropriate for women to wear, would have been unusual for an enslaved woman, even one who worked in the plantation house. Drawers or underpants were adopted by women in the United States by 1810. Drawers were knee-length and fastened at the waist with a drawstring or button. Petticoats were fashionable as well as necessary undergarments since the skirts of women's dresses gained fullness in the 1820s. "If a slave woman ever received a petticoat, it would have been a smaller, modified version of that worn by her mistress – minus the fashionably necessary horsehair padding or cage-like steel frame."[46] It would be more likely that a house servant had some type of petticoat whereas the enslaved woman working in the field would not.

An apron would also be an item of clothing for an enslaved woman to have and wear when needed, whether field hand or house servant. The apron and fichu were indicative of her status as a working woman. "An apron was the ultimate symbol of the working woman, worn in public only by the women who did not enjoy a high social position."[47] The fichu was a large square piece of plain or printed cloth, folded into a triangle, and worn over the shoulders. The pointed side placed on the back and the ends tied in front. The fichu was a fashionable accessory at the end of the eighteenth century; however, it became an accessory associated with working-class dress into the mid-nineteenth century.

Wearing jewelry was another way that enslaved women adorned themselves. Jewelry was obtained as gifts or reward of a job well done. Photographs of nurse-maids, ladies' maids, and other house servants show women wearing small dangle earrings, a pin or brooch, and sometimes a beaded necklace. Some portraits show tignons or turbans decorated with beading. Blue was a popular color for beads. Beads, although not found in abundance in excavations of slave communities, when found were blue in color. Blue may have been popular due to the Muslim belief that blue protected against the evil eye, thus kept one safe.[48] It was not unusual during this period for a house servant to emulate "her mistress in manner, the practice [of wearing jewelry] was apparently universal in the lower class of the period."[49] However, photographers at this time had props, like jewelry and even clothing, for someone to wear in a photograph. Since ownership of the jewelry worn by African American women is impossible to know, their evidence of wear in photographs "prove that is was not unusual for Black women to wear jewelry at the time."[50]

At the beginning of the nineteenth century women's shoes included leather and cloth slippers, made as straights rather than designated for the right or left foot. As the nineteenth century progressed ankle boots were introduced for women and became a daily alternative to the lightweight slipper. In addition, by mid-century shoes were made for the right and left foot. Enslaved women generally received some type of shoe once a year, in most cases this was a rough leather boot known as a brogan. These lace up boots were stiff, ill-fitting, and uncomfortable to wear. Many women went barefoot in the summer rather than wear the stiff brogans; others would apply grease to their feet and ankles to make wearing the brogans bearable.[51]

Historians Shane White and Graham White stated that "the appearance of slaves" was controlled, however, runaway advertisements demonstrate that slaves "fashioned their appearance" in different ways and "discovered an often surprising degree of social and cultural space."[52] On plantations where the fabric was woven and the clothing made by enslaved women, often under the direction of the plantation mistress, there were opportunities for enslaved women to "enhance the look of the cloth,"[53] through the art of dyeing the yarn or cloth with indigo, black walnut bark, berries, cedar moss, and other botanical products. Since enslaved women were not free to express their individuality in dress, how clothing is [was] worn may be as significant as what clothing is [was] worn. The significant point to be noticed is clothing behavior rather than clothing. If slaves were subject to more external constraints upon their dress than were free persons, they were nevertheless not quite devoid of choice both in how clothing was worn and to some extent in how it was cut [or restyled through the addition of fabric or color to the cloth].[54]

Other examples of the creative expression were accomplished through mending or patching the clothes, wrapping and tying the headwrap, and remaking handed-down clothing. Elizabeth Botume, a Northern school teacher to ex-slaves in South Carolina in the 1860s, wrote about the time "thirty new plaid worsted dresses showed up at the school," when the students "took the dresses home their mothers looked askance at them" for being too short and showing the feet and ankles which was not appropriate for women's skirts at that time.[55] So the students added old cotton fabric to the bottom of the skirts. Botume remarked that the finished skirt "looked like a modern crazy quilt" but "really not ugly."[56] White people in the area found the mix of colors and the quilt-like skirt odd; this attitude reflected the "cultural gap between black and white. What lay behind these differences was an African American aesthetic, the use not only of varied materials and patterns but also of contrasting colors in a manner that jangled white sensibilities."[57] The use of varied colors and patterns also reflects the creativity and need for individual expression in their dress that was prevented by having no choice in clothing selection; reworking the clothes gave the young women a creative outlet.

As the American Civil War was ending and the Thirteenth Amendment was signed into law, many African American men, women, and children left plantations to make their way to areas controlled by the United States Army. Many of these newly freed people left with only the clothes on their backs, while others managed to carry away hats, bonnets, and other items of clothing. Whichever the case, the future must have been exciting but daunting. Charlotte Forten, the daughter of free Blacks from Philadelphia, spent time as a teacher in Port Royal, South Carolina, at the end of the war. In letters to her friend, American poet John Greenleaf Whittier, she often wrote about the clothing and headwear of abandoned slaves:

> The next morning L. and I were awakened by the cheerful voices of men, and women, children [...] We ran to the window, and looked out. Women in bright-colored handkerchiefs, some carrying pails on their heads, were crossing the yard, busy with their morning work.[58]

In another letter to Whittier, Forten wrote about her recent Sunday attendance at the Baptist church. She stated that the church was filled and that everyone was "dressed in their Sunday attire," the women wore "dark frocks, with white aprons and bright-colored head-handkerchiefs."[59] After the church service all the attendees gathered outside; Forten observed women "in their bright handkerchiefs and white aprons [and] they made a striking picture under the gray-mossed trees."[60]

FASHION AND ADORNMENT 1865 TO 1920

In the years following the end of the American Civil War, formerly enslaved men and women found themselves searching for new homes, new work, and new lives. While some newly freed people remained on the plantations in which they were enslaved, assured of shelter and food, they continued to work and live under similar conditions endured under slavery.[61] Others left the rural areas for Southern cities, where some women found work as domestic servants, cooks, and laundresses.

African American women born into freedom rather than slavery before the American Civil War likely had better means to supply interest in fashion and adornment. They worked as cooks, seamstresses, and domestic servants and were paid according to their skill level. Some seamstresses and dressmakers had their own shops, worked out of their homes, or worked for other seamstresses, tailors, and dressmakers. Freed women were also gaining experience in millinery, a specialized trade that required creativity as well as the skill of shaping leather, felt, and straw into stylish hats.

Whether working in the urban or rural areas of the United States freed and newly freed African Americans "endured institutionalized segregation, state supported racism, poverty, and substandard living conditions,"[62] with their pursuits for a good and healthy life. Hairstyles, headwear, and clothing helped to identify freed women's new status. Women in rural areas were paid significantly less for their work, whether on the farm as agricultural workers or in the house as domestic servants. Some women might have headwear and clothing in pretty good shape at the end of the war. Dress historian Gerilyn Tandberg wrote:

> Perhaps because they [the women] took care of the cast-off clothing
> they had received before the war and made use of many items left
> behind by families fleeing occupied southern cities, many black women
> were better dressed after the war than their former mistresses.[63]

While some women, for the most part, were able to afford some good clothing, it is certain that they were still forced to economize in purchase of items of fashion and adornment.[64] However, hair was something most women could arrange in the latest styles without too much expense.

Hats continued to be a necessary item required of women to wear when outdoors; however, headwraps and turbans remained a style for rural African American women whereas a hat might be reserved for special occasions such as church and weddings.

Travelers to the South working for newspapers and magazines in major cities of the north and northeastern United States recorded living and working conditions in their journals. For example, Edward King, working for *Scribner's Magazine*, visited a former plantation in South Carolina. King wrote about the women working in the fields wearing "gay colors, with handkerchiefs uniting all of the colors of the rainbow, around their temples."[65] In another example, Charles Stern, a Northern teacher and philanthropist, purchased a plantation in Georgia after the American Civil War. In the 1870s he wrote about Margaret, a former slave on the plantation, wearing around her head "a large yellow handkerchief, with a few spots upon its surface."[66]

An examination of photographs of African American women in Georgia and South Carolina wearing headwraps revealed that both patterned and plain fabrics in four distinct styles were worn: (1) fabric wrapped around the head and fastened with a knot on top of the head, (2) fabric wrapped around the head and fastened in a knot at the back or side of the head, (3) fabric wrapped around the head and arranged so that a brim of fabric jutted out on the brow and a curtain of fabric hung at the back, and (4) fabric wrapped around the head and tucked under the cloth rather than knotted in place. Type 3 was both creative and functional with a brim to shield the eyes and a curtain to protect the back of the neck from the sun.[67]

Wearing of the headwrap became more obviously replaced by hats in the early twentieth century. Rossa B. Cooley started working at the Penn School on St. Helena Island, South Carolina, in 1904 and recorded the demise of the headwrap:

> The women used always to wear this bright colored headdress wound close to show the shape of the head. When we reached the islands nineteen years ago, bandannas had begun to go, the black and white head-cloths had taken their place and hats had found a place on top of the headcloths.[68]

If headwraps were worn, then hats were often worn over them. Julia Peterkin, writing about African Americans living on her family's plantation after slavery, observed: "the older women tie up their heads in headkerchiefs and wear Sunday hats perched upon them."[69] During the early twentieth century, hats replaced headwraps for many African American women. In many ways, these headdresses lost their significance until the late twentieth century when, according to Helen Bradley Griebel: "the enslaved and their descendants [...] regarded the head wrap as a helmet of courage that evoked an image of their homeland—be that ancient Africa or the newer homeland, America."[70] Work clothing was "cut with greater simplification than fashionable clothing of the period, reflecting the vast domestic and field responsibilities of the rural women."[71] Most clothing was still stitched by hand or with the help of the sewing machine. By the 1870s simple skirts and bodices and house and wash dresses could be purchased ready-made from local merchants or from mail-order companies. These dresses were made from cotton or wool, plain or patterned fabrics, dark in color, and likely related to fashionable styles without the fashionable close-fitting bodices, abundance of ornamentation prevalent on dresses in the 1870s. Instead, work clothes would be durable and easy to clean. Aprons were another common feature worn by working women, possibly made from "older, unserviceable garments" that were "well-worn and consistently tattered."[72]

As fashionable dress became available to more and more African American women, popular pastimes did as well. Bicycle riding was a popular and fashionable sporting activity for women in the late nineteenth and early twentieth centuries. A column in the *Atlanta Independent* about bicycling informed its women readers about the bicycle suit, "a double-breasted reefer and skirt of fine serge of marine blue."[73] Fashion columns like this in African American-owned and operated newspapers also informed women of the latest styles of hairstyles, headwear, and clothing. For example, a wedding announcement supplied fashion information in regard to wedding clothes:

> A very fashionable wedding was solemnized on Thursday, May 7. The bride wore white silk beautifully trimmed, and carried carnations and lilies of the valley. The groom wore conventional black. The bridesmaids wore white brilliantine and carried pink carnations and roses.[74]

Since little description is given about the bride's dress, it is likely that the bride wore a fashionable white wedding dress of the 1890s with large leg-of-mutton or balloon sleeves, fitted bodice with high collar, and full-length gored skirt. A veil would have completed the wedding ensemble and was usually of a fine tulle or lace. The brilliantine worn by the bridesmaids was a lightweight wool and silk or wool and cotton fabric blend made of a plain or twill weave. It had a lustrous finish so was often used for evening or special occasion dresses.[75]

Hats continued to be an essential part of women's wardrobe; in fact, hats were known to add to an outfit. Advertisements in newspapers documented the types of fashionable hats and clothing offered for sale. Some ads gave fashion advice. The Gate City Millinery and Dry Goods Company in Atlanta furnished the following: "Do you know the hat has more to do with your appearance than any other wearing apparel? Dress up my head and I am dressed."[76]

Fashion columns in African American newspapers gave attention to hats. For example: "The sailor hat is in as high favor as ever, but its shape is somewhat changed: the latest boasts bell curves and has a sharp angle at the upper and lower parts of the crown."[77] The sailor hat was a fashionable accessory for women since the late nineteenth century when men's hats became fashionable hats for women to wear for sporting activities such as bicycle riding or professional work activities. This hat style was worn in a straw or felt version depending on the time of year. Women also wore the female version of the fedora—smaller in size and softer than the menswear style. The sailor hat and fedora worn by women were usually less decorated than the fashionable hats of the late nineteenth century thus promoting their function as hats for wearing to work or for sports.

Hair was as fashionable as apparel and accessories. Hairstyles changed as frequently as skirt and bodice styles. In the 1860s hair was worn low at the back and encased in a snood at the back of the neck; in the 1870s ringlets at the sides added to the ornamentation of the total look as did the frills and ruffles on skirts and bodices. In the 1880s hair was worn up in a chignon to accommodate standing band collars. The highness continued in the 1890s as the standing band collar increased in height. The beginnings of the pompadour with fullness arranged around the sides and top of the face with a high chignon began in the 1890s and continued into the first years of the twentieth century. Hairwork was an important business. John T. Gassaway advertised that he had "opened a first-class colored barber shop." The advertisement continued: "Ladies' and Children's Hair Cutting and Shampooing a Specialty."[78] By the 1910s hair was worn lower over the ears with a low chignon. Photographs of African American women are good illustrations of how these fashionable styles changed from 1865 to 1920. White and White stated:

> by the turn of the century, the swelling black populations of northern cities had created an urban African American consumer market of some significance, and commercial beauty products—at first hair oils and later creams for the face—quickly became a regular item in the expenditure of many blacks, even those who were hardly well-off.[79]

Many of the new hair products produced for African American hair were created by African American entrepreneurs like Anthony Overton, Annie Turnbo Malone, and Madame C.J. Walker. The modern hair products permitted Black women to arrange their hair in the fashionable styles or create styles with their own innovative interpretation.[80] Straightening the hair "was a practical necessity if some sort of styling were to be accomplished, a preliminary to styling, not its end point."[81] Straightening the hair allowed African American women to produce fashionable styles or be more creative and design their own hairstyles.

Cosmetics were not in general use by most women in the nineteenth century; in fact, "cosmetics suffered from a dubious image in mid-nineteenth century America" associated with prostitutes and other women of questionable character.[82] Powder and powdered paper were available for use by the end of the nineteenth century; red pencils for lips and black for eyebrows, as well as skin creams, were available in the early years of the twentieth century.[83] By the end of the 1910s socialites were wearing heavy eye makeup, lipstick, and rouge. The adoption of cosmetics by the general public of women gained further acceptance in the 1920s as favorite actresses wore makeup in silent movies and fashion magazines promoted cosmetics through advertisements and fashion columns.

Another product available to African American women was skin whitener. Color discrimination was "an important and debilitating factor in African American life."[84] Young African American women used skin whiteners not to be like white women, "it was more often the case that they wanted the same freedom to construct their appearance that whites were allowed";[85] the opportunity to be different from their mothers and grandmothers and part of the modern age was important to all women.

Church was a principal venue for wearing one's best hat, hairstyle, and apparel. Work apparel worn throughout the week was exchanged for newer clothes reflecting the most fashionable styles. "Young women appeared 'very smart' in dresses and hats bought from local stores or obtained through mail-order catalogs."[86] Since having newer clothes and fashionable clothes and hats was a mark of success in the late nineteenth century, savvy retailers came up with ways that working-class Americans could purchase the newest hats and clothing. Clein's Installment House on Auburn Avenue in Atlanta, Georgia, explained an option:

> Let us explain to you how a little money will dress you in most fashionable wearing apparel for this season. Our credit system is the most reasonable ordered—a small payment opens an account with us; you enjoy the wear of your purchase while you pay for it in small weekly or monthly payments.[87]

The installment plan was not unusual. In fact, many apparel shops indicated that they had installment plans for their customers. Another retailer, the Royal Credit Outfitters, allowed customers to pay $1.00 per week to participate in "the sensible way to buy clothes."[88]

Fashion columns in newspapers also included the latest fashion news about styles and construction for dresses, coats, skirts, and other fashionable garments:

> Many ladies are having heavy black serge skirts made up without lining, as the serge can be washed. The waists are finished with a tailor's binding of black satin on the darts and edges, as satin relieved the dead black of the serge; a good quality of satin should be selected. Brocaded silks are among the samples shown for the season's wear both in black and colors.[89]

Participating in fashionable dress was an important symbol of status to the developing African American middle class in cities throughout the United States. Magazines carried articles of several pages in length that focused on fashionable apparel. An article published in 1901 gave the "prevailing styles for early summer."[90] Mme. Rumford, a dressmaker, wrote the article and provided illustrations of the fashionable styles. Her sketches showed hats with large brims and shallow crowns adorned with feathers and flowers. The dresses illustrated had the fashionable mono-bosom bodice with high standing collar, bishop sleeves, and the long, floor-length skirt of gored panels that fitted close over the hips and flared out to a fuller bottom that splayed out on the floor. All were fashionable features of early-twentieth-century dresses.[91]

Fashion and adornment has long been a way to show status, while many African American women after the American Civil War lacked the economic means to purchase fashionable styles of dress, these women participated in adornment through what and how they wore the clothes and fabric they had, whether a new or well-worn hat, the creative wrap of a piece of fabric around their heads, or the combination of clothing they wore. Fashionable and new items were usually reserved for Sunday or best dress for weddings and other events. If a woman worked in a trade that required fashionable dress and the knowledge of it, such as a dressmaker, tailoress, or milliner, then work clothes included fashionable styles toned down in ornamentation and frill. Although many women were undoubtedly hindered by economic and time restraints during the early twentieth century and wore functional styles of dress, many other African American women wore the most fashionable styles. African American educator Fannie Barrier Williams had concern in the early twentieth century that women were spending too much time and money on clothing. She cautioned the readers of the magazine *The Voice of the Negro*: "we are more or less at the mercy of the modist and the milliner. We go to them with all our vanities, our social ambitions and our envies, but seldom with any independent judgment or individuality of taste as to our pocket book limitations or to what becomes us."[92] Photographs from the period show African American women participating in the fashions of the day in all aspects: hair, headwear, and clothing. The continued use of the headwrap by some African American women likely reflected a functional and creative choice rather than the only option.

CONCLUSION

African American women participated in fashion and adornment as much as they could between 1800 and 1920, particularly after the American Civil War when there were more opportunities to participate in the wearing of fashionable hairstyles, hats, and clothing from their own devices of skill, work, and well-being. Enslaved women working in the fields had very little say so in their dress—fashion was not important; however, adornment constituted one way to express one's individuality in the creative wrapping of fabric for the multipurposed headwrap or in the mending of a skirt or dress. Servants working in the house as child-nurses and maids were better dressed, sometimes in fashionable styles or in less fashionable but newer forms of dress. After the American Civil War the headwrap remained a mainstay for the house servant as well. As style changes occurred in women's fashion and adornment, so did the types of hats, hairstyles, clothing, and accessories worn by African American women. Hair and headdress were as important as skirt, bodice, and accessories—to be fashionable reflected your knowledge of the subject as well as your skill to make it or means to purchase it.

CHAPTER FOUR

Production and Practice: Hair Harvest, Hairpieces, and Hairwork

SALLIE MCNAMARA

INTRODUCTION

I have a commission or two for you. I enclose a bit of my hair for you to hand over to Marshall as a pattern for a fillet of hair for the front; I have cut off my tail for comfort, and as my front hair is always coming out of curl in the damp summer evenings, and as I find everybody sports a false toupee, I don't see why I should not have the comfort of one too. I wish it to be as fashionable and as deceiving as possible. (Maria Josepha, Lady Stanley, 1802)[1]

Lady Stanley's comments at the start of the long nineteenth century are indicative of some of the practices relating to hair as she refers to the efforts involved in trying to be fashionable. While hairstyles were never as extravagant as those in the eighteenth century,[2] fashions throughout most of the period necessitated the use of a variety of hairpieces and ornaments; this only changed toward the end of the century and the beginning of the next. The references to "fillet of hair"[3] and "false toupee" indicate the artifice involved in achieving the required style, and, with the help of consumer products, some of the practices adopted. Also implicit, therefore, is the complex business that informs hair production and practice. The context for this Age of Empire was huge social change, a period where, as Eric Hobsbawm observes, the world economy was transformed and identified, for a brief period, with the fortunes of Great Britain, and the development of the contemporary world "temporarily identified with that of nineteenth-century liberal bourgeois society."[4] This is important to note: the "liberal bourgeois society" referred to by Hobsbawm informs not only trading patterns but also debates concerning class, race, and gender, as well as contemporary fashion. Hobsbawm also refers to patterns of trade, noting that the 1880s, compared to the 1780s, were genuinely global. Global trade and the latest technological innovations are important factors. Colonization and overseas trade brought access to new products; and technology helped with the development of consumer goods for an expanding market. For example, the development of the modern comb can be linked to both emerging technologies and new materials found in British colonies. This included gutta-percha, a natural latex/plant sap, which came from Malaysia and other Pacific Rim countries. Hard rubber combs became available after the 1850s, and, unlike wooden combs, were less likely to snap.[5]

Products thus have complex biographies, histories, and meanings;[6] this is obviously the case here, indicating a potentially wide-ranging discussion as different cultures have their own approaches to "hair care." With this in mind, this chapter will focus on production and practice in "the West," primarily Britain and the United States. "The West," as Stuart Hall argues, is a *historical*, not a geographical, construct, "a society that is developed, industrialized, urbanized, capitalist, secular, and modern" (emphasis in original).[7] This concept of "the West" functions in many ways, but important to note is that it provides criteria of evaluation against which other societies are ranked "and around which powerful positive and negative feelings cluster. [...] 'the West = developed = *good* = desirable; or the "non-West" = under-developed = *bad* = undesirable'. It produces a certain kind of *knowledge* about a subject" (emphases in original).[8] There are four points of discussion. The first, "Producing Hair," will consider the global trade, sources, and attitudes. In the context of changing constructions of masculinity and femininity, "Gender: Products and Practice" looks at popular approaches to hair care along with debates informing their use. "Practice: Hairwork" explores the passion for creating items such as jewelry and portraits, and Victorian popular culture's love of sentimentality. Finally, "Hair and Race" references African Americans and the practices employed by enslaved people, as well as postbellum developments in hair care.

PRODUCING HAIR

In the West there was an obsession with hair.[9] Some indication of the wide variety of products available for preparation and decoration is shown in this advertisement from a New York wig-maker in 1867:

> Hair Jewelry, Gold Mountings for Hair Jewelry, Gent's wigs and Toupees, Ladies' Wigs, Switches, Braids, Curls, Waterfalls, Frizettes, Coils, Bows, Fronts, Scratches, Bands, Hair, Partings, Whiskers, Beards, Mustaches, Puffs, Curling-Irons, Curling-Sticks, Crimping-Irons, Perfumery, Pomades and Creams, Soaps, Hair Brushes, combs, Hair Oils, Cosmetiques, Crimping-Pins, Face Powders, Rouges, French Enamel and Hair Powders–Diamond Powder, Gold Powder, Silver Powder.[10]

Wide-ranging as it is, the advertisement refers solely to adornments and products *for* the hair, and does not include jewelry and other crafts *made* from hair. It is also important to note that the products are not gendered solely for women. Secondly, implicit in this is a complex intersection of goods and commerce, manufacturing, and advertising, all of which contribute to the trade in hair.

Clearly all products made of hair require raw material, and the question is where does this originate; is it of human and/or animal origin? Two fictional characters, Jo March in Louisa May Alcott's *Little Women* (1868) and Marty South in Thomas Hardy's *The Woodlanders* (1887), separated by class, time, and continent, are united in that they both sell their hair in order to raise money.[11] Marty receives two sovereigns for hers,[12] Jo twenty-five dollars; tails of hair sell for forty dollars.[13] In Marty's case class and economic relationships are explicit and immediate as her hair is used to make a wig for a rich local widow. Class is less obvious in *Little Women*, but economic inequality is clear, as Jo wants the money to help her father, hospitalized while fighting in the American Civil War (1861–1865), and her act also concerns female sacrifice during a time of war. While their shorn hair is seen as challenging dominant notions of femininity and with implications for their personal identity, at the same time these examples draw attention to the point that one person's fashion can depend on the sacrifice of another. In western capitalist society privilege and poverty went hand in hand with inequalities of relations of production in this huge global market.

Hair came from Asia Minor, India, China, and Japan, as well as from Europe. It was described as being "harvested," bought and sold at markets across Europe, such as that at Morlans in the Pyrenees,[14] where the hair of poor peasant and serving women was cut and bought by hairdressers and traders, sometimes for money, sometimes for handkerchiefs, muslins, or ribbons.[15] Thomas Adolphus Trollope commented on the hair harvest that took place at a fair in Brittany in the late 1830s or 1840, showing sympathy for the young women on the loss of their hair, "an article which must be worth a sum of considerable importance to them" and criticizing the traders:

> The highest value given by these abominable hair-merchants is twenty sous, and the more usual consideration by far is a gaudy, but trumpery, cotton handkerchief, worth about twelve or sixteen sous [...] The profit thus netted by these hair-mongers, during a tour through the country, must be enormous.[16]

A sous was a very small amount, equal to 5 centimes and 10 centimes (equivalent to the UK penny and the US cent); women in the United States received a similar sum, "only about fifteen to seventy cents a pound,"[17] overall a far cry from that paid to the fictional characters as the suppliers received little for their "product." Alexander Rowland writing in 1853 estimated that a peruke (a man's wig, or periwig), which contained only three ounces of hair originally costing less than a shilling, "is frequently sold at the price of twenty-five to thirty shillings."[18] Trollope also suggested the women being dehumanized by the process as they were "sheared one after the other like sheep."[19]

As indicated, the hair trade was a huge business. Richard Corson notes that over a one-year period, 1859–1860, 150,000 and 200,000 pounds of hair, valued close to a million dollars (about £365,000 in 1965) was imported into the United States; in 1866 it was triple the amount.[20] The London *Times* stated in 1870 that 11,954 chignons were exported from France to England during the past year (Paris was the major hair market of the world) and also a sufficient quantity of hair for 7,000 chignons to be made up in England;[21] and in 1862 it was reported that about a hundred tons a year was bought in the Paris market.[22] Other major importers were Russia and the United States. While the reports do not make it clear as to whether this is *all* human hair, it is interesting to speculate on the numbers of women selling their hair for this to be achieved. Given its global nature, and the vast array of associated products, it is also interesting to consider how many people were involved in the trade overall. Some indication of the numbers employed in Britain was given by Alexander Rowland, who states Pigot's (trade) Directory for 1840 shows 950 hairdressers in London, and about the same in the provinces. The London Directory included:

> Three hair-merchants (large wholesale importers probably); seventeen hair-manufacturers; twenty-four artistes, or workers in hair—hair jewellers, or device workers, as they may be termed—who elaborate the hair of our deceased friends and relatives into such *memento mori* as rings, brooches, earrings, chains, and other fanciful ornaments; 650 hair-dressers, barbers etc. and twenty-seven wig-makers [...]. (Emphasis in original.)[23]

The connections to other associated businesses also discussed by Rowland are important to note as he refers to the silk manufacturers in Lyon, France, where silk linings and ribbons for a million perukes a year are made, as well as metallic clasps and fastenings, "to the amount of one hundred thousand francs yearly."[24]

Hair was thus commercialized and industrialized, detached from its use value, and prized for its exchange value.[25] However, products also carry symbolic value and are overlaid with social and cultural meanings. Perhaps most obvious is the discourse of fashion, be that relating to style, or color, and what is considered modish at any one time. For example, in the early part of the nineteenth century dark hair, especially black, was in fashion: "What spectacle, indeed [...] can be more seducing than that of jet black hair, falling in undulating ringlets upon the bosom of a youthful beauty?" wrote the anonymous author of *The Art of Beauty* in 1825.[26] In the 1860s golden and light tinted hair began to be favored, with gold and silver powder considered elegant in fashionable circles, and at this time hair from Germany, being lighter in color, was particularly valuable.[27] Less obvious, perhaps, but of no less importance, were discourses concerning race and issues around social order and disintegration.[28] In her discussion of nineteenth-century biological determinism, hair, and race, Sarah Cheang comments that in this period cultural differences between groups were thought to have had "a biological, and hence inescapable, origin in the body. However, the biological concept of race still involved cultural values and distinction";[29] not all hair was seen as "equal." That there was a value system relating to race was made evident in comments in the *Hairdressers' Weekly Journal* with a reference to "The woolly hair of the negro," the dry temperature in Africa changing the hair "into a kind of course wool."[30] Similarly, Robert Tomes, writing in the United States in 1870, criticized the chignon as a "tumor-like excrescence," going on to say that it was made from hair "which is mostly brought from Caffreland, where it is cut from the heads of the filthiest and most disgusting population in the world."[31] In the United States Asian hair was denigrated in the 1880s and 1890s with newspaper articles alleging it was the cause of the introduction of many diseases to Europe, was cut after death, and often carried the germs of the disease.[32] Hair did go through a cleaning process, for example, advertised in the 1880s by Osbourne, Garrett & Co. as "perfectly clubbed, clean and free from nits," diluted in nitric acid to remove the original color.[33] However, while issues of race were evident, there were also anxieties relating to public health, overcrowding, and sanitation, which were linked to outbreaks of three contagious diseases: cholera, typhus, and influenza. Some of these anxieties are perhaps also behind comments made by writers in magazines reporting on hair collection and storage; the *Ladies' Treasury* in 1868 reported on a visit to a hair workshop referred to the "close and fusty smell," and being assured that none of the hair was cut from corpses:

> There is a certain deadness and harshness which an experienced hand recognises immediately [...] the poverty, the sickness, the sorrow, the ignorance, and the vice, forcibly suggested themselves as we turned over mass after mass of human hair.[34]

The *Ladies' Gazette of Fashion* commented on scavengers wading through the gutter to hook up "every floating tangle of hairs." "Many hundredweights of these heads and tails, grimly characterised as 'dead hair', annually cross the Alps [...] on their way to our more Northern centres of civilisation."[35] The reference to the north as "civilized" is also important to note.[36] Further, as Galia Ofek argues, Victorian representations viewed women's hair as contamination;[37] the above comments on the production process are a long way from the slightly more bucolic image of the peasant girl, selling at the hair harvest, or indeed the literary references above.

GENDER: PRODUCTS AND PRACTICE

While the addition of hairpieces, of ornaments, combs, frizettes, curls, and ringlets, helped create volume, it took time to achieve the elaborate styles, as did the work involved in maintaining upkeep (i.e. washing, brushing, drying). Hairstyles throughout the nineteenth and early twentieth centuries were continually changing;[38] the search for novelty, for the new, was aided by the discourse of fashion being disseminated via the growing market for women's magazines in both Britain and the United States.[39] Magazines advised readers on a range of issues, including premature grayness, hair colors, and in 1873 in the *Young Ladies' Journal*, concerns raised about hair loss or thinning hair: "Try rum and castor oil mixed in equal parts, shaken together, and rubbed into the roots of the hair at night. It is stimulating and nourishing."[40] There was not always agreement on whether to wash or brush the hair, also whether it should be dyed. In 1830 *Godey's Lady's Book* recommended washing it daily "with warm soft water to which occasionally a portion of soap will be a very proper addition."[41] However, earlier in 1809, Alexander Rowland claimed hair washed with soap and water was "very pernicious to long hair, and sometimes turns it red."[42] Dyeing the hair was frowned upon by some, with Robert Tomes stating that "dyeing the hair is the most preposterous of all attempts at human deceit";[43] his concern perhaps related to notions of the individual, deception, and issues of identity. For Isabel Mallon, who wrote as Ruth Ashmore in the *Ladies' Home Journal*, its use had a class aspect, and while seemingly sharing similar ideas regarding artificiality, it perhaps also linked to anxieties and the *demi monde*, as she commented in 1892:

> It almost goes without saying that a well-bred woman does not dye her hair. If in some moment of, I was going to say temporary insanity, she should be induced to do it, although it would be mortifying and she will have to permit herself to look like a striped zebra for a short time, still it will be wisest to face the situation and allow her hair to grow back to its natural colour.[44]

One writer in *Leisure Hour: A Family Journal of Instruction and Recreation* viewed the practice as "silly, and worse, morally wrong," criticizing both women and men.[45] A scientific discourse, along with an appeal to vanity, was employed in the discussion as the writer refers to using a lead compound or a lead comb, and nitrate of silver—lunar caustic—which while effective can bestow "a certain play of iridescent colours, *which makes one look ridiculous*" (my emphasis).[46] He or she continues by commenting that whenever iron or any of its soluble preparations is used as a hair dye "the blackening sulphur agent must be artificially supplied, in the form of that abominably smelling compound, sulphide of ammonium."[47] It would thus be both obvious and potentially off-putting to others. However, publications provided recipes for those who wished to change their hair color, together with warnings as to its use, as evidenced by the following in 1825, which aimed to achieve the black hair fashionable at the time:

> Dissolve two drachms of nitrate of silver in six ounces of distilled water, add two drachms of gum water. Perfume it with any essence you choose, and wet the hair which you wish to dye black. It is dangerous if applied to the skin; and although it does darken the hair at first, the black colour is apt soon to become purple. It is often sold at a rack price.[48]

While being critical of using dye, some writers did not, perhaps, want to alienate those readers who might desire change, so suggested coloring the hair. To darken it, "Isobel," the author of *The Art of Beauty: A Book for Women and Girls*, recommended: "a mixture of rust and iron, oil of rosemary, and strong old ale (unsweetened), to be shaken daily for a fortnight, each shaking to be followed a few hours later by a decanting of the clear liquid."[49]

As the infrastructure improved in the West—roads and railways, for example—a growing number of commercial products became more widely available, further facilitated by the spread of the department store, the multiple shop, and advertising becoming an increasingly visible feature of an expanding consumer culture.[50] Consumer desire was no doubt also aided by the great, or universal exhibitions held in both European and American cities in the nineteenth century; six million people are said to have visited the Great Exhibition at Crystal Palace, London, in 1851.[51] Among the more curious exhibits at the London Exhibition was a "large vase composed of human hair: executed by J. Woodley,"[52] finger rings made of hair,[53] and a collection of "likenesses" of the Queen, Prince Albert, and the children,[54] while the Paris Exposition of 1855 displayed a life-size portrait of Queen Victoria crafted entirely from hair.[55] Among the more unusual exhibits at the New York Crystal Palace Exhibition of 1853 was a tea set made from hair shown by Linherr & Co., of 577 Broadway, New York City.[56] The tea set is not featured in the catalogue, though, which lists them as exhibiting "hair bracelets, breast-pins, rings and watch chains."[57] In what could be read as an early advertorial from *Gleason's Pictorial Drawing-Room Companion*, (figure 4.1) this magazine made several references promoting the artistry and abilities of Linherr & Co., including the comment "the bracelet and *tea set*—think of a tea set made of a lover's hair!—are really wonders of art, and must have required great labor to perfect them" (emphasis in original).[58] For Paris in 1855 Metcalf, Bingley & Co. of London produced a wide range of "articles for the hair," including products "to improve and beautify, to strengthen the roots and prevent it turning grey"; "Pure Bear's Grease. Carefully prepared and perfumed"; hair dyes "Instantaneous Liquid Hair Dye, warranted perfectly free from any unpleasant smell whatsoever," and the splendidly named "Crème de Sybarites."[59] John Mantel of Bedford presented "skin partings for wigs,"[60] while Eugene Rimmel advertised a "pommade" (*sic*), "Nutritive cream, a choice pellucid preparation."[61] W.H. Child of London displayed a new "Patent Friction Hair Brush" made to thoroughly clean "the Head from Dandriff [*sic*] and polish the Hair at the same time."[62]

One widely advertised commercial product in Britain toward the end of the century was Edwards' Harlene hair tonic, which made claims to both produce and restore hair. This product was aimed at men and women; the adverts show women with luxuriant Rapunzel-length hair (figure 4.2) and men with flowing locks and bushy beards, while the text states that among other things it is "the world-renowned remedy for baldness."[63] Many adverts presented a domestic setting and also aimed to promote its use at a very early age. In one from 1897 (Figure 2.2) a young girl, with long, shiny, beautiful hair, is pouring the product over the head of a baby, the text reading: "Harlene produces luxuriant hair"; while another features a girl sitting by her mother's dressing table watching her brush her long hair: "Mama, shall I have beautiful long hair like you when I grow up? Certainly, my dear, if you use Edwards' Harlene."[64] In the United States from the mid-1880s to 1924, the Sutherland Sisters produced a tonic that made similar claims to Edwards' Harlene. It was produced under the name of the Seven Sutherland Sisters Hair Grower from 1885, one slogan being "Remember! It's the Hair—not the Hat, that makes a Woman Attractive."[65] The Sutherland Sisters began their careers as singers with Barnum and Bailey's Greatest Show on Earth but their hair, which collectively measured thirty-seven feet (one sister's weighed about seven pounds), became the main attraction. The commercial potential of these products is evidenced by the profits they made: between 1886 and 1887 they sold $180,000's worth of the product, and when their business career finished in 1924 "sales had reached almost $3 million."[66] Changing fashions, primarily the popularity of shorter, bobbed hair, was the reason for production ceasing.

Possibly the most well known of all commodities in the period was Macassar Oil, the staining qualities of which gave rise to the "antimacassar," a small, decorative covering which adorned the arms and backs of Victorian and Edwardian upholstered furniture. Not everybody favored the product though; the author of *The Art of Beauty* suggested the public pay "hundreds, if not thousands, annually" for something composed of cheap materials, and along with other "receipts" (recipes) to beautify the hair, provided "the genuine recipe for its preparation."[67] However, the virtues of Macassar were extolled by Alexander Rowland in his pamphlet *An Essay on the Cultivation and Improvement of the Human Hair* in 1809. This publication, complete with testimonials from users, is a panegyric to Macassar as a panacea for all hair problems. He cites its benefits as helping to remedy "hair falling off,"[68] dryness,[69] grayness,[70] "Dandriffe" (*sic*) and "Scorbutic Humours" (i.e. scurvy) afflicting the "Heads of Children."[71] Gray hair, he suggested, arose from "ill-health, great anxiety, close attention to study; for intense thinking consumes the strength and exhausts the spirits."[72] To help with circulation, gentlemen who wear powder "should have the hair thoroughly combed with a fine tooth comb every week, in order to remove the powder and pomatum" as it would otherwise cause a headache, and possibly turn the hair gray.[73] Gender stereotypes are implicit as he asserts that hair loss in women "is generally owing to nervous and hypochondriac disorders—fevers and accouchements—disorders which convulse the human frame to that degree, as to cause

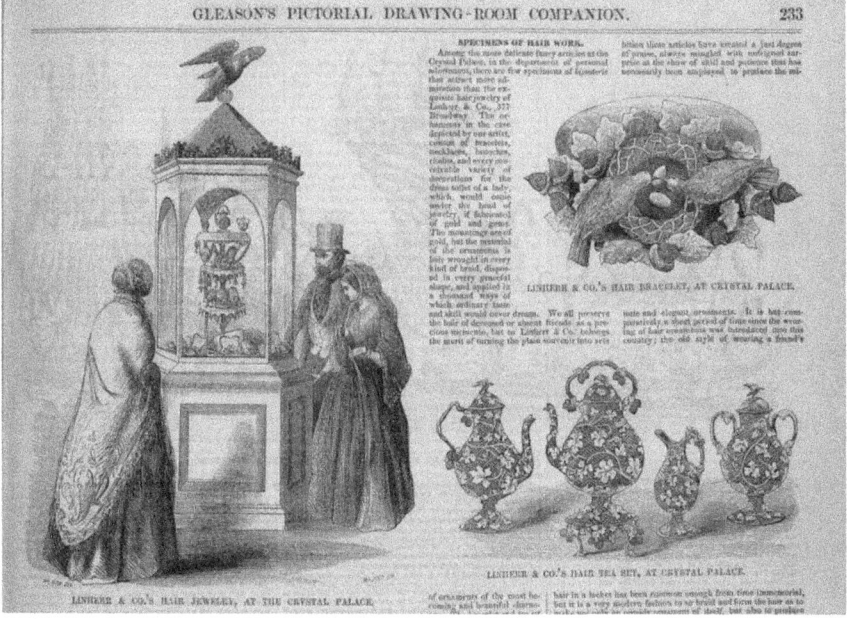

FIGURE 4.1: Hairwork by Linherr & Co., *Gleason's Pictorial Drawing Room Companion*, 1853. Courtesy Trustees of the Boston Public Library.

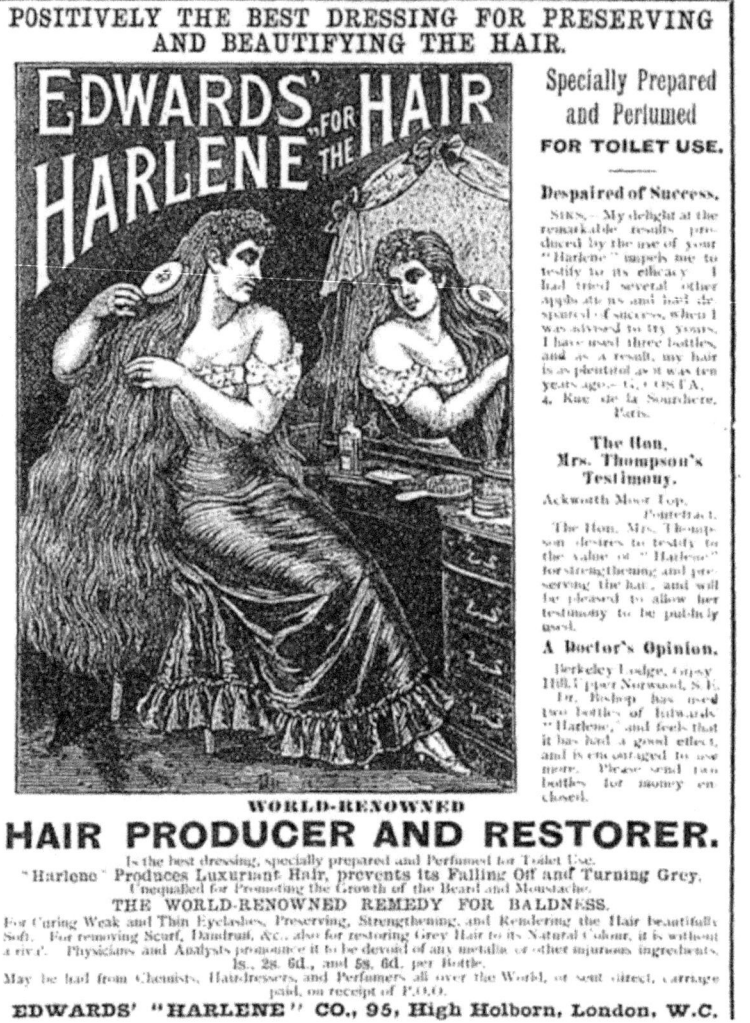

FIGURE 4.2: Advertisement for Edwards' Harlene, 1898. *The Shetland Times*, June 25, 1898.

a general relaxation of the pores."[74] He was in favor of brushing: women with long hair should use the hair brush frequently "especially if it is inclined to be damp, which is the cause of the dandriffe," and have their hair cut once a month by a person of experience. This, he stated, would help avoid split ends. That men experience hair loss and change of hair color (grayness) sooner than women was because of "perspiration, originating from violent exercise."[75]

As indicated, many products were not differentiated but manufactured for women and men alike, with writers and advertisers discussing similar problems experienced by both genders—hair loss and grayness, for example. Men also used hairpieces and dyes to create the right image; this was occasionally essential, particularly in some branches of the military where the mustache was necessary. If the recruit was unable to grow his own then fakery was resorted to, as evidenced firstly by the memoirs of Baron de Marbot and his experience when joining the 1st Hussars in France at the beginning of the century. He stated they all had to resemble one another: "the regiments of Hussars of that period had not only pig-tails, but long plaited tresses which hung from their temples and turned-up moustaches, it was the rule that everyone belonging to the regiment must have moustache, pig-tail and tresses."[76] As he had neither, both pig-tail and tresses were attached to his own hair. Further, having no mustache, his mentor used black wax to paint "an enormous curling moustache, which covered my upper lip and reached almost to, my eyes."[77] This apparently caused great discomfort while on guard duty where "the Italian sun sucked the moisture out of the wax of which my moustache was made, and, as it dried it pulled at my skin in a most disagreeable manner."[78] Some English regiments in the 1820s and 1830s also had regulations requiring mustaches which necessitated many young officers acquiring false ones in place of those they were unable to grow themselves.[79] Overall, these present interesting images, which undercut the hegemonic masculinity represented by the military.

The advertising discussed above, which included images of men with beards, is not coincidental as toward the middle of the century the beard began to symbolize trustworthiness and intelligence. Discourses relating to constructions of masculinity and gender politics as they inform fashion, thus linking to product use and practice, are important to note. In Britain in the early part of the nineteenth century, beards had been associated with political affiliations and were generally unfashionable.[80] However, as "the beard movement" developed from the 1850s, it was suggested they were integral to masculinity, symbolizing men's "natural" superiority over women.[81] As Alexander Rowland put it, the beard gave "that true masculine character indicative of energy, bold daring, and decision."[82] Beards and whiskers also became popular in the United States. When Abraham Lincoln took office in 1861, he became the first president to wear a beard; after the Civil War ended in 1865, "a more heavy-set and mature appearance for men was in vogue," one that included whiskers.[83] The beard, loved by many writers, including Charles Dickens, also received the following tender praise from the poet Robert Southey, together with suggestions for its care. He wrote, seemingly without irony:

> I myself, if I wore a beard, should cherish it, as the Cid Campeador did, for my pleasure. I should regale it on a summer's day with rose water, and without making it an idol, I should sometimes offer incense to it, with a pastille, or with lavender and sugar. My children, when they were young enough for such blandishments, would have delighted to stroke and comb and curl it, and my grandchildren in their turn would have succeeded to the same course of mutual endearment.[84]

Products such as Macassar, Edwards' Harlene, and the Sutherland Sisters' hair tonic, as well as false whiskers and mustaches, were, of course, important aids to the less hirsute.

The beard's popularity declined toward the end of the nineteenth century, with Oldstone-Moore suggesting concepts of hygiene may have played a part, but that more importantly "the virtues associated with beards lost importance in defining masculinity."[85] He states: "By World War I, a new construction of masculinity based more on group identity than domestic paternalism found its ideal image in the shaven face."[86] However, in the early part of the twentieth century the mustache was still favored by some, particularly the Kaiser mustache, with various suggestions given on how the shape could be achieved. In the United States the *Barbers' Journal* carried the following advertisement in 1904:

To obtain the Latest Fad in Facial Adornment, the Kaiser Mustache. Contains no grease. Simply dip into water and apply to mustache and beard. Will keep same in shape for rest of day. Now used and for sale by all leading barbers (Figure 4.3).[87]

The rather interesting Kaiser Mustache Trainer promised that if the device were worn for only five or ten minutes daily it would train the mustache to the shape desired. If worn all night for a few times it suggested the effect would be permanent.

FIGURE 4.3: Advertisement for the "Kaiser Mustache Trainer," 1904. Courtesy Trustees of the Boston Public Library.

There are complex arguments relating to changing fashions, notably the trend for being clean-shaven, and the role shaving technology might play here. Oldstone-Moore argues that improvements in shaving, particularly William Henson's hoe-type razor of 1847, and the safety razor, introduced at the end of the nineteenth century neither impacted the popularity of facial hair nor caused the beard's decline.[88] While his argument is compelling, it is probably also the case that both of the above products simplified the process of shaving; technology certainly has a role to play. King Camp Gillette, the mustache-wearing founder of the American Safety Razor Company in 1901, is credited with inventing the safety razor:

> I could see the way the blade could be held in a holder, then came the idea of sharpening the two opposite edges on the thin piece of steel that was uniform in thickness throughout, thus doubling its services; and following sequence came the clamping plates for the blade and a handle equally disposed between the two edges of the blade.[89]

Apparently sales of his safety razor were initially low: only 51 razors and 168 blades were sold in 1903, but by 1904 sales had risen to 90,000 razors and 123,000 blades. World War I and canny marketing further helped the product: when the United States entered the war in 1917, Gillette negotiated with the US armed forces to supply troops with individual "Khaki Sets" which contained a safety razor and blades which the men could take to Europe.[90]

PRACTICE: HAIRWORK

As discussed, the products exhibited in the great exhibitions, that is, jewelry and portraits, show there was a thriving trade in commodities that used hair; and while those on display were commercially made, there was also a flourishing "industry" within the home. Helen Sheumaker comments that in the United States most hairwork and jewelry was handmade until the 1870s; these were, as she puts it, "amateurs" making hairwork not for wages but as a hobby or home craft.[91] It is important to note women's unpaid labor here, and that this took place within the context of a growing bourgeois culture where female domesticity was lauded. Further, as already noted, in her discussion of the magazine market and its dissemination of the discourse of fashion, Margaret Beetham asserts: "the creation of a self through dress and appearance moved to the centre of feminine identity. Women's dress did not signify the productive labour of making commodities but [...] the labour of self-production."[92] Magazines, however, carry contradictory discourses, and Beetham identifies a tension between fashionable leisure and the duties of moral management, stating:

> The discourse of fashion represents a femininity located in appearance and display, old aristocratic values which—however revised—contradicted the bourgeois ideal of a femininity hidden in the domestic home and the female heart.[93]

The emphasis on female display links to Thorstein Veblen's argument concerning the conspicuous consumption, waste, and leisure of the (newly) wealthy bourgeoisie.[94] At the same time, female accomplishment within the home was highly prized, and while this included the more traditional pursuits such as painting and music, as shown by the many articles that extolled its virtues, hairwork was another such skill. The emphasis on crafts produced by women within the home shows evidence of a discourse relating to producing an identity which is not solely about display but about work, albeit unpaid, and creativity.

Hairwork was not new and had been produced in the eighteenth century, though, as Helen Sheumaker notes, with significant differences.[95] In the eighteenth century portrait miniatures were backed with hair and presented on small tables, and if displayed openly, to be picked up, this aided a *performance* of emotion. However, by the mid-nineteenth century these were replaced by items made entirely from hair, and these included watch chains, bracelets, brooches, rings, wreaths, as well as other decorative pieces for the home. Many items were made using the hair of a loved one, either as a home craft or with the hair taken to a jeweler to be made up into a piece of jewelry; products made also included what the US company E.C. Shriner described as "mementoes of the dead" including "wreaths made from Relics of Deceased Friends." This could include hair, as well as pieces of clothing, shrouds, and coffins.[96] It is important to set this passion for hairwork, particularly when using one's own hair or that of a loved one, in the context of the sentimental impulse that defined much of Victorian popular culture, the dynamics of which, unlike the more moralistic or inward-looking sensibilities associated with the eighteenth century and Romantic forms of feeling, can be regarded as a concern with the sharing of emotion, "the power and the pleasure of interactive feeling."[97] As Sheumaker observes, hairwork "made tangible the narrative of experience demanded by sentimentality (as laid out in countless sentimental fictional tales) because it physically embodied the emotional relationships between individuals."[98]

The practice of hairwork thus commodified emotions and relationships, and was deemed as appropriate work for women inside the home. It also helped in the creation of entrepreneurial activity, including the development of small businesses, one of which was run by a Mrs. Alexanna Speight. Speight was a hairworker in London who published a "how-to" booklet in 1871, *The Lock of Hair: Its History, Ancient and Modern, Natural and Artistic*. This, as the title suggests, included historical facts but also instructions on hairwork and how to make different designs, one of which was using palette-work to create the Prince of Wales' feather (Figure 4.4). Speight also sold kits containing all the tools necessary for working in hair, the details of which were provided in her book. They ranged in price from the "half-guinea," one polished cedar box; the "guinea box," one extra finished rosewood box, lined with velvet; and the "two guinea box," an extra finished silk velvet lined rosewood veneered box. Depending upon the price paid, tools included curling irons, scissors, tweezers, prepared gum, wire, porcelain palettes, and other items necessary for production.[99] Also Depending upon price, the number of tools increased and their quality improved—for example, one pair of tweezers in the half-guinea box; one pair of burnished gold and silver gilt tweezers for two guineas. Her mode of address is interesting; it is clearly for women, and more specifically aimed at the young: "If, after this little lecture, the fair and gentle reader will turn to diagram 17 (oddly coinciding, we have little doubt, with the number of her own tender summers)."[100]

Again with a youthful audience in mind, in 1890 *The Girl's Own Paper* described hairwork as "a highly remunerative employment for girls," and the skills could be "acquired by the youngest worker in a few moments,"[101] though the somewhat ambiguous reference to the "youngest *worker*" could indicate this as possibly something more than an accomplishment for young women. The article, written by "A.P.P." suggested it was "simple to learn" and over a period of three weeks, provided instructions, which included how to make a wooden frame, similar to a small loom, which would clamp onto a table. The tools for this could be obtained "from any village carpenter," and the lengthy tails of

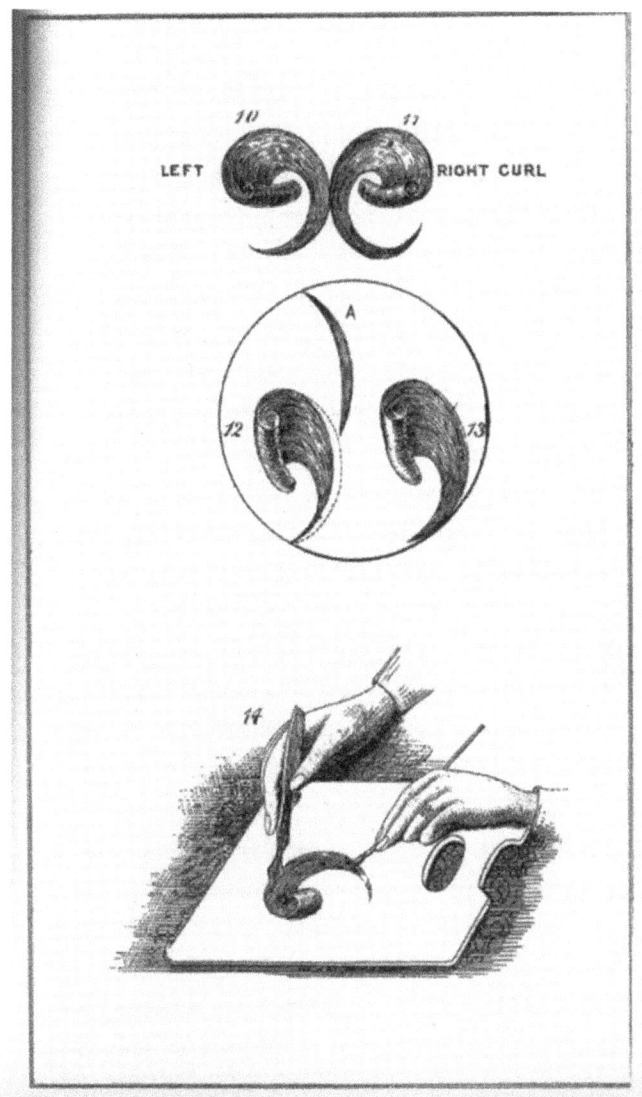

FIGURE 4.4: One step in palette-working hair. Alexanna Speight, *The Lock of Hair: Its History, Ancient and Modern, Natural and Artistic; With the Art of Working in Hair* (London: A. Goubard, 1871).

hair shown in the illustrations could be bought "by the ounce, of any length or colour."[102] A.P.P. refers to a range of possible items that could be made, including knotting to make the crown of a wig, designs such as the Scotch thistle with leaves and blossoms for the border of a sofa rug, and tambouring to make muffs, boas, and trimmings.[103] The making of the weft for this work, using wool and crimped silk, for example, is suggested as "a favourite occupation for children, girls or boys, on a wet day."[104] The final week of the series discussed the "Artistic Aspect of the Work," considering the importance of matching hair colors to individuals, and likening this to the work of a portrait painter.

The writer stated this requires a great degree of observation and discrimination, which "renders the work peculiarly suitable to ladies possessing artistic taste which they wish to turn to profitable account,"[105] an interesting comment, given history's celebration of *male* portrait painters. In an indication of the writer's ideological leanings, A.P.P. refers to "pure tints" such as chestnut and golden (Saxon), which cannot be artificially obtained; black and white hair, though similarly varied in tone, is not described in such terms. The skilled hairworker, the writer suggested, was able to obtain the "pure" tones by mixing tints, work requiring "the greatest nicety and care to be successfully accomplished."

Hairwork, therefore, lent itself to a variety of applications, as a home craft, as a pursuit for the less well-off to generate further income, and as small-scale independent production. It had the advantage of requiring little in the way of materials and stock, particularly for those unable to access capital and credit necessary to set up larger-scale factory production; artisan hairworkers in the United States included African Americans as well as north European immigrants.[106] This was one good source of employment for free African Americans in the ante- and postbellum years, and included Jared Gray in Chicago, and George and Elizabeth Stewart in Philadelphia among other professionals who made hair jewelry, as well as providing wigs, toupees, and hairdressing.[107] Even smaller scale is the work offered by the hairworker within the home, the woman presumably trying to supplement her income. This would appear to be the case in Helen Sheumaker's reference to a neighbor of diarist Harriet Smith. In her diary in 1863 she told of her neighbor offering to make items from horsehair: the woman asked fifteen dollars for "earrings, breast pin and head dress," but apparently could not supply an example of her work.[108]

Overall, hairwork was a time-consuming pastime, made more difficult if trying to collect hair to use in the project; despite A.P.P.'s statement that the practice was simple, it looks to be a somewhat complex and fiddly process. It was not a craft that survived long into the twentieth century; the British journal *Cornhill Magazine* announced it had ended as a fashion in July 1885, and while this statement was somewhat premature, it had all but disappeared from the market by the 1920s.[109] There were many reasons for this. Social, economic, political, and cultural changes at the *fin de siècle* obviously influenced the lives of men and women: as constructions of masculinity were changing, so too were discourses relating to femininity. Most notable were debates surrounding the "New Woman" toward the end of the century: the heroine of many novels of the *fin de siècle*, the sexually independent woman seeking opportunities for self-development outside of marriage.[110] There were complex narratives surrounding the New Woman, linked to women's changing social position and female emancipation. The birth rate dropped; secondary education for girls expanded; more women worked in paid occupations such as offices and shops; they played more sport, including tennis, cycling, and motorcycling; and they acquired greater freedom of movement.[111] These all impact the body. Although longer hair was still fashionable in the early part of the new century, shorter styles become popular in the second decade and post-World War I; Eric Hobsbawm comments that the postwar "jazz generation" "took over the public use of cosmetics, which had previously been the characteristic of women whose exclusive function was to please men: prostitutes and other entertainers."[112] Clothing became less restrictive, and women now displayed parts of the body, notably the legs (perhaps also helping to fuel the sales of safety razors). With this shift toward greater freedom for women, it is perhaps unsurprising that high-maintenance styles that required pads, combs, and false hair became less popular, along with time-consuming crafts such as hairwork. The issue of false hair being possibly unhygienic, together with notions of dirt and pollution, was, as already noted, of concern and perhaps another factor. Disquiet was voiced by six women interviewed by the *Ladies' Home Journal* in 1911. When they were asked, "Can a woman's hair be done simply?" all responded "*Yes!*" (emphasis in original), saying it was possible to wear their hair without using the "unsanitary and ridiculous" "rat" or "puff."[113] Further, questions regarding identity and "authenticity" had been voiced in the previous century,[114] and these anxieties, along with what was also the suggestion of a new spirit of openness, can be seen in the observation of one woman questioned by the *Ladies' Home Journal*: "I would infinitely rather go without hair if need be than live a lie to myself, my husband, and my children."[115]

The practice of adding false hair did continue, though, and the "postiche" was created for those who regretted bobbing their hair. In Paris in 1910 a Monsieur Perrin invented the Marie-Louise barrette, a bar-shaped clip or hairslide to connect two pieces of postiche. The French hairdresser Emile Long described it thus:

> [It is] a barrette pierced with little holes, into which is sewn a length of clubbed hair or two lengths [permitting short locks of hair to be connected seamlessly. It allows for the use of hair] obtainable cheaply, ornamented pleasingly and as long as may be desired to encircle the head for a coiffure *à la mode*. (Emphasis in original.)[116]

Other practices, which had their own histories, became more widespread. Waving the hair by using hot tongs, as well as creating curls or ringlets by using rags, was well known, but these approaches were not long-lasting. Although he was not the first person to devise a method for curling hair, German hairdresser Karl Nessler, later Charles Nestlé, is noted as inventing the permanent wave. He combined two earlier approaches—heat to curl hair and the use of caustic chemicals to curl wigs—and developed his own spiral heat method. It was demonstrated in London in 1906, and the procedure involved hair being soaked in an alkaline solution (allegedly mixing cow urine and water), with hair wound around rods connected to an electric heating machine; the rods were heated to curl the damp chemically treated hair.[117] Taking up to twelve hours to complete and costing around $1,000, it was both expensive and time-consuming, thus clearly only available to the wealthy, and given the potential for burning hair and scalp, presumably also only undertaken by the brave. Obviously the procedure was finessed and refined as the century progressed; but generally, for many women and the changing context of their lives, products that held out the promise of saving time carried more potential. Therefore, the complex interrelationship of social change and technological development is important to note. Progress in electrical engineering in the late nineteenth century and electricity becoming available in the home played its part in the development of new consumer products and the creation of new markets, the electric hair dryer being one such item. The "offspring" of the vacuum cleaner and the blender, the hair dryer was developed for sale in 1920, and has an intriguing history. Charles Panati notes that in the first decade of the century it was usual to promote several functions for a single appliance;[118] an advertisement for the Pneumatic Cleaner showed a woman drying her hair with a hose connected to the exhaust of a vacuum cleaner—a fascinating combination of the multifunctional, the labor-saving, and the time-saving.

HAIR AND RACE

The account so far has considered production and practice in relation to white women/men in the West, and it is clear that many of the histories of fashion, style, and adornment have privileged this group. However, there are other stories. The history of hair, and the connection with skin color and race, is complex; meanings shift and are subject to debate,[119] and its role in African American history and identity politics is important to note. Kobena Mercer argues hair is second only to skin color as a racial signifier. He states:

> when hair-styling is critically evaluated as an aesthetic practice inscribed in everyday life, all black hair-styles are political in that they articulate responses to the panoply of historical forces which have invested this element of the ethnic signifier with both personal and political "meaning" and significance.[120]

The hair practices of African Americans have to be set in the context of slavery, of biological determinism, which has invested hair with negative meanings,[121] and practices which have articulated an ideal based on white western standards of beauty.

Slaves in the American South devised various methods to maintain their hair, making use of whatever materials were available. Axle grease was used by men as both a dye and a hair relaxer;[122] chopped corn was rubbed into the hair to help remove dust and dirt; and kerosene was used to dry clean it by rinsing it through the hair repeatedly, or applying the kerosene to a rag and rubbing this over strands of hair.[123] Further, freshly churned butter or mutton tallow was used as a hair conditioner, while a "unique hair and skin conditioner was wild apple leaves and chicken fat boiled together."[124] Men who worked outside would shave their heads and wear hats, while the women would wear headscarves. Noliwe M. Rooks comments on portraits of slave women that show them covering their hair by wearing bandannas.[125] This practice was multifunctional as it lessened the chance of heatstroke, kept the hair clean, absorbed perspiration, and "trained" hair growth,[126] that is, kept it smooth. Slaves also created other haircare tools, including using wool carding tools to comb through tangles.[127] The comb is an important instance of product design suggested as the norm, that is, to be used by all, but only reflecting the dominant culture. African American hair historian Willie Morrow states enslaved house workers introduced the European comb, noting how it hurt, unlike when used on the hair of white children.[128]

Rooks's comment on "training" hair growth is important to note as this practice relates to smoothing out kinks in the hair, and draws attention to debates surrounding hair straightening and suggested conformity to hegemonic white culture. She identifies different meanings in the advertisements for hair straightening products in the period being discussed. For example, Ozonized Ox Marrow and Curl-I-Cure were marketed by white-owned companies in the nineteenth century, and aimed at African Americans; the advertisements argued for the desirability of African Americans *changing* characteristics such as hair texture if they wanted to fit into American society.[129] However, in the early twentieth century companies owned and operated by African American women started taking a different approach by challenging dominant ideologies and constructions of African American women; advertisements suggested they should strive for *healthy* hair.[130] Madam T.D. Perkins's adverts state she is a "Scientific Scalp Specialist" telling readers, "no matter how dark your skin is" the treatment "will cultivate, beautify and grow a persons hair, so long as there is no physical ailment which will prevent it."[131] Madam C.J. Walker, credited with "widely distributing and popularising the straightening comb around 1905,"[132] similarly suggested the health benefits of her products, including her Vegetable Shampoo and Wonderful Hair Grower.[133] However, from late 1914 she also linked her haircare products with ideas of independence and economic security for women by using her method of hair preparation while they also distributed the product: "Learn to Grow Hair and Make Money."[134]

I referred above to African American artisans and entrepreneurs involved in hairwork, wig making, or hairdressing, noted by Sheumaker, and others included Northern free women Cecilia Remond Putnam, Marchita Remond, and Caroline Remond, who owned the Ladies Hair Work Salon in Salem, Massachusetts, as well as the largest wig factory in the state. Their product, Mrs. Putnam's Medicated Hair Tonic, was marketed for dealing with hair loss; some sales were local, while most of their business was carried out via mail order.[135] Juliet Walker notes that many antebellum free black women capitalized on the haircare business, and given the poverty of many African Americans, their customers were predominantly white.[136] It is important to note that many of the companies started by African American women in the postbellum era, including Madam T.D. Perkins and Madam C.J. Walker, catered for women and men from within their cultural group.

Finally, it is important to look at comments that talk of the *pleasure* of curly hair. Juliette Harris and Pamela Johnson refer to the practice of "wrapping" the hair with thread or string, which continued into the twentieth century. Women used whatever was available to achieve a specific look; if store-bought thread was unobtainable they used the white string from cotton bags, "tobacco vines, or strips of stockings to wrap hair that had been oiled with lard or fatback grease. Keeping spring hair elongated and untangled, the technique somewhat smoothed the kinks."[137] Peter Clifton beautifully evokes the attraction for this in his memory of an enslaved woman's string-wrapped hair: "I meets Christina and seek her out for to marry. Dere was somethin' about dat gal dat day I meets her, though her hair had about a pound of cotton thread in it, dat just attracted me to her like fly will sail 'round and light on a 'lasses pitcher."[138] Another former slave, Amos Lincoln commented: "the gals dressed up on Sunday. All week they wear they hair all roll up with cotton ... Sunday come they com' their hair out fine. No grease on it. They want it naturally curly."[139]

CONCLUSION

Focusing on four areas—"Producing Hair," "Gender: Products and Practice," "Practice: Hairwork," and "Hair and Race"—this chapter has drawn attention to the complexity of the trade in hair in "the West" in the long nineteenth century. The context was a period of social change, global trade, technological innovation, and a developing liberal bourgeois society, informing discussions of race, gender, and class. Inequalities range across all areas, to include those selling their hair—poor working-class/peasant women receiving little reward—and preferences as to origin (predominantly European), this in turn linking to anxieties concerning hygiene, dirt, and pollution from an "other." Inequalities also apply to the products available for use and to product design only suitable for certain types of hair. The choices for enslaved people were limited and had to be improvised as they used everyday items, though the use of kerosene suggests potential dangers.

The hair trade was all-encompassing. Products were manufactured *for* the hair—ornaments, wigs, hairpieces; there were goods that *used* hair, testified to by exhibits at the universal exhibitions; and with hairwork it became a task, or accomplishment, predominantly for women, but one that led to the possibility of paid employment within the home. It is also interesting to note the many debates on product use, whether or not hair should be washed, and apprehensions over use of dyes. Such apprehensions over the use of dyes; the latter not necessarily concern over possible harm but implications relating to identity. These debates both conform to and perpetuate dominant notions of masculinity and femininity in the period, broadly male dominance and female passivity. However, product use is also subject to social transformation with changing lifestyles and technical innovation, just two areas that impact hair production and practice in the Age of Empire.

ACKNOWLEDGMENT

For Pam Chipperton.

CHAPTER FIVE

Health and Hygiene: "Monster top-knots and balloon chignons"

Purity and Contamination in the False Hair Trade

JANICE M. ALLAN

When a lady buys false locks she little knows the curious and mysterious tale each individual hair possibly could tell her. (*The London Review*, September 23, 1863)[1]

Topographically considered, the [price] list does, of course, supply the required information, but it affords no clue to the real source and mode of origin of a large proportion of the hair used in the English trade, which, startling as the assertion may appear, are intimately associated with one of the most difficult problems of hygiene and modern civilization. (*The Examiner*, November 28, 1874)[2]

Since the so-called "material turn" in nineteenth-century studies, it has become widely recognized that the profusion of "things" that dominated the Victorian imagination, no less than their parlors or the pages of their novels, is endowed with a degree of agency that challenges the Cartesian binary of subject and object. "Like human subjects," Katharina Boehm argues, "objects have been found to possess complex biographies and histories, social and cultural lives."[3] Writing the hidden histories of the "things" that sit at the heart of thing theory, early advocates such as Elaine Freedgood (2006) and John Plotz (2009) have revealed the social and historical, personal and imperial significance of seemingly mundane Victorian objects, demanding recognition for what is too familiar to register as meaningful. At the same time, such readings have foregrounded the extent to which nineteenth-century subjects depend on inanimate objects in the construction (and reconstruction) of classed and gendered identities. Adding to this growing body of work, this chapter will explore the histories and biographies of the false hair that was imported into England by the ton to create the elaborate coiffures that, together with the appropriate dress and accessories, created the appearance of genteel femininity in the 1860s and 1870s (Figure 5.1).

FIGURE 5.1: "The present fashions in hair, 1870." From a Private Collection.

Equally important, it will also consider how the use of such hair—sourced from the heads of peasant "growers" or less palatable sources—came to be, as suggested by the chapter's epigraph, "intimately associated with one of the most difficult problems of hygiene and modern civilization."

According to Mary Douglas's foundational reading of purity and pollution, the term "clean" designates that which is "proper to its class, suitable, fitting" while dirt, in contrast, "is essentially disorder."[4] So conceived, dirt is "never a unique, isolated event. Where there is dirt there is system. Dirt is the by-product of a systematic ordering and classification of matter, in so far as ordering involves rejecting inappropriate elements."[5] Thus it is hardly surprising that "references to dirt in nineteenth-century texts are generally informed by bourgeois ideas of order, respectability, and propriety. A morally charged notion of cleanliness was a crucial component of the self-image of the middle classes, who sought to set themselves apart from the working classes."⁶ Building on this construction of dirt as a relational rather than an ontological category—expressed most clearly in Douglas's assertion that dirt is "matter out of place"⁷—this chapter will argue that false hair can and should be read in the same way. As genuine human hair, as opposed to synthetic or animal-derived, such hair was "false" only in relation to the "real" hair to which it was added. Unlike dirt, however, the "place" of false hair is surprisingly difficult to determine. At the most basic level, where else might hair belong but on a head? If, however, matter "is conceived as dirt when it disturbs order and threatens to pollute what a social group cherishes as clear and pure,"⁸ false hair is, as this chapter will demonstrate, most decidedly "dirty."

In tracing the literal and symbolic relations between false hair and contemporary constructions of purity and pollution, it is important to be mindful of the caveat offered in Ian Hodder's appropriately entitled *Entangled* (2012), that the "'return to things' in the humanities and social sciences has not quite made it to the things themselves": "Things in themselves are skirted, always embedded in meaning and discourse."⁹ To test Hodder's assertion one need only recollect one of the many heightened representations of hair in nineteenth-century fiction—Maggie Tulliver urging her brother to hack off her heavy tresses in a moment of impulsive rebellion or the golden hair of one of Mary Braddon's sensational heroines coming loose and tumbling down in a moment of unrestrained passion¹⁰—to recognize how our understanding of hair has been "conditioned by the discursive environment" in which it is read, first and foremost, "as a signifier, encoding and creating meaning."¹¹ Consider, in contrast, the following description of a journalist's trip to a large hair emporium:

> we found the four walls of the sale-room lined round with shelves, reaching from the floor to the ceiling, on which were piled up chignons upon chignons of all qualities and all shades of colour, from raven black to the most delicate blond, done up in packets of six, the smallest number sold by the house, which does no retail trade [...] In an adjoining warehouse the raw material was lying in heaps upon the floor beside scores of young women, who were sorting and weighing out the chignons of the future, allowing so many grammes for one sort and so many for another. The place, in fact, was redolent of hair. There was hair in all the drawers, hair in cardboard boxes, hair hanging from the ceiling and clinging to the walls, hair upon the counters, upon the chairs, and in the very inkstand; there was even hair in the air itself, moving about as it were in clouds, which when you agitated them disagreeably caressed you.¹²

Removed from the "discursive environment" that renders it meaningful and possessing an uncanny agency and energy, this somewhat grotesque representation of hair has a dislocating effect that "interrupt[s] the habits with which we view the world, the habits that prevent us from seeing the world—to call us to a particular and particularizing attention" to the thing itself, in all its physicality (Figure 5.2).¹³ Crucially, for Hodder, it is only when the "gaze shifts to look more closely, harder at the thing" that the viewer can begin to recognize the extent to which "things are connected to and dependent on other things."¹⁴

In order to concretize these connections and dependencies, Hodder adopts the analogy of a house to foreground "the ways in which the front or visible parts of things often depend on back or hidden parts":

The front of a house often looks neat, tidy and self-sufficient, concerned with expressing status, order, wealth and so on. It is only at the back of the house that one sees all the electricity wires, flues, gutters and outlets, the air conditioners and the communication dishes. And hidden away behind walls and beneath the floors there are the drains and sewers, the ducts and piping. Digging down we would uncover the dependencies of things. Behind the scenes there are the flows that make the front of the house possible. Things at the back service things at the front.[15]

For the purposes of this chapter, the "front" corresponds to the finished coiffures that are presented to the public in an effort to both perform and demarcate class and gender status in increasingly anonymized urban centers. The real interest, however, lies "at the back," where it is possible to trace the "hidden" histories of false hair, from its dubious origins—

FIGURE 5.2: "Human hair sewn onto a braid foundation" (1850s–1880s) © Victoria and Albert Museum, London.

including the drains and sewers that were scoured by ragpickers for "dead hair"—to the point at which it is braided seamlessly into the natural hair of its "owner."

This journey, "from poverty, tears, and parting kisses, to riches and ball-rooms" was, as noted by a writer for the *Hairdressers' Journal*, a "sad subject for contemplation."[16] According to this same journal, moreover, "no less than two hundred thousand pounds weight of human hair, or a little under one hundred tons" makes its way into Paris each year.[17] And from Paris, "the hair—manufactured and unmanufactured, prepared and unprepared, sorted in lengths and as it comes from the head, clean and dirty, lustrous and ragged—streams to all parts of Europe, nay, to all parts of the new and old world."[18] Given the potential for class and racial contamination within this process—far more dangerous than a case of chignon fungus—it is hardly surprising that the traffic in hair was also an increasingly anxious "subject of contemplation" as the contemporary press alternately denied or exaggerated the threat it represented.

"A NECESSITY OF MODERN SOCIAL EXISTENCE"

Before turning to the origin stories of false hair and its trafficking in the 1860s and 1870s, it is important to establish the extent of its use; for what was true in 1854—"that only a small number of persons are really aware of the extent and the curious nature of this traffic"—remains true today.[19] Writing in 1874, the physician Andrew Wynter announced that the "fashion of wearing false hair has become so universal, that the exception of the few persons contented with the crop Nature has supplied simply serves to prove the rule."[20] A similar view is offered by *The Times*, whose correspondent claims that "almost every woman wears, more or less, false hair, either in the shape of luxuriant locks, which the rich only can command, or in the shape of frizzets, or the foundations for those monstrous excrescences which are deforming the beautiful contour of the head in the shape of chignons."[21] While hardly a disinterested source, the *Hairdressers' Journal* rejoices that "the variety of hair-shapes is almost without end, and their number is of course daily increasing. Are there not fronts, bags, ringlets, coronets, rolls, plaits, plicaturas, and countless others, and has not each of these forms its many varieties? (Figure 5.3)"[22]

All the Year Round remains neutral and simply accepts the use of false hair "as a necessity of modern social existence."[23] Focusing on the financial and trade dimensions, other sources astound their readers with relevant facts and figures. Reporting on the French trade returns for 1877, the *London Reader*, for example, announces that "from 12,000 to 15,000 chignons of false hair are annually imported into this country from France alone, and at the same time enough unmade hair to furnish 10,000 more. The total value of the hair exported from France is set down at £88,000, of which by far the largest portion is paid by the ladies of this country."[24] The "vast rise in its price," according to the *Daily News*, is attributable to "the enormous quantities of false hair used by ladies," explaining that this "has gone up 400 percent within the last dozen years, while four times as much is used now as at that period. Sixteen times as much money is consequently spent upon this article of adornment in the present year as was devoted to it in 1856."[25]

To explain such demand one need look no further than the hairdressers of the 1860s and 1870s who had a vested interest in promoting the increasingly elaborate styles that complemented the evening wear of the period. Intricate coiffures that could not be executed by a lady's maid, let alone the lady herself, kept hairdressers in business. Thus a correspondent of the *French Hairdressers' Journal* makes a formal complaint to its editor about the lack of new styles within its pages:

FIGURE 5.3: Advertisement for "Postiches, nattes et crêpes." *La mode illustrée, Journal de la famille* 22 (May 31, 1863): 174.

For the past two years we have seen nothing but the same immortal head-dress which varies only in name [...] Mind I don't find fault with the coiffure, only it is so old that most ladies can dress it for themselves—and those who can't can easily find ladies' maids who will. I expect daily to see this style on the head of the next fish-wife.[26]

Nor is it irrelevant that the fees charged by hairdressers were relatively modest in comparison to the income generated by the sale of false hair; its many varieties displayed on waxen shop window dummies before being transferred to the heads of the customers inside. It is, therefore, hardly surprising that this same correspondent is quick to specify

HEALTH AND HYGIENE

that any new style must have "plenty of false hair in it,—for you are right when you recommend the use of false hair. We pretty well live on it."[27] It is unlikely that the English *Hairdressers' Journal* would provoke such complaints as each issue contains two specially prepared plates representing the latest English and French styles, together with detailed instructions for their execution.

Looking through these instructions, it becomes clear that the use of false hair is both routine and extensive. Figure 5.4, for example, representing a style that is recommended "as one very becoming to English faces, and easy of execution," requires an unspecified number of "small frizzettes […] a false curl for each side, and a set of three curls for the

FIGURE 5.4: "English plate." *Hairdresser's Journal* 1, no. 4 (June 1863): n.p.

back hair."[28] Another style, christened the "NŒUD PSYCHE," requires only two pieces of false hair but one of these must be no less than 26 inches in length.[29] Such requirements were in no way atypical.

Coiffures made of the highest quality of manufactured hair bought "on foot" and imported from France or Germany were limited to women with sufficient income and leisure to enjoy them.[30] There were, however, alternative sources of cheap inferior hair which extended its use all the way down to the most common maid-of-all-work. As noted by the *Daily News*, false hair was "manufactured to meet the wishes and the purses of all classes of society, from the sixpenny frizett sold to fill out the sparse locks of the servant-of-all-work to the ten-guinea head of hair made up to aid the beauty of a Duchess."[31] Although restricted to the use of inferior hair, servants and other members of the working classes were just as much affected by the climate of social emulation as those above them and did their best—much to the disgust of contemporary social commentators—to imitate the coiffures as much as the dress and manners of their so-called betters. As an anonymous commentator complained in 1863:

> we allow our lady's-maids to abandon the neat and suitable distinction of caps, and to wear either their hair well *coiffé*, or to stick on a ghastly bit of black lace, or a net; so that it is wholly impossible to know whether the good lady who condescends to bring up warm water for our toilet is madame, at your service—or ma'amselle—fish or fowl, mistress or maid.[32]

As a style designed for the elite market grew familiar and open to imitation from below—"Miss Lofty plaits or curls her aristocratic locks; in emulation so also does Biddy, the maid-of-all-work"[33]—it became as necessary to the customers as the hairdressers themselves that it be replaced by something new. As a result, hairstyles became increasingly elaborate and voluminous, and dependent upon more and more false hair. This pattern continued until the inevitable backlash, which can be dated to around 1880, when the hairdressers begin to "view with dismay, not unmixed with indignation, the present fashion of dressing the hair simply and without ornament. The absence of curls, the disappearance of plaits, the neglect of the once popular chignon, they regard as so many slights offered to themselves."[34]

ORIGIN STORIES

> I have provided half the young ladies in Paris with false tresses, and not one has ever asked me the slightest question as to how or where they were obtained. ("The False Hair: A Tale," 1862)[35]

In order to meet the ever increasing demand for false hair, it was procured from a range of sources and the contemporary press appeared to delight in regaling its readers with both sanitized and sensational origin stories. As the *Saturday Review* recognized, "the subject of hair possesses our newspapers."[36] One of the earliest and most often cited of such stories comes from Thomas Adolphus Trollope's *A Summer in Brittany* (1840), which offers an illustrated account of the annual hair harvest that took place in the months of April and May (Figure 5.5).

In the immediate description of the process—that which was most often reproduced within the periodical press—it appears fairly benign. Attributing the girls' willingness to part with their hair to the use of the close Breton caps that hide its absence, Trollope

FIGURE 5.5: "Fair at Collinée." From chapter 18 of Thomas Adolphus Trollope's *A Summer in Brittany*. Edited by Frances Trollope, 2 vols. (London: Henry Colburn, Publishers, 1840), vol. 1.

describes how he saw "several girls sheared one after the other like sheep, and as many more standing ready for the shears, with their caps in their hands, and their long hair combed out and hanging down to their waists."[37] Most important within this description is the suggestion of free choice—there is no imputation of coercion or violence—and the connotations of cleanliness and health associated with the unadulterated country life of the peasant girls. While the price of hair fluctuated according to its length and quality, as well as the changing fashions that saw shades fall in and out of favor, Breton hair—and within the trade it was accepted as "a fact that there seems to be as much *breed* in hair as in other matters"[38]—retained its value. Ostensibly, this was because of its inherent qualities, including its fineness and pristine state (protected as it was by the peasants' traditional caps) but there is no evidence to suggest that the hair of this district was, in any way, quantifiably superior to that of others. Interrogating its privileged status within the trade, *Bentley's Miscellany* acknowledges that it is "not because their hair is particularly long or fine [...] they have no more of it than their neighbours."[39] Thus it is entirely plausible that it was the benign nature of its origins, as represented by Trollope and disseminated through the press, which played a key role in establishing and maintaining its market value. There is certainly no question that the various versions of this origin story that circulate throughout the 1850s, 1860s, and even 1870s concentrate on the quaint, even amusing, aspects of the harvest. Noticeably absent are Trollope's descriptions of the peasants themselves—not only "ragged and filthy" and "wretchedly poor" but also "invariably ugly [... and] very subject to scrofulous affections"[40]—that would call into question the health and hygiene of the hair itself.

To appreciate the appeal of this particular origin story, it may be helpful to return, if only briefly, to the discursive environments in which hair is read, first and foremost, "as a signifier, encoding and creating meaning." As already suggested, one of the most important of these environments is that concerned with literal and metaphorical, as well as personal and social, constructions of purity and contamination. It was within this particular framework that hair was, as Galia Ofek argues, "invested with an over-determination of sexual meaning."[41] Clean and carefully arranged hair, most obviously in the well-ordered upswept day style adopted by middle-class married women, connoted modesty and a controlled and properly directed sexuality.[42] Excessive or uncontrolled hair, in contrast, suggested unruly, even aggressive appetites. Such constructions were, however, rendered infinitely more complex by the addition of false hair. As Ofek suggests, the "increasing popularity of artificial hair and very large and elaborate hairdos in the 1860s and 1870s could be interpreted as a central route to constructing a sexual subjectivity."[43] While the agency implied by this act of self-construction was troubling enough, the notion of a "sexual subjectivity" dependent upon the marketplace brings the wearer of false hair dangerously close to the prostitute. Through the public display of their coiffures the wearers of false hair came to resemble a thing-like commodity: an object on display for the male gaze and a "creeping sense of unease results from boundary ambiguity, as a most private and personal part of the woman's body—her hair—is presented in public, for public admiration."[44] There is, moreover, little to choose between the living models used in hair contests and demonstrations, in which they sat immobile as an artist manipulated the "raw material" into the "realization of a Dresden china ideal,"[45] and the wax dummies of the hairdressers' windows, especially as described by *The Speaker*:

> There is a hairdresser (be his name accursed!) who advertises [his] wares on a mechanical model. Beauty (in wax) publicly lifts a certain appurtenance to her brow,

to show with what ease and grace it can be fixed and detached! Throngs of women watch the movement with fascinated gaze [...] But man, brutal opponent of women's suffrage though he may be, hurries by with a sinking of the heart at such a monstrous exhibition. To him the thing is unspeakable [...] the wax image, moving its false hair to and fro with monotonous mockery.[46]

Part-subject, part-object, wearers of false hair were also open to charges of adulteration, making themselves more attractive through the addition of questionable material and thus participating in what Tammy Whitlock characterizes as a "growing retail culture of 'fraud'."[47] As the *Quarterly Review* demands: "From what source issue those pendant tresses gleaming in the background, with which the blooming belle, aptly entangling their snaky coil with her own, tempts our eligible Adams?"[48]

Thus the trade in false hair appeared to dehumanize those involved, reducing its sellers to "purveyors of the raw material"[49] and its wearers to commodities, and positioning both within a contaminated and contaminating marketplace that involves "the substitution of real relationships and people for artificial objects and commercial transactions."[50] Consider, for example, the language used within the following report of "hair crime"—an increasingly common problem as the price of hair reached record levels:

> Human hair, amounting in weight to 87lb., and in value to about £400 [...] has recently been stolen from the premises of Mr. Schletter [...] The hair stolen comprises nearly all the choicest specimens cultivated by Swedish girls for the market, and varies in length from 24in. to 33in., the latter, if of good quality, realising about a sovereign an ounce [...] It is alleged that the accused sold 9lb. of the valuable material to a local hairdresser at a price considerably below that paid to the actual "growers" themselves.[51]

Within such a climate, it is hardly surprising that Trollope's idealized representation, in which the preference for bartering meant that money rarely changed hands, was particularly appealing to its audience.

Before turning to the sensationalized origin stories that became increasingly prominent in the later 1860s, as the craze for false hair reached, quite literally, new heights, it is worth pausing to consider "The False Hair: A Tale" (1852) another early, reassuring narrative that was published within the morally instructive and uplifting *Chambers's Edinburgh Journal*. Although this source predates the marked expansion in the use of false hair, it effectively preempts the anxieties associated with the commercial dimension of the practice as just described. The tale focuses on a young and wealthy Parisian woman, Adelaide de Varenne, who is convinced by her hairdresser to supplement her own sparse tresses with "a long lock of soft golden hair."[52] While the practice itself is represented as commonplace, Adelaide's perception of it is not. Rather than viewing the hair as a commodity, she constructs it as a memento that cannot be disassociated from the woman who sold it. As she informs the hairdresser, "I shall be thinking of her continually" and, as her "thoughts were fixed upon the young girl whose beauty had been sacrificed for hers, [...] an unconquerable desire to learn her fate took possession of her mind."[53] In adopting this view of the hair, Adelaide effectively removes it from the marketplace and places it within a "gift economy." As Babette Bärbel Tischleder explains in *The Literary Life of Things*:

> Unlike the circulation of commodities, which is constituted by one-time transactions regulated by the market, the exchange of gifts entails a perpetual cycle of exchange, whereby objects function as social media between persons. The reciprocity between

the giver and the recipient is the vital principle of the gift economy, in which things figure as connectors, actualizing the relations between groups or individuals through the cyclical processes of giving, taking, and returning.⁵⁴

It is significant that when Adelaide fortuitously locates the young girl whose hair she wears, the donor is revealed to be as moral as she is beautiful, thus allaying any fears about symbolic contamination. Even more significant, however, is the fact that Adelaide reciprocates the "gift" of hair not with money—dragging it back into the commercial realm—but by clearing the name of the young woman's betrothed and securing him a position within her father's service. Thus the story ensures that the cycle of reciprocity that began with the "golden hair" is able to continue. Functioning as a "connector" between the two young women, the titular hair thus negates the imputation that its use dehumanizes and objectifies those involved.

Both *A Summer in Brittany* and "The False Hair" were written before the use of false hair came to be perceived as "universal"; it appears that while the practice was limited, the press could afford to be lenient. Moving into the mid to late 1860s, however, commentators became increasingly vocal about what they saw as the *abuse* of false hair, now constructed as a "mental and moral disease [...] inherited from the remotest ages":⁵⁵

> there is something repulsive as well as grotesque in the idea of decking one's head with other people's hair, and arraying living beauty with the spoils of the grave; but though chignons change their shape from time to time with Protean readiness, and shift from the nape of the neck to the crown of the head and back again, as fashion decrees, with wonderful uniformity, they do not appear to grow any smaller or more becoming. They are not used to replace the defects of nature or the ravages of time—the only intelligible pleas that could be advanced for such a custom—but solely and simply to disfigure nature by increasing the apparent proportions of the head, and overbalancing the figure; so that a small or short woman, whose hair is dressed in the height of the fashion, not unfrequently presents the appearance of a magnified tadpole, all head and no body, and, in less extreme circumstances, may be easily mistaken for the victim of a severe attack of water on the brain [...] Monster top-knots and balloon chignons are hideous enough when they are native, and to the wearer born: when they are the spoils of other scalps they are altogether intolerable.⁵⁶

Far from enhancing its charms, false hair infects and distorts the female body, rendering it grotesque. In so doing, it reveals its ability to transgress bodily limits, collapsing the boundaries between subject and object. At the same time, its use represents a form of regression as the women who wear "the spoils of other scalps" come to resemble a "savage" racial other. A similar view is put forward by *The London Review*, which claims that the women of Africa wear chignons "not at all unlike what may be seen any day in Regent-street or Piccadilly." Indeed, the only "difference between the Ishogo and the English lady is that the former manufactures the chignon out of her own hair and head while the latter buys it ready-made in the shops."⁵⁷

In addition to the use of overt ridicule and palpable disgust, (see, for example, Figure 5.6) the press published a series of increasingly harrowing and sensationalized origin stories in the hope that, if "anything could check the fashion, it would be the impossibility of dissociating it from thoughts of disease, putrefaction, and decay."⁵⁸

To appreciate this change in climate it may be instructive to compare "The Lock of Hair" to "The First Coiffeur of his Age," again from *Chambers's Journal* but published

NEXT HIDEOUS "SENSATION CHIGNON."

FIGURE 5.6: "Next Hideous 'Sensation Chignon.'" *Punch* 53 (November 30, 1867): 219. Artist: Edward Linley Sambourne.

at the height of the false hair craze in 1869. This narrative relates the story of the titular coiffeur, M. Gastelet, in his attempt to obtain a rare shade of hair to fashion a wig for a Russian princess who, significantly, suffers from an infectious medical condition that requires her head be routinely shaved. Having searched high and low using all legitimate channels, Gastelet resorts to employing a questionable agent—"a dark-complexioned, dwarfish, monkey-like man"—to procure the unusual shade for him, promising to pay a high price and ask no questions about its source.[59] When the agent returns with the hair after an absence of several months, Gastelet, although doubtful of its provenance, creates the wig that allows the princess to join the fashionable elite of Paris. Ensconced within a select box at the theater with her "lace and satin-covered hoop, at least four yards in circumference, [and] her towering coiffure, a pile of curls and a blaze of diamonds,"[60] the princess' reign of power comes to an abrupt and sensational end when "a long bony hand" with "claw-like nails" appears out of nowhere and tears the wig from her head, revealing the artificial nature of her beauty.[61] As time passes and the crime remains a mystery, rumors begin to circulate that the hair was obtained by murdering some unfortunate young woman whose ghost has returned to reclaim its rightful property. M. Gastelet is arrested for the crime and is saved only when an old priest arrives in Paris with a young woman who is in possession of the stolen wig. As the priest explains, she is an insane *crétine* cared for by his convent where Gastelet's unscrupulous agent tricked her into a neighboring forest and forcibly robbed her of her hair. "Remarkable for more than ordinary cunning, dexterity of hand, and the pride she took in the uncommon-coloured hair," this young woman traveled to Paris in search of her stolen locks and, having spied them on the head of the princess, managed to conceal herself in the theater to retrieve her property.[62] Although Gastelet is set free, his reputation is left in tatters and he is forced to retire. Fallen from her pedestal, the princess retires to Vienna where she loses herself to cards and gaming. The moral of this cautionary tale is clear. In sharp contrast to the idealized "cycle of reciprocity" established between two beautiful and virtuous women in "The Lock of Hair," the history of the princess' "towering coiffure" is characterized only by violence (including a symbolic rape), deceit, and disease. Female readers are thus encouraged to pause and consider the hidden dependencies and connections that may well link their own chignons, frizettes, and curls—weighing down their heads as they read the story—to such contaminated and contaminating sources.

Moving from the realm of fiction to "fact," the contemporary press of the 1860s and 1870s tended to focus on two of the least palatable sources of false hair where the potential for contamination was writ large for all to see. While there is no doubt that English women relied heavily on false hair imported from the continent, this was supplemented by a limited native supply derived from convents, paupers, hospitals— where "fever lays its contribution daily, hourly, in the hands of the manufacturer"[63]—and, primarily, prisons. As was widely reported, "the majority of the long English tresses come from the heads of criminals."[64] Even after the Prison Act of 1865 legislated against the practice, the shearing of female convicts remained routine until the end of the century.[65] Ostensibly undertaken on the grounds of hygiene, the act was also a significant element of the prisoners' moral reformation. According to Elizabeth Fry, the cutting of felons' hair was "a certain yet harmless punishment; and would promote that humiliation of spirit, which, in persons so circumstanced, is one indispensable step to improvement and reformation."[66] As described by contemporary commentators, however, the operation appears anything but "harmless":

> The first inexorable rule to which the new prisoner has to submit, and which is a trial that is always one of the hardest to bear, is that of having the hair cut [...] Women whose hearts have not quailed, perhaps, at the murder of their infants, or the poisoning of their husbands, clasp their hands in horror at this sacrifice of their natural adornment—weep, beg, pray, occasionally assume a defiant attitude and resist to the last, and are finally only overcome by force [...] On such occasions the guards on duty in the outer yards, or in the men's prison, are summoned to put the handcuffs on, while the necessary ceremony is gone through. In [one] case it required three men to secure her wrists whilst her hair was cut the requisite length, she struggling, and cursing, and swearing long after the operation was over.[67]

Commenting on the use of hair sourced in this manner, the *London Review* insists that those who resort to its use "should at least be informed that [it is] never obtained without oaths, prayers, and blasphemous imprecations upon the despoilers, which the drawing-room belles little dream of, as those purchased tresses dance pendulous upon their cheek in the heated saloon."[68] The explicit reference to touch within this warning—especially within the context of an overheated saloon—suggests an inappropriate intimacy between the pure and the impure. If, moreover, Lucia Zedner is correct in asserting that the cutting of the felon's hair "served the symbolic function of divesting the woman of the tainted character of her former life,"[69] the women of England were, in a particularly worrying form of adulteration, assuming the symbolic taint of their unfortunate sisters.

Even less palatable than prison hair was the so-called dead hair upon which the lower end of the hair market depended. Contrary to what is implied by its name, dead hair was not sourced from corpses—although such practices did exist on a limited scale[70]—but, rather, from the natural shedding of hair that occurs as it is being groomed. Dead hair could easily be distinguished from its more expensive counterpart, sourced "on foot," by the presence of the root or bulb, showing that it had been pulled rather than cut from the head. Many women collected their own dead hair, saved within the ornate hair catchers that graced their vanity tables, in order to make the "rats" (rolls of hair) needed to achieve extra height or volume in their coiffures. And, when conducted on a personal scale, the use of dead hair was one of the least threatening and most hygienic ways in which a woman might source false hair, as its origins were both known and "safe." When conducted for trade purposes, however, the harvesting of dead hair—conducted primarily in Italy and contributing an estimated 80,000 lb. of hair to the English market per year[71]—is positively harrowing in its potential for contamination. As described in *The Examiner* in 1874, it involves three distinct steps:

> The Italian women, like their sisters in other parts of the world, have the practice of twisting into a coil all the hairs which become detached from the heads in the operation of combing or brushing. These coils, in the total absence of house drains, are thrown with other refuse into the open gutters, which seldom fail to supply an Italian household with a near and ready means of disposing of the offcastings of their habitations. This is the first step in the proceeding. The next is affected when the scavenger appears on the scene with his springless cart, and, like another Neptune, trident in hand, wades through the gutter, and hooks up every floating tangle of hairs. These he carefully consigns to a separate receptacle, and keeps by him—for he well knows their value—till the hair pedlar, technically known in the trade as "the Cutter," makes his next round and gathers in the season's harvest, which is forthwith conveyed to Genoa and other seaport towns, where the coils are disentangled, and separated by children who are employed in the business [...] It is said that of late years many hundred-weights of these heads and tails, grimly characterised as "dead hair," annually cross the Alps, or round the Rock at Gibraltar, on their way to our more northern centres of civilization, where existing systems of drainage present insuperable obstacles to the retention and utilization of refuse coils of hair.[72]

Returning to Hodder's notion of entanglement in which "the front or visible parts of things often depend on back or hidden parts," the use of dead hair establishes a direct connection between genteel English femininity and its lowest other: the refuse of the foreign and filthy gutter. Although this hair was "washed with bran and potash, carded, sifted, classed, and sorted" before being fashioned into a marketable hairpiece, the symbolic taint of its origins is not so easily removed.[73]

No discussion of the potential for contamination harbored within false hair would be complete without reference to the microscopic parasites, known as gregarines, which were discovered by a Russian scientist in 1867. As was widely reported by the press, including *The Lancet*, this research claimed that three-quarters of the Russian hair used to produce chignons for export was infested with gregarines deposited by lice. Although *The Lancet* suggested the need for the results to be verified, it did not hesitate to engage in what amounted to scaremongering and, like many other sources, focused in upon the purported effect of a heated ballroom on the parasites, causing them to "revive, grow, and multiply by dividing into many parts—so called germ globules; these fly about the ballroom in millions, get inhaled, drop on the refreshments—in fact, enter the interior of people by hundreds of ways."[74] The *Daily Telegraph* was quick to capitalize on the resulting furor after a correspondent identifying themselves as an "Investigator" reported the results of his own experiments—involving strands of false hair being wound around the neck of a live chicken to mimic the heat generated by a woman's head—in order to describe how "when heat gradually warms their gelatinous envelope, they increase, get antennæ, feet, organs of all kinds, and start upon their travels."[75] Here, as with Italian dead hair, a direct connection is made between high and low, pure and impure, as the public is forced to consider, albeit mistakenly, that "those glossy hypocrisies at the back of ladies' heads could be nests of unmentionable animalculæ, bred in the unclean huts of Mongol or Calmuck peasants, and hatching, like eggs in a hydro-incubator, on the warm necks of our ladies."[76] The piece ends with a final plea, suggesting that if "nothing can kill what comes over with the chignons, let the chignons die out themselves."[77]

The potential for contamination did not end with the sourcing of false hair; as the plaits passed from hand to hand—from the ragpickers and cutters to the agents, dealers, and wholesale merchants through to the hairdressers—they became entangled, quite literally, with equally tainted or troubling locks. Describing a trip to a large hair warehouse, a reporter for the *Daily News* describes how "huge canvas sacks, each weighing 150 lb., and containing about 600 heads of hair, were standing unpacked in one of the workshops. These give out a close and fusty smell, suggesting some furrier's establishment where none but coarse and common furs are sold."[78] When one of these sacks is opened for his perusal:

> a strange variety of matted, greasy, unpleasant-looking hair is seen. Here is the iron-grey of middle-life, the snowy white of old age, the brown and black and flaxen of comparative youth, all roughly twisted up together like so many piebald horses' tails. Some of the hair is long, some short, some coarse, some fine, some neglected and dirty, some carefully combed and clean.[79]

Defying all notions of classification and order, this tangle brings together the hair of the old and the young, the clean and the unclean, and of different nations and regions. Sharing the odor of animal skins and resembling horsetails, it also challenges human/animal boundaries. Such disorder, moreover, is mirrored in the individual chignons, which are constructed by "mixing together, in certain proportions, hair of the same tint and slightly varying in length. To arrange a grand chignon the hair-worker will at times employ the spoils derived from the heads of no less than thirty women."[80] Foregrounding the racial hybridity of chignons, the merchant goes on to explain that hair from the South of France is "too coarse to use alone, though it worked up very well mixed with other kinds." Spanish hair, in turn, is "too decidedly black, too sombre, to suit ordinary complexions;

it was therefore requisite to mix this also, to soften it, in fact, with hair of a more delicate shade; the same with the tow-like tint of the Flemish hair, which had to be made more sunny-looking by the addition of German hair of a richer blond."[81] It would be difficult to imagine a more complex representation of symbolic miscegenation than that presented by the seamless intertwining of these hybrid hairpieces—"these abominable nests of foreign horrors"—into the natural hair of English women.[82]

CONCLUSION

Rationalizing the popularity of false hair during the period, Ofek explains that:

> As Victorian fashion emphasized the grooming of women's hair, the latter seemed to transform from a chaotic, wild and natural growth into a well-trimmed, man-made and decorative bower [...] The demands for both order and artificiality were compatible, as both suggested an advanced state of cultivation, sophistication and civilization, and distanced hair from its organic, untidy origin. As a result, false hair became fashionable, and ladies used enormous quantities of it.[83]

While there is no doubt that well-groomed hair connoted order, the assertion that "order and artificiality were compatible" is based on the erroneous assumption that false hair is, in Douglas's terms, "clean," that is, "proper to its class, suitable, fitting." What Ofek's argument fails to recognize—and what this chapter has attempted to demonstrate—is the extent to which the origins and "secret histories" of false hair undermine, at both a personal and a social level, the "advanced state of cultivation, sophistication and civilization" that middle-class Victorians aspired to. Whether sourced from scrofulous French peasants, English convicts, or Italian gutters, false hair bears an indelible trace of its origins and, therefore, disturbs the systems of classification and order upon which cleanliness depends. Gathered from "the most objectionable and repulsive sources," it establishes a direct connection and dependency between the morally and physically pure body of English femininity and its most polluted others.[84] In an age of sanitary reform, where cleanliness was a marker of middle-class status and "the dichotomy of purity and pollution cohered around, and produced the meaning of 'woman' with particular intensity," it is hardly surprising that the contemporary press adopted a series of increasingly sensational strategies to discourage its use.[85] More surprising is how the extraordinary volume of false hair used by English women has itself been caught and tamed by discursive frameworks that mask its material complexities. The process of untangling these complexities has only just begun.

CHAPTER SIX

Gender and Sexuality: Tresses Adorned and Adored, Locks Coiled and Cut

SARAH HEATON

Rapunzel had radiant hair, as fine as spun gold. Each time she heard the fairy's voice, she unpinned her braids and wound them around a window hook on the window. Then she let her hair drop twenty yards to the ground, and the fairy would climb up on it. (Brothers Grim, "Rapunzel," 1812)[1]

INTRODUCTION

When Rapunzel let down her hair in the 1812 Brothers Grimm version of the fairy tale the tropes of the Victorian period were set. Here is the abundant golden hair of innocence made sexual; here is the man mounting her hair; here is the mother figure who weighs heavily on Rapunzel's sexual identity and, unwilling to gift her daughter to the prince, castrates her as she "snip, snap" cuts the hair off.[2] Much has been written about the links between women's hair and body politics in the Victorian period and how it is used as form of social control, in particular the progression from presexual to postsexual. Freud's suggestion that female hair is the site of her femininity is frequently invoked and the psychoanalytical model has illuminated the fetishization of hair.[3] Victorian hair is thus read as a sign of sexuality linked to the castration complex. While Foucault's reading of sexuality as a historical construct offers up a paradigm for understanding hair as a symbol in the exploration of gendered power exchange. Both of these approaches are clearly evinced in the fairy tale *Rapunzel* and combining them suggests the tangled discourses woven into narratives of hair.

In Victorian society the body, particularly the female body, was a site of patriarchal control. There were clear rules and codes of hair dressing which set out to organize not simply the female body but female sexuality. Such regulatory codes sketched out the various permissible stages of sexuality: a child's loose hair was symbolic of her innocence and purity while the married woman's postsexual state was controlled and contained in braided and coiled styles which were often covered. In contrast uncontrolled, loosened hair in the sexual female was threatening. According to the literary critic Galia Ofek "haircuts and hair rules differentiated men from women. While male hairstyles grew short and less ornate, men emphasized their manliness by boasting impressive beards—an unmistakable badge of masculinity [...] Concomitant with Victorian sexual over-determination of women's hair were hair rules and conventions."[4] The symbiotic link between hair and female sexuality is at its most explicit in literature and painting. The strict rules surrounding the styling of hair according to sexual age proved key to the changing of the name of Renoir's *Promenade (Mother and Children)* to simply *La Promenade*. The art historian Sinead Furlong-Clancy notes that: "In spite of the loose hair of the eldest female figure, the painting was assumed to represent a mother and her daughters [...] For a nanny, the eldest figure seemed [...] too richly dressed, but her loose hair, emphasized by Renoir strongly resisted the description of mother" (8).[5] In 2012 infrared reflectography revealed underpainted figures, one of whom has her hair clearly worn up and is the mother figure while the central figure of the painting with her abundant loose dark hair had her status as adolescent sister restored. Jan Marsh says: "Loose hair was only worn by children [...] its appearance in art has therefore an intimate, erotic significance."[6] This significance is important to the understanding of how hair is represented in art and literature during a period in which explicit sexual reference became the focus of the growing pornography industry. Because of the public reifying of women's hair in Victorian culture and the allusion to sexuality hidden in its strands, this chapter will focus on women's hair in literature and art. For Ofek:

> [Victorian] fashion dictates and social mores prohibited bare hands, legs and other parts which were covered for modesty's sake [...] hair was almost the only exposed, visible and distinctly feminine body part in a lady's appearance. Thus the association of hair and the female sex intensified as the rest of woman's body was covered, and as a result, hair was invested with an over-determination of sexual meaning.[7]

The explicit social rules and conventions which control the public display of hair demonstrate aspects of femininity and female sexual desire but they also, as this chapter will suggest, illuminate aspects of masculinity and male sexual desire.

COILING AND UNCOILING HAIR

For a character such as Jo in Louisa M. Alcott's *Little Women* hair becomes a contested site. Her hair needs "the united exertions of the family" to get it up and nineteen pins to stay it.[8] Meg, her older sister, regularly exhorts Jo to control her hair to fit with society's ideas of constructed femininity, while Jo herself is often pulling, twisting, and giving it a "wrathful tweak."[9] The "wrathful tweak" occurs at the thought of Meg's impending sexualization, exposing her anxieties about not just the social constructions of femininity but also female sexuality and that she will be next. One of Jo's most significant moments of freedom both from prescribed gender roles but also a freedom in terms of feminine sexuality comes when she runs down the road with Laurie: "Jo darted away, soon leaving hat and comb behind her, and scattering hair-pins as she ran [... Laurie's] Atlanta came panting up with flying hair, bright eyes, ruddy cheek, and no signs of dissatisfaction in her face."[10] The scene suggests that their relationship will be consummated but Alcott notoriously did not give the reader the satisfaction. Here the uncoiled hair remains innocent and rather liberates her from social constraints of gender performance. This unpinning of her hair is given further expression of her New Woman sensibility when she cuts it off in exchange for cash to help pay for her mother to visit their sick father. She cries momentarily but recognizes her vanity at the loss as a social construction.[11] Arguably Jo does "castrate" Meg's sexuality when she tries to fashion her hair with irons and burns it off. When Meg is "successfully" done up by the Moffat girls in the latest French fashions with "crimped and curled" hair for the ball in the chapter pointedly titled "Meg goes to Vanity Fair" she does attract male attention but according to the male guests they have "spoilt her entirely; she's nothing but a doll."[12] Where Jo's hair becomes a contested site which challenges social constructions of femininity, Meg's hair becomes a site where power exchanges over her sexuality are played out. That she is overdone alludes to the conflict between natural and artificial beauty with a suspicion of the latter firmly endorsed.

In Nathaniel Hawthorne's *The Scarlet Letter* Hester's hair is used to explore social constraints over both femininity and female sexuality. The "adulteress" Hester wears her hair hidden under a cap to accord with Puritan society sensibility: "her rich and luxuriant hair had either been cut off, or was so completely hidden by a cap."[13] That it might have been cut off accords with the Puritan society's desire to castrate her; that she keeps it hidden suggests the broader exchange of power exerted in the figuration of the embroidered letter A. Ordered to wear a scarlet letter A on her breast to signify her adultery the richness of her embroidery makes it an object of beauty ensconced in its significations of sin, while the self-imposed covering of her hair hides its burgeoning luxuriousness. The only time she removes her cap is in the forest with Arthur Dimmesdale, her lover the priest: "she took off her formal cap which confined her hair; and down it fell upon her shoulders, dark and rich."[14] Not only are they outside the confining boundaries of "civilized" society; they are lying together on the forest floor in a state of sexual desire. The contrast between the controlled female sexuality and released sexual desire finds its locus in her hair.

In Elizabeth Barrett Browning's *Aurora Leigh* Marion Erle's overabundant hair appears to obscure her small face: "The hair, too, ran its opulence of curls / In doubt 'twixt dark and bright, nor left you clear / To name the colour. Too much hair perhaps / (I'll name a fault here) for so small a head."[15] The overwhelming weight of her hair causes her head to "droop,"[16] and when her mother lets down her hair to offer her to the squire it "blinds her," so that it not merely obscures her identity but makes it waver from side to side.[17] The hair suggests an overabundant sexuality over which she has little control; here her sexuality is being actively exchanged by her mother in the letting down of her hair. In contrast the upper-class Lady Waldemar appears to have an active control over her hair and sexuality in her open pursuing of Romney. But her hair while styled is still difficult to control in its abundance: "Her maid must use both hands to twist that coil / Of tresses, then be careful lest the rich / Bronze rounds should slip—she missed though, a gray hair / A single one."[18] For both these women their hair is abundant suggesting an abundant sexuality. For one the hair is naturally overflowing and she has little control over her sexual life. For the other there is the attempt at control and styling of her sexual life.

These opposite extremes of female sexuality play out in Aurora. Her sexual passion comes alive through her hair when she uncoils and displays it to Romney:

My long loose hair began to burn and creep,
Alive to its very ends, about my knees:
I swept it backward as the wind sweeps flame,
With the passion of my hands. Ah, Romney laughed

> One day (how full the memories come up!)
> "—Your Florence fire-flies live on in your hair."
> He said, "it gleams so." Well, I wrung them out,
> My fire-flies; made a knot as hard as life
> Of those loose, soft, impracticable curls.[19]

Here her hair contains within it her sexual desire, but also her jealous passion. When Romney recognizes the sexual desire for him in the memories of Florence she immediately knots her hair up again, the tightness suggesting that this is the last display of her sexual desire and that ultimately she has control over it; she is coiling up her sexual desire, very different to the display of enticing coils which Lady Waldemar displays. Further, the sexual desire which is predatory in Lady Waldemar is displaced by the female friendship between Marion and Aurora, a friendship which allows Aurora to come to terms with her sexual identity. Earlier in the poem tightly controlled curls are associated with a lack of not just sexuality but also life. Aurora's aunt is described: "She stood straight and calm, / Her somewhat narrow forehead braided tight / As if for taming accidental thoughts / From possible pulses; brown hair pricked with grey / By frigid use of life."[20] But Aurora's coiling up of her own hair becomes associated with female friendship, an intellectual life, and the choice to become a poet.

While the coiling and uncoiling of hair is a literary trope which repeatedly suggests constrained and unconstrained female sexuality, it is who exerts agency over the coiling and uncoiling which suggests a more nuanced reading. Ultimately it can be argued that Aurora, Hester, Jo, and even Meg finally determine a control over their hair, their sexual desire, and sense of self.

CUTTING HAIR: A LOCK OR A SHEATH

The lock of hair was fetishized in all sorts of ways during the Victorian period, in lockets and rings, framed and displayed on walls, or sequestered away hidden among other keepsakes. These treasured locks memorialized, fetishized babies and were lovers' tokens but they were also symbolic of moments of exchange in which power and agency, specifically sexual power and agency, shifted. Time and again women gave away locks of hair. Caroline Helstone in Bronte's *Shirley* pushes a lock onto Moore insisting on one of his own, while Marianne Dashwood in Austen's *Sense and Sensibility* gives a lock to Willoughby before they are engaged. These women have given part of themselves to these men and offered their sexual availability. Unlike the locks of hair both fade when they are then rejected by the men. When a woman takes another's hair it is more complex. Clearly Rapunzel's "mother" is taking her sexual identity; elsewhere we find women shearing girls of their hair as punishment for sexual activity. But when a woman treasures another's lock of hair there is the suggestion of female unity which questions simplistic concepts of power exchange in narratives of desire.

It is well known that Freud saw a woman's hair as the site of her femininity.[21] If Victorian social mores saw loose abundant hair as equating to loose sexuality and if that abundant hair for Freud is the phallic substitute which asserts castration then by giving a lock of hair to her lover the female is actively castrating herself. When the lock is cut from a woman's head by a man he is actively castrating her to ensure that he is not. The cutting and exchange of locks in Thomas Hardy's *Far From the Madding Crowd* shows such shifting power dynamics. When Troy cuts off Bathsheba's stray lock with his sword he is taking her body. It is the culminating act after his private performance of masculine prowess when he demonstrates his sword skills to her. The phallic symbol is clear and that he uses it to cut her hair off affirms that she has been sexually taken. Further, he "castrates" her as it marks the moment when she loses any sense of agency and becomes subject to his masculine desire as his scared wife. In contrast her young admirer the shepherd Gabriel Oak's attempt to "shear" Bathsheba fails because he brands his sheep putting his capital in her name and emasculating himself. Whereas Troy does "shear" her, taking ownership and treating her like livestock.

It is the taking of another woman's lock of hair which restores Bathsheba's power. The lock of hair reveals to Bathsheba Troy's affair with Fanny and leads to his eventual death. By owning the lock Troy had owned Fanny, just as he owned Bathsheba, but he had forgotten about the lock and she became a fallen woman. In a Victorian culture which fetishized hair, from lovers' keepsakes through to memorializing objects, for a man to cast aside the precious token is damning. When Bathsheba finds it she decides to treasure the "little coil of pale hair [...] in memory of her, poor thing!"[22] Here the now memorializing lock serves not only to restore Fanny's place beside her lover in the grave but restores Bathsheba's sexuality that had been taken from her by Troy. The two taken locks, one pale one dark, which have tamed the women via female sexual subjection now link the two women bodily to restore Bathsheba's sexual and feminine identity. She may need a man, Boldwood, to kill Troy but her powerful sexuality represented by her "soft lustre" and "dark hair" returns.[23] This coming together of two women through the exchange of hair suggests an important fissure in dominant patriarchal discourses which sexualized Victorian women's hair. Although clearly Fanny is dead and arguably Bathsheba has taken her hair rather than being given it by Fanny, it does still suggest a significant female bond.

While many of the cultural figurations of female Victorian hair are authored by men, Jo's hair is an example of a female authoring the unpinning of the constraints on hair. Certainly it appears that Elizabeth Gaskell has absorbed and cannot step away from Pre-Raphaelite renditions of the fallen women but she seemingly shifts the paradigm just enough to raise the question. Gaskell's Ruth finds a sensuous pleasure in everything around her that borders on the spiritual: in the "stately white lilies, sacred to the virgin" which are aligned to the "floating golden-tressed laburnum boughs."[24] Putting these two states, purity and sensuality, together causes a disjuncture in expected figurations which suggests Gaskell's questioning voice. Further, there is the repeated taking of her sexuality, first when Mr. Bellingham "places his flowers in her hair," flowers which are so heavy that they cause her hair to "droop" and become "disordered,"[25] to Sally's cutting of her hair "in a merciless manner [...] Ruth was still and silent, with meekly bowed head, under the strange hands that were shearing her beautiful hair."[26] The "shearing" reinforces her "innocent" passivity but also links her directly to prostitution. Yet Sally takes Ruth's cut hair and keeps it because of its beauty. Predominantly the giving of a lock of hair binds one to a suitor but here the shearing means it is a prostitute's locks which would not be something to be treasured. It is then in this keeping of the shorn hair that Gaskell critiques the rigidity of social convention and also restores Ruth's innocence, an innocence which leads to her downfall, so that her contemplation of flowers comes from the same sense of innocence rather than being opposites of femininity which society would suggest.

A similar restoration of femininity and sexuality through sisterly solidarity can be seen in Christina Rossetti's "Goblin Market," which is all about pre- and postsexual femininity in what can be considered a morality tale. Laura, when the Goblins stop in front her with their entreaty to "come buy" their fruit, quickly cuts a lock of hair in exchange for the fruit. "'You have much gold upon your head,' / They answered all together: / 'Buy from us with a golden curl.' / She clipp'd a precious golden lock, / She dropped a tear more rare than pearl, / Then suck'd their fruit globes fair or red."[27] The lock of hair is explicitly linked to gold here when it is exchanged for the fruit. It is also explicitly linked to Laura's sexuality. According to the literary critics Sandra Gilbert and Susan Gubar when Lizzie gives the Goblins a lock of her hair in exchange for fruit, the giving of the lock represents the giving of her virginity (566).[28] This ties female sexuality to a cash nexus through golden hair just as elsewhere the shearing of hair has associated the female with prostitution. Certainly Laura becomes the fallen woman as she is driven by her sexual desire and continues to consume and be consumed by the desire for the fruit. The fruit is withheld from her as the "men" only offer it to virgins. When Lizzie seeks to save her sister by getting some fruit for her she is beaten by the Goblins for resisting their fruit penetrating her. She saves her sister by allowing her to "Eat me, drink me, love me."[29] Here Laura cleanses Lizzie of the Goblins' juice, in effect saving her savior, suggesting a female solidarity which then finds the fruit of men tastes "bitter."[30] Her female sexuality is also restored to her, her body and hair coming alive again "Writhing as one possessed she leaped and sung, / Her locks streamed like the torch / like a caged thing freed."[31] / But it is an anguished bodily experience with phallic metaphors torn down as she seemingly orgasms having tasted the juices now become bitter: "Like the watch-tower of a town / Which an earthquake shatters down, / Like a lightning-stricken mast, / Like a wind-uprooted tree [...] She fell at last; / Pleasure past and anguish past, / Is it death or is it life?"[32] She lives, unlike Jeanie, because her desire is satisfied. Further it is satisfied after tasting the juices of the fruit from the female body. That the two sisters are seemingly indistinguishable in hair and body, "Golden head by golden head / Cheek to cheek and breast to breast,"[33] / means that they each stand for the other, the innocent and the fallen existing side by side as one. The female sanctuary at the end of the poem, both are married but the husbands are absent from the poem, suggests a restoration of normative female sexuality on the one hand—they have both had children and are teaching them to avoid the "haunted glen"[34] of female sexuality which is out of control—but on the other suggests a sapphic/autoerotic sexuality as restorative—when Laura licks the juice of the Goblins off Lizzie the phallic symbols all fall.

THE GOLDEN-HAIRED ANGEL IN THE HOUSE

Golden hair is everywhere in Victorian culture and in its many figurations becomes a symbol which represents different femininities and stages of female sexuality. Golden hair is fawned over, fought over, fetishized, and forbidden. In George Eliot's *Silas Marner* Eppie's golden hair suggests a virtuous femininity, certainly she redeems Silas, although even here golden hair becomes associated with economic exchange when Silas associates Eppie's hair with his stolen money. But the economic exchange is made redundant in the context of Silas's hoarding of his money for its own sake. The literary critic Galia Ofek explores how it is a form of fetishism: "Eppie, the perfect woman, who was drawn to Silas by the light of the fire in his hearth, is thus described by Eliot as the god of Silas's fire and family life, and her hair symbolises the light of the fire and homely happiness, and Silas's salvation from the worship of gold."[35] Eliot, like the other female authors considered here, takes the expected reading and makes a step sideways. The golden hair symbolizes female innocence when the child first arrives: "'Anybody 'ud think the angels in heaven couldn't be prettier,' said Dolly rubbing the golden curls and kissing them."[36]

Even the dirty rags cannot hide her purity and her being drawn to Silas as a child confirms it as a natural instinct. The next stage of femininity finds Eppie described: "there is the freshest blossom of youth by his side – a blond dimpled girl of eighteen, who has vainly tried to chastise her curly auburn hair into smoothness under her brown bonnet: the hair ripples as obstinately as a brooklet under the March breeze, and the little ringlets burst away from the restraining comb behind."[37] And the "good-looking youth" by her side rather than taking her away from the father figure joins the family at Silas's fireside specifically because he "doesn't want Eppie's hair to be different."[38] Importantly Eppie does not fashion her hair with a comb, the symbol of feminine control and deception in its artificial weaving of hair, so reinforcing her naturalness and innocence; her hair escapes not sensuously in erotic terms but like a "brooklet." While Eliot may have restored golden hair to its innocent, natural origins away from a male fetishism linked to either cash or sexual desire, in the postsexual woman arguably she does so only to restore the Victorian ideal of the angel in the house tying Eppie to the hearth.

The child angel is a difficult ideal to protect from the sexualized gaze. Recent critical assertion of sexual desire as the driving interest that Ruskin had in his "girlies" appears to have some veracity when his letters to Kate Greenaway are reread. Such exhortations as, "*I think* we might go to the length of expecting the frocks to come off sometimes – when it was very warm? you know" make her drawings, which have become idealized icons of innocence, appear to have a darker subtext.[39] Greenaway's desire to court Ruskin via her drawings aside, if they are analyzed together with her poems they appear to be all about the conflicts and anxieties in the move from pre- to postsexual femininity.

This conflict is played out more explicitly in Hawthorne's *The Scarlett Letter* in the character of Pearl. While she is introduced as "innocent life" she cannot, either by the Puritan community or by the reader, be anything other than associated with Hester and Dimmesdale's sexual desire and consummation.[40] Further dressed in her elaborately embroidered red dress she becomes the letter A itself: "the scarlet letter endowed with life!"[41] She is therefore the manifestation of Hester's sexual desire. Hester's hair is a "deep-glossy brown, and which, in after years, would be nearly akin to black" is in contrast to Pearl's golden hair which suggests Hester's virginal vagina at the point which Dimmesdale makes love to her.[42] There is an interplay between innocence and knowing; she is at once elf-child, "airy sprite," "demon off-spring" asking the knowing question: "why does the minister keep his hand over his heart?"[43] Such interplay between knowing and innocence is similarly demonstrated in Zane Grey's *Riders of the Purple Sage* in the child Fay who's "crown of her childish loveliness was the curling golden hair."[44] Grey complicates the presexual innocence with Fay's flirtatious "seducing" of the gun-man Lassiter: "She laughed with glee as she ran her little hands down the slippery, shiny surface of Lassiter's leather chaps. Soon she discovered one of the hanging gun-sheaths."[45] That Jane Withersteen uses her feminine wiles to try and stay the gun-man Lassiter's hand, and that the scene of greatest sexual tension and desire is when Jane also reaches for Lassiter's guns is not insignificant.

STRANDS OF RED IN THE GOLDEN FLEECE OF HAIR

In *Lady Audley's Secret* golden hair brings together a peculiar pre- and postsexual femininity more explicitly in one person—Lady Audley. Throughout her qualities of childlike innocence are dwelt upon but also questioned: "The innocence and candour of an infant beamed in Lady Audley's fair face [...] the rosy lips, the delicate nose, the profusion fair ringlets, all contributed to preserve to her beauty the character of extreme youth and freshness [...] as girlish as if she had but just left the nursery."[46] But she is also all abundant and disordered feminine sexuality "with her disordered hair in a pale haze of yellow gold."[47] The link to gold, the cash nexus, is made explicit as it is her looks and childlike qualities which attract money. The novel's plot also hinges on two locks of hair which should stand in for each other but don't:

> He found nothing but a bright ring of golden hair, of that glittering hue which is so rarely seen except upon the head of a child—a sunny lock which curled as naturally as the tendril of a vine; and was the very opposite in texture, if not different in hue, to the soft, smooth tress which the landlady at Ventnor had given to George Tallboys after his wife's death.[48]

Clearly the suggestion is that not all golden hair is the same. While it is her "childish beauty [...] with large clear blue eyes, and pale golden ringlets" which identify her, rather than her being the pure angel at the hearth found in Eliot, she

> twined her fingers in her loose amber curls, and made as if she would have torn them from her head. But even in that moment of mute despair the unyielding dominion of beauty asserted itself, and she released the poor tangled glitter of ringlets, leaving them to make a halo around her head in the dim firelight.[49]

She might be at the hearthside but she is not center of the home. Further, the restoring of the halo on her head does not assert her innocence but links her to her image of her mother. When Lady Audley, or rather Helen Tallboys, is taken from her boarding school to the asylum, from the pre- to the postsexual institutions of controlled femininity, to meet her mother she finds "a golden-haired, blue-eyed, girlish creature [...] who skipped towards us with her yellow curls decorated with natural flowers."[50] The asylum preserves the mother figure in the presexual phase so that she cannot pass on, endorse, and legitimize her daughter's female sexuality. The mother and daughter are mirror images of each other, fearing she will become her mother when Lady Audley reaches her asylum she "plucked at the feathery golden curls as if she would have torn them from her head."[51]

While Lady Audley's hair is luxurious and glitters her servant, and double, Phoebe's "pale hair was as smoothly braided." And the point is it glitters. When Robert Audley suggests that the hair in her portrait could only have been painted by a Pre-Raphaelite there is a hint of the question about how far she is in control, how far her childlike persona is duplicitous and manipulative, and how far it is innocent: "peeping out of the lurid mass of colour, as if out of a raging furnace [...] the red gold gleaming in the yellow hair."[52] The red, which is usually hidden, is here exposed telling us that she is not a virgin but has been married before, she is not innocent but a criminal, that in fact her golden hair was a "shining snare" to catch the moneyed Audley. But it is less the red hair of Ofek's "smouldering sexuality,"[53] and more revealing the woman who "jerks her head form under the hairbrush, or chafes at the gentlest administration of the comb,"[54] and is struggling to fit with society's expected femininities. Lady Audley recognizes the artifice in constructing beauty when she tells Phoebe: "you *are* like me [...] Why, with a bottle of hair dye, such as we see advertised in the papers, and a pot of rouge, you'd be as good-looking as I any day."[55] The red hair in the portrait suggests the duplicitousness; Lady Audley does after all disguise herself but it is her natural attributes, her hair, body, and face, which also reveal her. As Ofek points out contemporary critics of Lady Audley's hair were concerned that "such representations of women's hair would influence female readers and change their habits of consumption, their looks, and their definition of womanliness."[56] Even outside the text golden hair is linked with economic concerns and any "smouldering sexuality" suggested by the red hair is more to do with her own narcissistic desire which is all about financial gain and lifestyle.

There is a similar linking of the childlike with natural instinct aligned to a "smouldering sexuality" and a narcissistic desire in Émile Zola's Nana whose golden-red hair "looked like an animal's fleece."[57] Throughout she is associated with animal desire. Over the two novels in which she appears she moves from prostitute to courtesan and throughout there is a narcissistic power which emerges from the display of her body and hair:

> This was Venus rising from the waves, with no veil save her tresses. And when Nana raised her arms, the golden hairs in her arm-pits could be seen in the glare of the footlights [...] All of a sudden, in the good-natured child the woman stood revealed, a disturbing woman with all the impulsive madness of her sex, opening the gates the unknown world of desire. Nana was still smiling, but with the deadly smile of a man-eater.[58]

The presence of her body hair in the text suggests animal fur: "Nana's body was covered with fine hair, reddish down which turned her skin into velvet."[59] She is referred to as the "Golden Beast" and "her mane of loosened yellow hair covered her back with the fell of a lioness."[60] All the male characters are consumed with desire for her yet she desires herself and her "boy-child" lover George. Further it is when she is in the natural environment of the country rather than the corrupt city that her own childlike qualities emerge.

The association of an animalistic desire with female sexuality is even more apparent in Zola's The Kill in which Renée, filled with ennui, makes love to her stepson, Maxine, in order to break the boredom. She has "strange, fawn-coloured hair,"[61] and childlike qualities. When Maxine, her stepson, casts his desiring gaze upon her: "her rumpled little face looked adorable under the rain of golden curls that fell down over her eyebrows."[62] For Maxine it is both that she is dressed as a boy and that the childlike curls are gender-neutral which feeds into his sexual desire. The desire in their first sexual encounter is further stimulated by Renée's "delicious uneasiness" at the thought of other women's hair and toilette which has taken place in this room: "the limpid, cynical mirror [...] had helped in the adjustment of so many false chignons."[63] When she tries to restore her own hair their failings are hers: "standing in front of the mirror, she clumsily tried to refasten the ribbon, but her chignon had slipped down, her little curls had flattened on her temple."[64] The waiter offers her "the comb" to civilize her hair only for it to make clear that all the women who use it are complicit in their subjection: "Renée suddenly understood. The room had a comb that formed part of its apparatus [...] she could see [...] the tortoiseshell teeth in which Laure d'Aurigny and Sylvia had left their fair hair and black."[65] These two motifs, the loosened chignon and the comb, directly associate women's hair with sexual activity. The chignon, which stands in for the women's pubic hair, slips. The dirty comb, which weaves together the dark and fair hair, loses its sense of being a tool of a woman's agency, "weaving" her hair to entice male sexual desire, and becomes a tool of subjection.

COILING SNAKES OF RED HAIR

A comparison of the color palette used in Gabriel Dante Rossetti's painting *Lady Lilith* of 1866–1868 and the altered version in 1872–1873 shows explicitly the move from hair of a golden hue to the far more fiery red tone commonly associated with the Pre-Raphaelite woman. The subtleties of difference in color suggest the shades of meaning which complicate the idea of appearance depicting character and or character traits. Red hair in the Victorian period was often associated with ugliness in such as the young girl in *Jane Eyre* whose red hair marks her out: "'*what* is that girl with curled hair? Red hair, ma'am, curled—curled all over?' And extending his cane he pointed to the awful object, his hand shaking as he did so."[66] The offending natural curls and shade is ordered to be cut off because "we are not to conform to nature."[67] Yet toward the end of the century the Pre-Raphaelites brought in a fashion for red hair: "Victorians generally considered red hair unsightly, but Pre-Raphaelites adored the fiery shade. If not blessed by nature with red hair, the artistic type could dye their hair with henna."[68] Richard Altick suggests that it is "artifice—unmitigated, unwomanly deceit—rushed in to supply the lack" and quotes Justin McCarthy writing in 1876: "How did all these Pre-Raphaelite girls manage to come to life so suddenly? Were they all born with that red hair … ?"[69] So even though the shade became fashionable it still retained a residue of unease. McCarthy is not quite pointing the finger and saying cut it off, but there is the sense that artifice used to comply with fashion suggests a female control over sexual desires which is uncomfortable for the male commentator in particular when, as Jessica Lenihan notes: "red hair in particular – with its fiery attention-grabbing vivacity – suggested what Ofek has termed 'smoldering sexuality'."[70] Further, there is a lack of containment not merely of the hair itself but of the hair as signifier in its continually shifting dependence on who has control of it.

Such a loss of ownership extends to narrative in the various stories surrounding Lizzie Siddal's hair. Married to Rossetti she was model, artist, and poet, painted time and again by the Pre-Raphaelites. On the one hand owning a lock of Lizzie's hair gives a sense of power, but it is only control over a cut lock, as her hair lives on. Certainly it does live on in the rumors, and of course the rumors suggest that her hair lived on, continuing to grow after she died. While Rossetti further added to those rumors in the published lines "Lies all that golden hair undimmed in death,"[71] and according to Ofek "imaginatively endowed his wife's hair with an independent power,"[72] he had already done so in the many renditions of her hair in both poetry and painting. Here the tension evinced in hair between the public and the private comes to the fore. Further, it is a tension between the older symbolic readings and the new, between the traditional rendition of femininity and the New Woman. Ofek elucidates in Rossetti's "Body's Beauty":

> Lilith's enchanted and ensnaring hair is conceptualized as a feminine trap, a net, a web and a noose ("bright web she can weave") wielded by the forerunners of the women's emancipation movement. They use their dangerous female power to plot against man and entrap him, eventually leaving his "straight neck bent/And around his heart one strangling golden hair" (ll. 4, 7, 14).[73]

Again and again the Pre-Raphaelites depicted women's hair as ensnaring, linking Victorian women's hair to Medusa's snakes. Because the fiery red hair is linked to female sexuality it can be suggested that the male artists are authoring their own anxieties. In the earlier Rossetti painting of Lilith the more golden tone links more explicitly to an innocence lost to the later fiery hue (see Figures 6.1 and 6.2).

The accentuated paleness of the skin and reddening of the lips suggest the artifice of beauty as do the additional folds in her dress. While the whitening of the roses surrounding her as well as her expression suggest that even though she is displaying her sexuality with the spreading of her hair and her availability in the absent corset and uncovered shoulder

FIGURE 6.1: Dante Gabriel Rossetti, *Lady Lilith*, 1866–1868 (altered 1872–1873). Oil on canvas, 97.5 cm × 84.1 cm. Delaware Art Museum Wilmington, USA/Samuel and Mary R. Bancroft Memorial, 1935.

FIGURE 6.2: Dante Gabriel Rossetti, *Lady Lilith*, 1873. Oil on canvas. Rossetti, Dante Gabriel Charles (1828–82) / Universal Images Group North America LLC / Alamy Stock Photo.

it is a cold and sterile sexual offering. The passionate red rose is plucked for her own pleasure and the red cord tied around her own wrist all reinforce the narcissistic gaze of self-desire unavailable to the male viewer of the painting. Finally, the daisy garland is not worn but symbolically placed to suggest a figuratively unbroken or perhaps rather unbreakable hymen; Lilith would, after all, not be subservient to Adam. The mirror in the background rather than containing her demon daughter contains nature. Rossetti's picture with all its sensuousness foregrounds the link between hair and sensuality in the Victorian cultural consciousness and explores the relationship between innocence, artifice, and female sexual desire. Lenihan points out that Rossetti altered the painting on the request of the purchaser as the blonder tone was too "sensual and commonplace" reminding us that blonde hair, as has already been seen, is equally mobile as a signifier.[74] The changes made depict the tensions within the picture that refuse an easy reading of simple enchantment. The lines in the poem point to the tension: "And, subtly of herself contemplative, / Draws men to watch the bright web she can weave, / Till heart and body and life are in its hold."[75] She is simultaneously sexualized and empowered. Lilith here is depicted combing her hair, the comb becomes linked simultaneously to the weaving, styling, authoring of the self, and sexuality. The tension in the painting suggests the male anxiety of desire mixed with fear of the empowered sexual feminine.

A similar development can be seen in the earlier studies and the final painting of William Holman Hunt's *The Lady of Shalott*. In the earlier *Study for the Lady of Shalott* (1850) her hair is tied at her neck suggesting that her hair and her arm offer little resistance to her fate. The drawing suggests a chasteness. Even in the mirror image she is turning away from Sir Lancelot while the roundel which shows his face is closest to her suggesting his complicity. Art historian Sharyn Udall questions "why this high-born lady described by Hunt as 'intelligent', condemns herself to a life lived at second and then, in a defiant about-face, rashly invokes the threatened curse."[76] And it is this questioning which begins to emerge in the illustration in the Moxon edition of the poet's work. Tennyson was famously unhappy with Holman's Moxon illustration, suggesting that it had moved away from the lines of the poem. "Why did you make the Lady of Shalott, in the illustration, with her hair wildly tossed about as if by a tornado? [...] Why do you make the web wind round her like the threads of a cocoon?"[77]

In the drawing (Figure 6.3) and subsequent painting (Figure 6.4) her hair is free with Christ in the background depicted on the cross. The Lady of Shalott appears caught in her weaving and the addition of Lancelot's bugle and lance all point to her as a fallen woman. The painting suggests that she is caught in her own sexual desire and Sir Lancelot is unseeing, riding away from that desire. Usually the fallen woman is depicted as innocent, then seduced and abandoned but here, as she looks out of what is now suggestive of a window rather than the earlier mirror, she looks directly at Sir Lancelot's bugle and lance: it is her desire which has led to her fall. In the later paintings the effect is further exaggerated.

Her wild hair takes over the upper half of the paintings as does her erotic desire. In one she is surrounded by images of a worldly Christ who is in agony in the Garden of Eden, while in the other painting the roundel depicts Mary praying over the newborn Christ while Hercules is taking an apple from the tree in the Garden of Eden invitingly looking over his shoulder. In both she has taken off her shoes, her arms are naked, and her skirt is raised, tangled in her weaving. The paintings are full of movement and chaos, her desire swirling round her in her hair, and rather than being submissively trapped by the feminine pursuit of weaving she appears to be fighting it, the color of the threads around her skirt

FIGURE 6.3: William Holman Hunt, *The Lady of Shalott*, 1857. Wood-engraved illustrations from the Moxon edition. Engraver J. Thompson.

FIGURE 6.4: William Holman Hunt, *The Lady of Shalott*, 1886–1905.

tying the weaving to her hair. This is far removed from the earlier mirrors which suggest a "truth" and the roundels depicting her life: here it is her hair which, with the tapestry, is weaving her desires.

The many images of abundant red hair from the Pre-Raphaelites suggest something more than a mere fetishization. There is a desire that is mesmerizing and through the many renditions it appears that the artists are trying to understand and take ownership of the hair that continues to elude them. In *Lady Audley's Secret* Robert Audley says that: "the painter must have been a pre-Raphaelite. No one but a pre-Raphaelite would have painted, hair by hair, those feathery mass of ringlets with every glimmer of gold."[78] Because the Pre-Raphaelite hair is all about female sexual desire on display this suggests that the male is trying to contain a woman's sexual desire but cannot. Finally, in these paintings the women rarely engage the male viewer's gaze so female sexual desire remains other.

DROWNING IN ABUNDANT TRESSES

In contrast Charles Baudelaire in the poem "Her Hair" immerses the self in the lover's hair. Importantly the female is sexually engaged with the man who subsumes himself to the cosseting effects of the hair. Baudelaire's poem explicitly reveals that "my desire may never find you deaf."[79] Because the desire is mutual the hair becomes a safe haven from the world: "O fleece, tumbling in waves upon the neck! o curls! o perfume heavy with carelessness! Ecstasy! To fill, this evening, the dark alcove with memories sleeping in this head of hair."[80] Her hair "carries" him, "strong tresses, be the sea that bears me away!" and nurtures him, "blue hair, enclosing tent of darkness, you bring back to me the measureless round sky."[81] So while the hair is imbued with an erotic seductiveness it is also womblike, a retreat from the world and a giver of strength; the female's hair empowering his masculinity. For Edgar Allan Poe in his poem "For Annie" her hair gives him peace and is restorative in the face of illness: "Drowned in a bath / Of the tresses of Annie."[82] Poe's feelings for Nancy Richmond, who nursed him, (she changed her name to Annie when her husband died) finds the apotheosis of platonic desire in her hair while the narrator in the poem arguably finds fulfillment of erotic desire in the tent of hair. Elisabeth G. Gitter points out that enveloped in hair the poetic persona finds solace: "Embraces are there, of course, but the hair tent is not primarily a bower of sexual love: it is a retreat from the world, a refuge for the poet, a cocoon."[83] Even in this figuration the hair retains a sense of enchantment and rather than emasculating the male the hair restores masculinity in that it operates both as sanctuary from the world and as permitting freedom of thought.

In Robert Browning's poem "Pauline" hair similarly surrounds, protects, and allows the male freedom of being: "And loosened hair and breathing lips, and arms / Drawing me to thee – these build up a screen / To shut me in with thee, and from all fear; / So that I may unlock the sleepless brood / Of fancies from my soul, their lurking place."[84] There is a sense here that femininity evinced in such natural hair nurtures masculinity free from the restraints of societies dictates of gender. Even Rossetti can in words get to where he cannot in painting: "Beneath her sheltering hair, / In the warm silence near her breast, / Our kisses and our sobs shall sink to rest; / As in some trance made aware / That day and night have wrought to fulness there / And Love has built out nest" ("The Stream's Secret," lines 79–84).[85] Again there is a womblike resonance to being inside her hair which nurtures their love and he is returned to her mothering breast. Their sexual desire for each other is becalmed by her nurturing instinct and the hair becomes a sign of protective fertility in their nest. This is taken further in "The Blessed Damozel," a poem he worked on throughout his life, when the Damozel is leaning out from heaven and the persona reclines looking up to her. His painting of the poem reinforces the spatial separation which denies physical interaction in the fulfillment of desire. While the Damozel dreams of being with her beloved, female sexual desire is absent and male desire has become purely spiritual: "Surely she lean'd o'er me-her hair / Fell all about my face."[86] The persona here is reflecting on his dreamlike vision of the Damozel from heaven, central to that conscious reflection is that "surely" he must be within the sanctuary of her hair. Gitter suggests that in these figurations of female hair the "woman herself is without individuality, silent and spiritualised."[87] Certainly this male desire to be subsumed into a woman's hair appears to be less about femininity and more about masculine desire which needs to deny female sexual desire. Certainly this appears to be the apotheosis which the endless working on "The Blessed Damozel" moves toward. Where Baudelaire may call for his poetic persona's lover to engage with his erotic desire, they are making love, the other renditions prefer a passive and even largely absent self with the hair taking precedence.

WHITE HAIR

In a culture which has fetishized hair in all sorts of different ways, in a range of hues, women's gray hair gets scant attention. One of the most startling images of female sexual desire is evinced in the white hair of Miss Havisham in *Great Expectations*: "And she had a long white veil dependent from her hair, and she had bridal flowers in her hair, but her hair was white."[88] The narrative tension derives from leaving the revelation that her hair is white to the final clause of the sentence. The disorientating juxtaposition of the wedding hair adornment and the fact that the hair is white leaves the reader uneasy precisely because the veil and the flowers offer up the presexual woman. They are motifs of fertility while her hair suggests otherwise. It also underscores that white or gray hair is not simply about aging for the female but is also about her waning fertility. While it is too easy to read Miss Havisham as declining and weak, in many ways she is not. Any agency she does have is not located in potential procreation but that her sexual desire still motivates her.

In contrast to Miss Havisham's dissipated body withering from her never consummated desire, Catherine Vernon's hair in Margaret Oliphant's *Hester* is "white and beautiful, her figure ample, but graceful still" further "her eye was not dim, nor her natural force abated. She had a finer colour than in her girlhood."[89] Not perfect but she is still full of physical vigor, arguably sexually attractive, and certainly powerful. And it is her womanly power which is pitted against the younger Hester's. While just after the end of the Age of Empire Edith Wharton's reading of white hair is perhaps even more interesting in *The Mother's Recompense*. Here the white-haired mother is figured as more youthful, in both dress and attitude, than her daughter. She also retains her sexual energy even if the younger man who is the focus of her desire chooses her daughter. But the younger Captain Fenno is as conservative as the daughter Anne who braids her hair in a "memorial manner,"[90] while Kate, the mother, dresses in a youthful style so when she is faced with returning to New York and the conservative fashions she has a crisis of age. However, she draws on her understanding of adornment to reconstruct herself as a middle-aged woman:

> She drew herself up with dignity. "A daughter of twenty-one; I'm joining her in New York next week. What would she think of me if I arrived in a hat more youthful than hers? Show me something darker, please: yes, the one with the autumn leaves. See, I'm growing gray on the temples – don't try to make me look like a flapper. What's the price of that blue fox over there? I like a gray fur with gray hair."[91]

She understands that when a woman ages society suggests she should look to autumnal color and, as she is returning to Old New York, the fox-fur trim will attest to a financial security she does not have and she understands the social codes in the styling of her hair. She is reconstructing herself as the middle-aged mother acceptable to New York replacing the fashion-forward woman of the Riviera. "In the end she stalked out, offended by the milliner's refusal to take her gray hair seriously."[92] When she arrives in New York she desires the young girl's body and hair as much as Anne desires her mother's. "And what a beautiful mother you are! And nobody wears their clothes as you do" and "all that lovely hair."[93] The young Lilla offers an interesting parallel to Anne in that she is wearing the latest fashions yet Kate is appalled by her youthful fashion and "that impudent stripped version of herself, with dyed hair, dyed lashes, drugged eyes and unintelligible dialect."[94] The abjection here is not merely Kate's lost youth but the artifice of femininity and the constructing of sexual desirableness. It is also the abjection in that Kate has carried on desiring Fenno, her young lover, who rather than choosing the woman with abundant flowing hair which is graying at the temples, marries Anne who dresses and braids her hair with stifling Old New York middle-aged etiquette. Here Wharton not only gives a sympathetic reading of feminine aging and the conflicts of sexual power but asserts it as preferential when she leaves Kate in the "slant of the Riviera sun," desirable and empowered, comfortable with her hair and in her fur: "she came back handsomer, better dressed—yes my dear, actually sables!—and she offered them cocktails and Mah-Jongg in her won sitting-room (with a view of the sea thrown in)."[95]

CONCLUSION

Throughout the Age of Empire hair has been fetishized and is abundant. The hair sits at a fascinating boundary between public and private desires: from the social codes of hair which call for it to be increasingly restrained to the fashions for hair and color which are all about public display even while they suggest more private idealizations of a public self. There is a tension in the level of permissible artifice to achieve those fashions and that social control. Finally, there is the tension between the natural innocence of childhood flowing locks and the fear of unrestrained tresses. For both genders hair is a site of contested discourses and power relations, and this is most ardently played out when the hair comes to represent sexuality and sexual desire.

CHAPTER SEVEN

Race and Ethnicity: Strands of the Diaspora

Black Hair in the Americas, 1800–1920

ELIZABETH WAY

AFRICAN ORIGINS

The cultural significance of hair for African Americans in the nineteenth and early twentieth centuries is rooted in African cultural practices of the same and earlier periods. Africa is home to thousands of ethnicities and cultural groups, each with their own hair practices, styles, and meanings that developed independently within ethnic groups, through interactions between various African groups, and through contact with the wider world. The significance of hair practices within individual African communities comprises a vast area of research, even when concentrating on just the customs of West and Central–West Africa, the geographic origin of most African Americans. Yet despite these countless variations and divergences, West and Central–West African ethnic groups have shared common attitudes toward the cultural importance of hair and its function as a means of communication.

Diaspora historian Gwendolyn Midlo Hall identifies the ten most prominent ethnic groups that were sold into slavery in the Americas over the four-century span of the slave trade as the BaKongo (from present-day Democratic Republic of Congo and Angola); the Mandé (Upper Guinea); the Adja, Mina, Ewe, and Fon, grouped together as the Gbe speakers (Togo, Ghana, and Benin); the Akan (Ghana and Côte d'Ivoire); the Wolof (Senegal and Gambia); the Igbo (southeastern Nigeria); the Mbundu (Angola); the Yoruba (southwestern Nigeria); the Chamba (Cameroon); and the Makua (Mozambique).[1] Among these groups and others, well-groomed hair was central to ideals of beauty for both men and women. According to African art scholar Niangi Batulukisi, hair in sub-Saharan Africa developed into "a cultural element of social communication" being "perceived as the expression of a cultural identity, a social status, or of a profession," yet:

> Hair care in traditional Africa is above all aesthetic in its goals. There is in black Africa an undeniable link between coiffure and beauty; a well-attended head has always been a criterion of beauty, a source of admiration, a reason for pride [...] the transformation of hair shows the human desire to modify nature, to create.[2]

Hairstyles throughout the fifteenth through nineteenth centuries were inspired by both tradition and changing fashions and might include braids, plaits, tufts, crests, frizzed styles, shaved patterns, locks, wigs and weaves, and other sculptural styles. Treatments were created with oils, fats, clay, powders, herbs, madder, and minerals. Hair ornamentations could incorporate beads, shells, coral, precious metal charms, magical amulets, amber, feathers, fabric, thread, and finely crafted combs of wood, bone, and ivory. The breadth of African hairstyles, and their creativity, was astounding, an expression of a wider African worldview and African art forms that emphasized innovation, visual rhythms, and improvisation.

Hair grooming constituted important social activities in many African societies, often separated by gender. Complex hairstyles could take a great deal of time to assemble, time in which social bonds were formed and maintained among peer groups and social norms were passed on to the next generation. Only during extreme situations, such as mourning for a close relative, would hair not be groomed into a specific style. Ungroomed or unwashed hair indicated insanity, criminality, or evil influences. Because hair styling emphasized social interactions, unkempt hair could also be a sign of social ostracization. Hair was generally viewed in West Africa as an essential representation of the person; therefore, only trusted individuals would be chosen to style one's hair, and clippings were carefully disposed of to prevent enemies from using them to cause harm.

Hair also emphasized important periods in the life cycle. For example, in many African cultures children's hairstyles differed from those worn by adolescences beginning puberty and from married people. African hair scholar Esi Sagay describes the traditional hairstyle that young Igbo women took on when seeking mates, noting a change in style every year for eight years, culminating in a wedding style in which "the hair was usually coated generously with a mixture of charcoal, clay, and oil and was then moulded into a crest, which was decorated with coils of hair, coins, and brass ornaments."[3]

In the Yoruba culture well-groomed hair was essential and hair styling played a large role in defining status and power within communities because of the centrality of the head in Yoruba religion. Nigerian art historian Babatunde Lawal explains:

> The Yoruba creation myth traces the origin of the human body to an archetypical sculpture (*ere*) modeled by the artist-deity Obatala, after which it is activated by the divine breath (*emi*) of Olodumare [the supreme being], located in the sculpture's head [...] According to the myth, every individual, before being born into the physical world, must proceed to the workshop of Ajalamopin, the heavenly potter, to choose one out of several undifferentiated, ready-made *Ori Inu*, the "inner head" on display in Ajalamopin's workshop. Each "inner head" contains Olodumare's ase (enabling power), and the one chosen by an individual predetermines his/her lot (*ipin*) in the physical world.[4]

The Yoruba also used hairstyles to designate age groups, distinguishing small boys and girls from each other and from those who had entered adulthood through initiation rites (Figure 7.1). Yoruba men tended to shave their heads, leaving patterns of hair that indicated royal or military status, or prowess as a hunter. Women wore their long hair in more elaborate styles to "honor their inner head" and in keeping with cultural standards of beauty.[5] Women's hairstyles also denoted marriage status. Priests, both male and female, and royal messengers wore specific hairstyles to indicate their profession and convey their power. Hair styling was a community activity, though it could also be professionalized. Authors Ayana D. Byrd and Lori L. Tharps note in *Hair Story*:

In the Yoruba tradition, all women were taught how to braid, but any young girl who showed talent in the art of hairdressing was encouraged to become a "master," assuming responsibility for the entre community's coiffures. Before a "master" died, she would pass on her box of hairdressing tools to a successor within the family during a sacred ceremony.[6]

Some of these traditions are maintained into the present day throughout West Africa.

FIGURE 7.1: The Smithsonian Museum of African Art describes the hairstyle of this Yoruba figure as "cone-shaped [...] with cylindrical projections [indicating] stylistic traits from the Oyo and Owo regions." Female figure, Yoruba peoples, Nigeria, mid-nineteenth century. Ivory, black stone, 30.2 cm × 5.3 cm × 8.6 cm. Acquisition grant from the James Smithson Society and museum purchase, 85-9-1. Photo: Franko Khoury, National Museum of African Art, Smithsonian Institution.

ENSLAVED IN THE AMERICAS

In *The Atlantic Slave Trade*, Herbert S. Klein determines that from 1700 to 1808, over six million African people were brought to the Americas, accounting for roughly two-thirds of all African slaves imported to the New World over the span of the slave trade. The highest volume of Africans arrived in the late eighteenth century—the 1780s saw 75,000 new Africans enslaved in the Americas each year, though another 2.3 million would arrive, mostly in Brazil and Cuba, by the mid-nineteenth century. This influx of slaves was absolutely critical for the development of the American economy: "Except for precious metals, almost all major American exports to Europe were produced by Africans."[7] The importation of slaves from Africa to the Americas was abolished throughout the first half of the nineteenth century—the United States legislated against the transatlantic slave trade in 1808; Brazil followed in 1831, though it did not effectively enforce the law until the 1850s. This meant that for African Americans during the early 1800s, new arrivals from the home continent continually reconnected and reminded them of their African traditions. As this influx slowed and stopped, the developing African American cultures of the nineteenth century came to rely on remembered and adapted African traditions, while creating new American hair practices.

In Africa, systems of hairstyles specific to ethnic groups acted as markers of social order and provided visual communications of the assigned place of each member in society. The social and individual repercussions that slavery presented created an enormous rupture in these traditions in the Americas. Europeans introduced new hierarchies among slaves, based on skills and capacities for labor. The freedom and eventually the knowledge to maintain complex African expressions of social systems through hair styling was fundamentally obliterated, yet hair remained a culturally significant manifestation of creativity, personal adornment, pride, and even entrepreneurial opportunity among African Americans throughout the nineteenth and early twentieth centuries.

When slaves were captured in Africa and made ready for exportation to the Americas, their heads were typically shaved. Although the procedure was deemed practical in preparation for the unsanitary conditions of the slave ships, the removal of the elaborate and ethnically specific hairstyle that marked one as a member of his or her community and detailed his or her place within it amounted to stripping away one's identity. Byrd and Tharps attest:

> The shaved head was the first step the Europeans took to erase the slave's culture and alter the relationship between the African and his or her hair [...] Arriving without their signature hairstyles, Mandingos, Fulanis, Ibos, and Ashantis entered the New World, just as the Europeans intended, like anonymous chattel.[8]

Yet Africans proved resilient in maintaining their traditions of adornment. Author of *Hair: Public Political Extremely Personal*, Diane Simon, quotes an eighteenth-century observer who noted that slaves, newly arrived in Suriname on the northeast coast of South America, had shaved figures of moons and stars into their heads with broken glass and soap during the Middle Passage.[9] Far from frivolous, this styling was perhaps a critical expression of both individuality and community that helped these people survive the horrific journey. By the time slaves arrived in the Americas, their hair was an important indicator of health and age that would influence prices at auction. Simon also notes that slavers would remove gray hairs or dye slaves' hair black, masking his or her age to fetch a higher price.[10]

Enslaved people, especially evident in the historical references to male African Americans, continued to use their hair as an expressive medium during the eighteenth century. However, by the nineteenth century creative hair styling was largely absent, due perhaps to the severing of fresh ideas from Africa's vibrant hair culture as fewer Africans came to the Americas, a more controlled attitude toward slave appearance by slave owners, and a shift in mainstream (white) hair fashions to shorter styles for men and less elaborate styles for women, which would have had an impact on slaves' hairstyles. In *Stylin': African American Expressive Culture from Its Beginnings to the Zoot Suit*, Shane White and Graham White use runaway slave notices in US newspapers to compare the creativity and ostentation of long and elaborate hairstyles frequently used to describe the mostly male runaway slaves advertised during the eighteenth century to the comparative lack of any hair descriptions in nineteenth-century runaway notices.[11] African American cultural historian Kennell Jackson also describes the inventive and vibrant African American hairstyles of the eighteenth century that drew on traditional African styles, such as braiding and decorative shaving, while incorporating long Native American and upswept European styles: "Exhibiting an African taste for hair novelty and comment, some men shaped their hair to mimic high-status [European] wigs."[12] These ostentatious styles were not as prevalent during the nineteenth century as slaves' hair, both male and female, was generally cut short.[13] White and White note that the lack of documentation of hairstyles in runaway notices in the early nineteenth century makes it difficult to track changes in black hairstyles, "However, the appearance of photographic studies of slaves in the 1850s confirms that there had been a shift to shorter hair among African American males, and at least among those females who appear in photographs with heads uncovered."[14] The importance of hair grooming and styling, however, persisted.

In many parts of Africa hairdressers maintained a high social status as skilled artisans. Dressing the hair included cleansing, combing with specialized combs, oiling with conditioners such as palm oil, and then styling into a coiffure that may take several hours to prepare.[15] Slaves in the Americas were not afforded time or their traditional tools to care for and style their hair, yet they tried as best they could to maintain their appearance and the social bonds that were created through communal hair care. On Sundays, usually the only day slaves were given to themselves, men shaved each other and combed and styled each other's hair, as depicted in the 1797 painting *Preparations for the Enjoyment of a Fine Sunday among the Blacks, Norfolk* by Benjamin Henry Latrobe. Here four men assist each other in their haircare rituals, utilizing a fenced yard as a barber shop and barrels as barber chairs. Women washed and set their hair, drawing on a combination of African traditions and contemporary European hair fashions to style plaits or cornrow braids, straighten their hair, tie it with thread, or wrap it in eel skin or cotton to create curls (Figure 7.2). These styles would be covered in headwraps during the week to be unveiled and finished for Sunday church services or special occasions. Slaves working in the plantation house might wear their styled hair uncovered all week. The adults also tended to children's hair, combing, styling, and delousing.

Slaves created hair products from improvised sources, such as axle grease and available animal fats, and invented homemade chemical straighteners from lye and potatoes.[16] The finely crafted combs used in Africa were replaced with cards, the wire brushes designed to align cotton or wool fibers before spinning that were ominously nicknamed "Jim-crows" by slaves in the United States.[17] Martha Harrison, who was about twelve years old during the US Civil War, recalled that on her home plantation:

FIGURE 7.2: This photograph is captioned "The Givers," and it illustrates the social bonds created through hair care on slave plantations. Photograph album: "Rose-mary. A Plantation Home" (ca. 1890–1910), Edward Ward Carmack Papers, 1850–1942. From the Southern Historical Collection, Louis Round Wilson Special Collections Library, University of North Carolina at Chapel Hill. (Original image has been cropped.)

> Chillen was just as lousy as pigs. They had these combs that was just like cards you "card" cotton with, and they would comb out your head with them. That wouldn't get the lice out, but it would make it feel better. They had to use larkspur to get 'em out; that would always get lice out of your head.[18]

In *The Language of Dress: Resistance and Accommodation in Jamaica 1760–1890*, Steeve O. Buckridge studies how dress—defined by anthropologists Mary Ellen Roach-Higgins and Joanne B. Eicher to include hair styling and other body modifications—was a vital component of survival for slaves in Jamaica in the late eighteenth and nineteenth centuries. Slaves expressed both resistance and accommodation through their dress choices and thereby preserved their cultural and personal value: "African cultural features were retained and nurtured in Jamaica because they guaranteed the survival of Africans and their descendants despite European attempts at cultural annihilation [...] Cultural expression as a survival strategy played an integral role in the daily lives of African slaves."[19] Buckridge illuminates hair styling as a vital part of the expression of resistance to slavery and in slave women's survival:

Hairstyles consisted of plaits or braids or of combing the hair into "lanes" or "walks" like the "parterre of a garden," as is done in West Africa. This display of African aesthetics in dress served as a marker to keep these women, the members of the slave community, separate from the world, and to identify those who did not belong. This separate sphere for slave women, as mirrored in their dress, became a site, as bell hooks describes it, that "One stays in, clings to even, because it nourishes one's capacity to resist. It offers to one the possibility of radical perspective from which to see and create, to imagine alternative new worlds."[20]

White people during the nineteenth century noted the care and pride that black people took in their hair—an important counterpoint in the discourse on African American self-hatred created by the slave system. Traveling in Mississippi during the 1830s, Joseph Ingraham, for example, described his observations of slaves' Sunday routine: "the women arrayed in their gay muslins, are arranging their frizzy hair, in which they take no little pride."[21] Yet this pride could be used against slaves to humiliate them—especially mixed-race women whose hair embodied European beauty standards and therefore threatened white females' beauty supremacy. White and White cite several examples, including James Brittian's grandmother whose long, silky hair inspired jealousy in her owner's wife, likely due to the owner's sexual attentions to his slave. The wife had Brittian's grandmother whipped and her head shaved.[22] The authors describe this particular form of abuse by white women of black women as "a result of the warped sexual dynamics of antebellum plantations, the mutilation of an African American woman's hair was usually an action directed at white men rather than the victim herself, although doubtless its import was not lost on the slaves in the quarter."[23]

WHITE PERSPECTIVES ON BLACK HAIR: SCIENCE, SATIRE, AND ART

African American hair during the nineteenth century drove arguments in science and politics, fueling the abolitionist and anti-abolitionist debates on the equality of African peoples. Hair was considered as important a characteristic as skin color in differentiating blacks from whites, and for some, the texture of black hair—termed wool—served as a central piece of evidence that people of African descent were inferior to Europeans. James Prichard, a British medical doctor and ethnologist, refuted the claims that black and white men were of different species in *The Natural History of Man*, first published in 1843. He specifically addresses the centrality of hair in the assumption of inequality:

> The nature of hair is, perhaps, one of the most permanent characteristics of different races. The hair of the Negro has been termed woolly: it is not wool, and only differs from the hair of other races in less important aspects. It may be seen that the texture of the hair affords in the animal kingdom no specific characters. In mankind, we find it in every gradation of variety; and if we take the African nations [...] we shall discover among them every possible gradation in the texture of the hair.[24]

He goes on to deduce from his lengthy study of the physical and cultural characteristics of different ethnic groups around the world that "mankind, whether white or black, are placed by nature nearly on an equal footing."[25]

Others refuted Prichard's conclusions. Peter Browne, described by John Campbell in his 1851 book *Negro-mania* as "a scientific gentleman of Philadelphia, who is well qualified to give a decisive opinion upon the subject,"[26] wrote an essay which appeared in Campbell's book titled "The Classification of Mankind, by the Hair and Wool of their Heads, with an Answer to Dr. Prichard's Assertion, that 'The Covering of the Head of the Negro is Hair, properly term, and not Wool:' by Peter A. Browne, Esq." Browne determined that the cross-sectional shape of individual strands of hair were unique among Europeans, Native Americans, and those of African descent, indicating that "These are three *species* [original emphasis]."[27] His observations on various growth angles, cortex canals, and scales of hair led him to conclude: "The inference is irresistible. The hair of the white man is *more perfect* than that of the Negro [original emphasis]."[28] Although Browne's observations break down into subjective judgments of beauty, these standards and their seemingly scientific backing had powerful repercussions on black Americans. Byrd and Tharps note that slave owners and other whites used this pseudo-scientific "proof" to justify slavery, "White slave owners sought to pathologize African features like dark skin and kinky hair to further demoralize the slaves, especially women."[29]

Among free blacks in the Americas and for slaves freed after emancipation, hair styling became an aspect of accommodation to white culture that marginally helped insulate them from racist discrimination. White and White state:

> The early years of freedom opened relatively few opportunities for aesthetic expression, and ahead lay a racial climate so oppressive that any sign of ostentation would have been perilous, and an era of hair straightening in which the potential of African American hair for stylistic innovation was largely denied.[30]

Yet Buckridge notes "accommodation in itself is a form of resistance [...] part of a subtle and complex survival strategy and adaptive mechanism."[31] Blacks in the northern United States generally dressed and arranged their hair in a conservative style reflecting the beauty standards of white America. Buckridge observes the same occurrence among freed blacks in Jamaica, yet this conservative mainstream style should not be read as denying blackness: "Some women [...] saw accommodation and adaption of European cultural standards not as reflecting a desire to be like whites but as resistance in itself, because to accommodate was a political act that marked them as not slaves."[32]

The general white population refused to acknowledge that black people could fit into their dominant standards of beauty, and hair was often an excuse. Buckridge references E.A. Hastings, a visitor to Jamaica in the late nineteenth century, who described black women in their Sunday best as: "Big hulking negresses [who] were attired in gorgeous silks and satins, and truly wonderful hats with broad brims and feathers and ribbon [...] The wooly locks under all this fashionable headgear were pathetically ludicrous."[33] Popular culture in the United States expressed similar denigrating attitudes through minstrel shows. The theatrical form in which white actors depicted racist stereotypes of African Americans while wearing blackface makeup and fright wigs was extremely popular in the mid-nineteenth century.

E.W. Clay's "Life in Philadelphia" series published from 1828 to 1830, also presents derogatory images of African Americans through caricatures of the black bourgeoisie. Clay mirrors Hastings's statements by illustrating black women as large and clumsy in garish versions of the latest French fashions. In number thirteen of the series he shows a black couple at a ball (Figure 7.3). The woman's hair references the fashionable style of the time, which involved parting the hair at the center front and styling it into cascading curls or braids at the temples. However, Clay depicts the woman wearing two unflattering puffs of hair over her ears. Her partner's hair forms a high peak, again not

FIGURE 7.3: Aquatint cartoon, drawn and etched by E.W. Clay. Philadelphia. Published by S. Hart & Son, 1829. The Library Company of Philadelphia.

quite achieving the piles of loose curls popular for men. Clay's illustration mocks and disparages middle-class African Americans for partaking in mainstream fashion, clearly implying that elegance and style are not within their grasp.

White and White state that during slavery and afterwards, white Americans did not understand African American hairstyles, clothing, and gestures. Their confusion most often manifested as "mockery of black pretensions and lack of 'taste'. What whites failed to detect were the signs of an emerging African American culture, a series of borrowings and blendings which, always changing over time, at least obliquely challenged the hegemony of blacks' oppressors."[34] Though slave owners may not have understood African American aesthetics, Monica Miller, author of *Slaves to Fashion: Black Dandyism and the Styling of Black Diasporic Identity*, notes they did understand these sartorial displays "had significance beyond functionality—at stake was nothing less than a sense of freedom, a display of the difference between purported essence, self-worth and aspiration."[35] She quotes political scientist James Scott, explaining these creative sartorial impulses as cultural resistance and "not at all trivial; they are acts that enable everything from survival to more overt forms of protest."[36]

French artist Jean-Baptiste Debret traveled to Brazil in 1816 and also illustrated African Americans. However, his motive was to exoticize Brazilian slaves for the fascination of European audiences, publishing a portfolio of prints, *Voyage pittoresque et historique au Brésil*, in 1834. Debret's intention in many of his illustrations—to emphasize the "otherness" of his subjects—must be taken into account when observing his images. He most likely took liberties to make his subjects seem as African as possible and his sitters may have been given extraordinary time and tools to prepare their appearances for his benefit. "Difffèrentes nations Nègres," for example, illustrates several men wearing

FIGURE 7.4: Jean-Baptiste Debret, "Esclaves nègres, de différentes nations." Print. One of 153 hand-colored lithographs on 140 sheets for Jean-Baptiste Debret, *Voyage pittoresque et historique au Brésil, ou Séjour d'un artiste français au Brésil, depuis 1816 jusqu'en 1831 inclusivement*, 3 vols. (Paris: Firmin Didot frères, 1834–1839), ii: pl. 22. Hickey and Robertson, Houston/Menil Foundation.

various elaborately shaved motifs in their hair. These hairstyles, very interesting to European viewers, would have been hard to maintain on a daily basis for laboring slaves. Yet even accounting for these manipulations, prints such as "Escravas negras oriundas de diversas tribos africanas trazidas para o Brasil" (Figure 7.4) of sixteen African Brazilian women, provided astounding examples of creolized, adaptive hairstyles.

The women depicted in the print are shown expertly blending European and African elements in broadly ranging hairstyles. The women all wear fashionable European clothing and some show scarification marks that might indicate African birth. The central figure in the top row wears her hair parted down the center front and the hair is amassed at the crown, adorned with rows of protruding flowers—likely local Brazilian flowers, again exemplifying creolization. Floral hair ornamentation would not have been uncommon in Europe, however, the woman drawn two places to the right of the central top figure places flowers in her hair to form a central crest, a silhouette often seen in West and Central-West African hair styling. Some of the women wear their hair unstraightened in short styles, or simply pushed back from the face, while others wear turbans or more obviously European curls. However, several of these hairstyles incorporate unique shapes and adornments revealing an African sense of improvisation and creativity. Brazil imported seven times the number of slaves that were brought to the United States, and in some parts of the country the number of Africans outnumbered both Europeans and Native Brazilians. Therefore, it is not surprising that African aesthetic traditions would have strong influence on African Brazilian hair styling in this period.[37]

These hairstyles concur with what Buckridge explains as "the emergence of a Creole dress as part of Creole culture [that] did not represent the abandonment or the entrenchment of African dress customs among slaves but rather led to new creations that were strongly influenced by African aesthetics."[38] Buckridge continues:

> Creole dress was subversive by nature. In fact, Creole dress was fundamentally radical because it defied easy categorization. In essence, it visually and symbolically challenged the colonial regime's apparent deep-seated desire to divide the colonial world into clear-cut opposites of black and white, or European and African.[39]

Whatever artificial constructions Debret may have implemented in these images, it can be assumed that he did not wholly fabricate these hairstyles. These African Brazilian women used hair as a medium to negotiate their identities and status in earlynineteenth-century Brazil, revealing their hair as highly visible sites for creolization, cultural expression, and individuality.

BLACK HAIR ADVANCING TOWARD FREEDOM

As American slaves gained their freedom during the later nineteenth century, accommodation and creolization in hairstyles and dress further developed as part of respectability politics, a way for black Americans to distance themselves from slavery, find a new place in society, and try to gain respect as citizens. Yet visual culturist Kobena Mercer asserts that:

> When hairstyling is critically evaluated as an aesthetic practice inscribed in everyday life, *all* black hairstyles are political in that they each articulate responses to the panoply of historical forces which have invested this element of the ethnic signifier with both symbolic meaning and significance. [Original emphasis.][40]

Given this idea and Miller's statement that "blackness [is] always already 'performed,'"[41] even when African Americans straightened their hair and styled it in accordance to contemporary mainstream fashions, it always differed from white styles because black people wore it. While self-hatred was certainly a part of the mental scars left by slavery, black Americans styled their hair in different ways for different reasons throughout the nineteenth and early twentieth centuries. Some simply desired to look neat or fashionable, while other African Americans proudly embraced their hair as symbolic of their race.

Frederick Douglass, the internationally famous abolitionist, writer, and speaker, was a particularly revealing example of the variety of hairstyles worn by African Americans for various reasons. Douglass's portraits show that he followed the fashionable men's hairstyles as a young man, which in the 1840s was long, in the Romantic style. Two photographs dated to the 1840s and 1847 to 1852 show his hair styled in a deep side part with volume formed at the section at the forehead, in keeping with the popular style that lasted from the 1840s through the mid-1860s.[42] Yet the texture of his hair—which he did not alter by straightening—was distinctly African in origin, creating a coiffure that was visibly different from white men wearing the same style. Douglass styled his hair in keeping with contemporary fashion, yet he did not in any way deny his blackness.

Propelled to fame and visibility in 1845 with the publishing of his autobiography, Douglass visited England to avoid the dangers of re-enslavement in the United States. Biographer John Stauffer states that Douglass loved England for its lack of racism:

> [Douglass] went so far as to suggest that being black was a social advantage in Britain, "I find I am hardly black enough for British taste, but by keeping my hair as woolly as possible I make out to pass for at least half a Negro at any rate," he half-jokingly wrote to one friend.[43]

Here Douglass articulated the commonly and deeply held idea that hair embodied race, yet his hair was a flexible medium that he could manipulate to influence others' impressions.

By the early 1860s, when Douglass was financially secure and had settled into writing at his home in Rochester, New York, he grew his hair long, experimenting with the look of a radical intellectual (Figure 7.5). Stauffer explains:

> For many white intellectuals hair was a sign of self-expression, an outward manifestation of one's inner spirit. Muttonchops, footlong beards, goatees, mustaches that drooped below the chin, and hair that stood on end, suggesting a mind so electric that its current coursed through the skin and split the hair ends, were all common styles of the day. Even with his new goatee and long hair Douglass looked rather staid compared to many of his friends. He did not want to go too far with his new look, did not need to draw any more attention to himself and risk being alienated from white bourgeois parlors.[44]

Again Douglass manipulates his image, playing on mainstream conceptions of hair. Although his style had strong associations with white intellectual culture, it also recalled the radically full and creative styling of eighteenth-century slaves who were well documented in runaway notices for their full, "bushy" hairstyles combed into crests and high waves. White and White noted that both the eighteenth-century styles and Douglass's coiffure were a complete break from West African hair culture, which favored more controlled arrangements. These full hairstyles "emphasized and even flaunted [their] distinctive texture [and] may have been an affirmation of difference and even of defiance, an attempt to revalorize a biological characteristic that white racism had

FIGURE 7.5: Frederick Douglass, ca. 1865. Photo: J.W. Hurn. Library of Congress, Prints and Photographs Division (LC-USZ62-24165).

sought to devalue."[45] Douglass's friend Richard Greener, a prominent African American lawyer and professor, emphasized Douglass's expression of black pride through hair in the February 1917 edition of *Champion Magazine*. He asserts that Douglass modeled his hairstyle after the French author Alexandre Dumas. When prompted by Douglass, Greener noted that Dumas wore his hair, "long and conspicuously." Douglass responded: "That is why I imitated him. He was not ashamed of 'fleecy locks and dark complexion,' was he? They did not 'forfeit nature's claim.'"[46]

FIGURE 7.6: Studio portrait of an unidentified African American woman, no date. (The vintage photograph is a carte de visite with the imprint of J.H. Smith, 769 Broad Street, Newark, NJ. A later copy print made by R.H. Beckwith, photographer, Helena, MT, is on a cabinet mount.) Montana Historical Society Research Center Photograph Archives, Helena, Montana.

Douglass was a highly visible example, but not an exception. Many African Americans experimented with different mainstream, innovative, or more "natural" hairstyles, especially when being photographed. In *The Face of Our Past*, Kathleen Thompson and Hilary Mac Austin show three black women's 1890s photographs, side by side. In Lily Armstrong Shaw's wedding photo, she wears her shoulder-length hair loose and parted in the center in a "remarkably natural [style] for the period."[47] A photograph of an unnamed woman in Montana shows her hair styled in glossy elongated curls, flattened around her forehead with the remaining length in a chignon at the crown, topped with a round ornament (Figure 7.6). Her hair is straightened, but styled creatively compared to mainstream examples. Lastly, Ethelyn Taylor Chisum, a high school dean in Texas, was photographed wearing her hair in the most fashionable mainstream style of the period, piled high in a Gibson Girl up-do. All three women wore fashionable clothing, showing that they were fluent in the mainstream styles of the period. Their hairstyles were deliberate expressions—especially chosen to be captured in a photograph—of their personal tastes and the legacy of black hair in America that helped shape them. These women are a tiny sample, exemplifying the broad range of choices black Americans made using hair styling as a tool of self-expression.

HAIR WITHIN BLACK COMMUNITIES: BEAUTY STANDARDS AND BUSINESSES

Black people were generally treated as second-class citizens all over the Americas, and color hierarchies within black populations further denied opportunities in education and employment to those with darker skin and "kinky" hair. Buckridge notes that in Jamaica, for example, mulatto slaves held themselves above African slaves and did not associate with them.[48] The privileges that mixed-race slaves obtained due to their kinship with whites and their closer adherence to European beauty standards included domestic work as opposed to agricultural work, training in skilled professions, education, and possibly freedom. Byrd and Tharps state that: "By 1850 in the South [of the United States], free mulattoes outnumbered slave mulattoes by two to one."[49] Americans, both black and white, carried this hierarchy into the post-slavery period.

In the northern United States, the elites of free black communities tended to exhibit light skin and straight hair. After slavery ended, these communities of highly educated, middle-class blacks sought to differentiate themselves from other African Americans within their community institutions, using skin color and hair texture as a standard for acceptance. In an extreme anecdotal example, Byrd and Tharps described: "In some churches a fine-toothed comb was hung from the front door. All persons wanting to join the church had to be able to pass the comb smoothly through their hair. If their hair was too kinky, membership was denied."[50] Less blatant, though no less impactful, measures privileged lighter skin and straighter hair in black colleges, social clubs, and skilled employment. For latenineteenth- and earlytwentieth-century African Americans seeking a respected place in mainstream society, especially among those emigrating from rural areas to urban centers, straightening their hair was often a first step to social acceptance within metropolitan black communities and to employment within white households or companies. The Great Migration in the United States began around 1910, eventually moving six million black Americans to northern cities.

> Cornrows, plaits, and other styles that were common in the 1800s were now found only on older rural women in the South. As large groups of Blacks moved to northern cities, they made sure that their hair was done in the latest straight styles so as not to look "countrified" in their new urban homes.[51]

Supporting these stylings was a thriving beauty industry in the United States and other American countries, selling products, especially hair straighteners and skin lighteners, to African Americans. Yet hair straightening was a highly debated topic among black Americans. Noliwe M. Rooks studied white- and black-owned, latenineteenth- and earlytwentieth-century beauty companies' advertisements aimed at African Americans. She stated: "In public discussions of the societal consequences of hair straightening, manufacturers of the products urged African Americans to straighten their hair to foster societal acceptance. However, many African Americans, even then, argued that straightened hair amounted to a disavowal of African ancestry."[52] Rooks notes that white-owned beauty companies from the 1830s regularly played on socially accepted ideas on the inferiority of African Americans in their advertisements, marketing their products as "cures" for blackness. These hair straightener advertisements used a "before and after" format, in which "before" images showed curly hair that was unkempt and completely unstyled, while "after" images showed neatly coiffed, straight hair on models with more distinctly European features. These companies played on the very real African American fear that without straight hair, one could not advance socially, economically, or even romantically.⁵³ An advertisement for Plough's Hair Dressing that appeared in the African American newspaper *New York Age* in 1910 read: "Race men and women may easily have straight, soft, long hair by simply applying Plough's Hair Dressing and in a short time all your kinky, snarly, ugly, curly hair becomes soft, silky, smooth, straight, long and easily handled, brushed or combed."⁵⁴

While fears, pressures, and outright racism from mainstream society certainly encouraged black people to straighten their hair, there were other reasons for straightening. White and White state that straightening was an established part of both African American and African hair practices, used as "a preliminary to styling, not its end point."⁵⁵ Indeed hair that was simply straightened and not further arranged would not have been viewed as a fashionable style in this period. In the late nineteenth and early twentieth centuries, stylish female hair was swept up into large volumes atop the head and high chignons were popular. For men hair was typically cut above the ears and parted, worn either straight or waved (Figures 7.7 and 7.8). White and White conclude

FIGURE 7.7: This man's hairstyle and facial hair are typical of fashionable men's styles at the turn of the twentieth century. Young African American man, 1900. Part of W.E.B. Du Bois's albums of photographs of African Americans in Georgia exhibited at the Paris Exposition Universalle 1900. Library of Congress (LC-USZ62-121113).

FIGURE 7.8: This class photograph of college-aged women shows a variety of women's hairstyles worn at the beginning of the twentieth century, some more elaborate and fashionable than others. Junior normal class of Fisk University, Nashville, Tennessee. Images collected by W.E.B. Du Bois and Thomas J. Calloway for the "American Negro Exhibit" at the Paris Exposition of 1900. Library of Congress (LC-USZ62-112357).

that straightening the hair and even wearing the fashionable hairstyles of the day was not "necessarily an admission of perceived inferiority. Straightening the hair may be seen not as a sign of a defective black consciousness but as an integral part of a time-honored creative process."[56]

Certain black intellectuals would have disagreed. African Americans entering the twentieth century, seeking a valued place within mainstream society, termed themselves New Negroes to distance themselves from a past dominated by slavery and degradation. Leaders of this movement, such as Booker T. Washington and Nannie H. Burroughs, generally styled themselves and their hair conservatively, while rejecting the overt valorization of European beauty standards. Washington expressed his condemnation for beauty manufacturers who promoted white standards of beauty by banning all beauty instructors from teaching at his African American training school, the Tuskegee Institute.[57] Burroughs, a prominent African American educator, activist, and feminist wrote a 1904 article entitled, "Not Color But Character," stating:

> Many Negroes have colorphobia as badly as white folk have Negrophobia. You say this is not true. Then, what does this wholesale bleaching of faces and straightening of hair indicate? From our view it simply means that the women who practice it wish they had white skin and straight hair.[58]

While Burroughs advocated for black women to focus on education and practical training, founding the National Training School for Girls and Women that educated women for domestic service in Washington, DC, in 1909, photographs of her also show that she modeled her appearance on the beauty standards of the day, wearing her hair upswept and topped with a stylish, but not overly elaborate, hat (Figure 7.9). Burroughs's views walked the line between creating an acceptable, neat appearance that would encourage ease among white society to gain employment and respectability while avoiding extreme measures to erase the physical traits of blackness.

FIGURE 7.9: Nannie Helen Burroughs, 1909. Photo: Rotograph Co., New York City. Library of Congress, Prints and Photographs Division (LC-USZ62-79903).

Although hair straighteners were controversial, hair care proved a lucrative business area for African Americans. Caring for the bodies of whites was common practice throughout the Americas, making professional hair care an acceptable occupation for blacks. African Americans worked as barbers and hairdressers since the colonial period, some becoming quite successful. Pierre Toussaint, for example, was born a slave in Santo Domingo in 1766, and rose to become a respected New York hairstylist in the early nineteenth century. "As a hair-dresser for ladies, he was unrivalled: he was the fashionable coiffeur of the day; he had all the custom and patronage of the French families of New York. Many of the most distinguished ladies of the city employed him; we might mention not a few who treated him as a particular friend."[59] Toussaint earned enough money to support his widowed owner, buy his and several other slaves' freedom, and to become a significant philanthropist, giving generously to the Catholic Church.[60]

Owing to increasing fears of black male sexuality, black barbers were more common in the United States in the mid-nineteenth century than black men who styled white women's hair. Juliet E.K. Walker points out in *The History of Black Business In America*, "In both the North and the South, barbering enterprises that catered to wealthy whites emerged as one of the most prosperous businesses for blacks and placed their owners among the occupationally elite in antebellum black America."[61] She notes several black men in the early to mid-nineteenth century who owned multiple barber shops, adeptly reinvested their money into expanding enterprises, and served as black community leaders. William W. Watson, for example, was bought and freed from slavery by his brother-in-law, a barber in Cincinnati, Ohio. Watson trained as a barber, repaid his debt to his brother-in-law, and opened his own shop. He was eventually able to purchase family members from slavery and rose to become a prominent Cincinnati citizen, donating money to build black churches. Even in the south, free blacks could earn distinction as barbers; John Stanley of North Carolina earned enough as a barber to purchase sixty-four slaves, including family members, who he freed.[62] In a period when the overwhelming majority of African American men worked as slaves in agriculture, white hair care provided opportunities for entrepreneurship that could lead to not only freedom, but also wealth.

African American women seized the same opportunities, as Adia Wingfield notes in *Doing Business With Beauty: Black Women, Hair Salons, and the Racial Enclave Economy*, "turn[ing] 'gender-based domestic and manufacturing activities into business enterprises'."[63] Many black female slaves were trained as hairdressers, especially in southern cities, a practical investment for white slave mistresses who would have had their hair dressed daily. These skilled slaves could also be hired out to provide even more income for their owners, and some kept a portion of their earnings.[64] In the north, black women could take fuller advantage of hair styling skills. Wingfield states: "As early as 1838, the Pennsylvania business register lists hairdressers as the most populous entrepreneurial venture operated by black women."[65] The Remond sisters, Cecilia, Maritcha, and Caroline, established the Ladies Hair Work Salon in Salem, Massachusetts, in the mid-nineteenth century, as well as a wig factory, catering to white women. They also sold Mrs. Putnam's Medicated Hair Tonic by mail order throughout New England.[66]

Black women had created tonics, treatments, and salves for their own hair throughout the nineteenth century and earlier, adapting remembered recipes from West Africa to incorporate American ingredients. However, during the early twentieth century, a black haircare boom propelled a few black female entrepreneurs to outstanding wealth and prominence. As white-owned hair product producers were quick to exploit, the majority of African Americans used some sort of hair treatment to maintain the health of their hair, to encourage it to grow to long lengths, and to style it into fashionable coiffures. Many black women and men invented effective treatments in their own homes and some established companies to market their special formulas. In 1900, Annie Turnbo Pope Malone began to commercially manufacture her own recipe for Wonderful Hair Grower in Lovejoy, Illinois. She expanded to St. Louis, Missouri, two years later and hired agents to sell her expanding product line door to door.

Malone provided an effective hair product to black women, copyrighted as Poro in 1906; yet more significantly she and other black female hair entrepreneurs helped change the negative beauty culture that berated black American women. Rooks states:

> While African American intellectuals were either downplaying the importance of outward physical beauty or raging at those who imitated white beauty, agents for hair-straightening systems were actually going door to door to sell these products. Often, agents were members of the community in which they were selling and served as images of African American female beauty.[67]

Malone's advertisements did not promote ideals of white beauty or degrade black women's hair, but engaged her audiences with inclusive messages of her products' effectiveness. A 1907 Poro advertisement that ran in the *St. Louis Palladium* pictured Malone and another Poro user and stated: "We grew our hair, now let us grow yours with Poro."[68] This was a very different message from the one sent by the 1910 Plough's Hair Dressing advertisement. Malone also established beauty schools and sent her agents to the Caribbean, South America, Africa, and the Philippines, setting an international model for success that would be famously perfected by Madam C.J. Walker, widely credited as the first African American millionaire.[69]

Much has been written on Walker, her prosperous haircare company, and her successful efforts in building up black women through employment, education, and self-empowerment. Though she popularized the straightening hot comb starting in 1905, she never maintained that black women should straighten their hair to adhere to white beauty standards. Walker also challenged gender and class norms of the early twentieth century by encouraging working-class black women to gain financial independence from black men, an idea that rankled male intellectuals of the black middle class who strove for a financial position within the black family that allowed women to remain at home. Booker T. Washington, for example, showed his disdain for Walker by continually snubbing her at the 1912 meeting of the National Negro Business League, refusing to recognize her until she finally addressed the crowd without his consent.[70] Despite this lack of support from the black elite, Walker was the most outstanding example of the monetary success that hair entrepreneurship could provide, becoming a celebrity in the international black press. She also illustrated the ways that black hair could be a force for social change for working-class women. In 1916 and 1917 she attempted to legitimize beauty and hair care as a viable career path for middle-class women by establishing programs at African American colleges and providing scholarships for students to attend.[71]

CONCLUSION

African American hair in the nineteenth and early twentieth centuries was an enormously charged cultural symbol used by both blacks and whites in the struggle to define black beauty, worth, and social standing. Though black hair remained a loaded cultural point throughout the twentieth century and into the present day, mainstream beauty culture changed in the 1920s, shifting away from nineteenth-century ideals to herald in a twentieth-century modernity that embraced artificiality:

> The look of a young African American woman, whose features were clearly made-up and whose hair had been straightened, bobbed, and dyed red, was not some pathetic and inept attempt to imitate white mores. What it did signify, however—and here there was a clear similarity between what young white and black women were doing, although who was imitating whom could be difficult to work out—was difference from the "natural" look of their mothers and grandmothers.[72]

Indeed what could be further from both traditional African and nineteenth-century European hairstyles than the glossy, cropped coiffure of Josephine Baker? One of the most famous black people in the world in the 1920s, Baker helped change standards of both black and white beauty. *Vogue* magazine, the bastion of white American fashion praised: "Her hair, which grows in tight curls, was plastered close to her head with white of egg and looked as though it were painted on her with black shellac. This woman is like a living drawing by Aubrey Beardsley or Picasso."[73] Baker was recognized by mainstream culture as the modern model of black beauty, and she was no less aware of the power of black hair than her predecessors—she quickly marketed her famous hairstyle into a product, Bakerfix pomade. It was one of her most lucrative business ventures.

CHAPTER EIGHT

Class and Social Status: "The more you have the better"

Or, the Politics and Economics of Hair

ELIZABETH CAROLYN MILLER

Scholarship on the cultural history of hair in nineteenth-century Britain has primarily focused on hair as a signifier of gender, exploring the crucial work that hair does to establish sexual difference and to stage changes in men's and women's gendered roles throughout the period.[1] And yet, hair was also a potent marker of class: it was a site of social aspiration and abnegation, and a setting for the display of wealth or the disgrace of poverty. Hair's important role as a status marker may be less visible to students of the period today, but close attention to nineteenth-century literature, print culture, and visual culture demonstrates the complex class politics of hair for both men and women. These complexities may seem surprising, since there was no inherent difference between the hair of the upper classes and the hair of the working classes. Unlike nineteenth-century gender and racial differences, which could be underscored by visible variance in hair texture, color, or growth patterns, the distinction between rich hair and poor hair is entirely cultural. Material conditions of living could and did, however, make for highly visible class distinctions in nineteenth-century hair. To take the most glaring example, close-cropped hair was associated with institutionalization: with the workhouses, hospitals, and prisons that marked their subjects as poor, diseased, or abominable. Changing notions of cleanliness produced another means by which nineteenth-century class was visible through hair: the wealthier had easier access to warm water and facilities for washing the hair, which led to different standards of cleanliness, particularly after washing the hair, as opposed to brushing it, became the normative hair-cleaning regimen around 1840.[2] The services of haircare professionals made for another key difference among the classes. Middle- and upper-class men could afford to visit the barber regularly for haircuts or shaves, whereas for working-class men, such personal care was typically done at home.[3] Hair care for women of all classes was usually undertaken at home in this era, but access to a lady's maid who "understands hairdressing," as the classified advertisements put it, made for highly visible distinctions among classes of women in terms of the types of hairstyles available to them.[4] These examples highlight some of the key ways that social class and social status played out in the nineteenth-century politics of hair, a topic that this chapter will endeavor to survey from a literary, historical, and visual point of view.

HAIR, HAIRLESSNESS, AND THE WORKHOUSE

If hairstyles had a social hierarchy in the nineteenth century, close-cropped hair was at the bottom rung, marking its wearer as at best gravely ill, at worst a destitute dependent of the state. With the advent of the New Poor Law in 1834, governmental provisions for the impoverished now emphasized "indoor relief" (institutionalization in the workhouse) rather than "outdoor relief" (provision of money, goods, food, or clothing), and fear of the workhouse consequently animates much writing by, for, and about the working classes in this period. A typical expression of such fear can be found in H.J. Bramsbury's novel *A Working-Class Tragedy*, which ran in the socialist newspaper *Justice* from 1888 to 1889: a character describes seeking relief from the Poor Law Board and being told that the "best thing we could do would be to go in the workhouse. I told him I would sooner starve first, and he said, of course we could do as we liked about it."[5] Close-cropped hair was a visible symbol of the humiliating dehumanization that was central to the nineteenth-century workhouse experience. Figure 8.1, for example, depicts boys at the Crumpsall Workhouse ca. 1895, with their close-cut hair and nearly uniform clothing. The workhouse was meant to be as unpleasant and shaming as possible, as a supposed deterrent for falling into poverty, and admission to the workhouse represented a much-feared descent from the working classes to the destitute. Any consideration of hair and social status in the nineteenth century must begin, then, with hairlessness, or the specter of hairlessness, which carried great emotional weight for many in this era.

Although there was no official rule that those admitted to the workhouse had to have their hair cut off, and in fact there seems to have been legal protection against cutting paupers' hair without their consent, in practice many of those admitted had their hair cut off as a sanitary measure against lice and against diseases such as ringworm. Peter Higginbotham writes that "children in a union workhouse could be compelled to have their hair cut, [but] the same was not true for adults unless required for medical reasons."[6] And yet practices seem to have varied. Margaret Drinkall, for example, writes of Rotherham Workhouse: "On admission to the workhouse the pauper's hair would be cropped by the workhouse barber, the same haircut given to men and women. Men would also be shaved by the barber on a regular basis."[7] Cutting another's hair against their will is an act that has, from the biblical Samson to Alexander Pope and beyond, been likened to a kind of symbolic rape, an appropriation of another's body. This is no doubt part of the reason why the cutting of paupers' hair in workhouses, and legal cases focusing on such events, received interested attention in newspapers throughout the period. One such case in Croydon prompted a letter to the editor of *The Times*, which ran in the November 19, 1841 issue, arguing sarcastically that "the admirable 'elasticity' of the New Poor Law has practically made the Commissioners a legislative body," making it a "difficult matter to decide what they may or may not authorize to be done by virtue of their 'rules, orders, and regulations'."[8] The letter's author, W.B., maintained that it was deemed illegal in an 1830 case to crop the hair of workhouse inmates without their consent. And yet such cropping continued to happen, whether because of ignorance of the law, knowing violation of the law on the part of the workhouse officers, or the difficulty in determining "consent" in the context of such an extreme power differential as existed in the workhouse.

FIGURE 8.1: Boys at Crumpsall Workhouse, ca. 1895–1897. Source: https://commons.wikimedia.org/wiki/File:Children_at_crumpsall_workhouse_circa_1895.jpg.

Some cases, unsurprisingly, involved contradictory statements about workhouse hair cutting and consent. An 1887 inquiry into the death of James Gardiner, aged seventy, in the Poplar Workhouse, for example, received a long and detailed account in *The Times*.[9] The account described how Gardiner left the workhouse complaining of being "unable to get warm" after having been given a cold bath in the workhouse, having had his hair and whiskers cut off, and having been put into the workhouse uniform of cotton rather than flannel.[10] The workhouse hairdresser Simon Lewis testified at the inquest that he "attended the Poplar Workhouse twice a week," and "remembered closely shaving deceased," but "did not remember cutting his hair. It was not customary for inmates to be shaved or to have their hair cut."

Whether or not Gardiner's hair was actually cut, it is clear from this and other reports that workhouse hair cutting was perceived as a kind of ritual humiliation for new initiates, particularly objectionable when it came to the elderly such as Gardiner. The satirical tone in W.B.'s letter, quoted earlier, represents a common discursive response to such practices, also evident in an article titled "A Fine Idea" that ran in the satirical magazine *Punch* in 1843. Here, "Punch presents his compliments to the Poor Law Commissioners and begs their acceptance of an idea": that since the "object of the New Poor Law is the prevention of Poverty," and since poverty "is a heinous crime" and "an offence against the purse of Society," the "horrors of the workhouse" must be made less "invisible."[11] Workhouses, *Punch* suggests, should heretofore be built of glass, so that those outside can see the "wretched objects" within. "Each pauper is to be attired in the Union uniform, the males having their hair cropped very close, or shaved."[12] Hair was one of the most visible bodily features in nineteenth-century Britain—since, at this time, hair, hands, and face were often the only exposed body parts available for public view—so *Punch*'s emphasis on making workhouse horrors "visible" relies on close-cut hair as the mark of humiliation for workhouse residents.

If close-cut hair was a class marker in the extreme, it was one that was also inflected by gender. Not only boys and men had their hair cut when given over to the power of the Poor Law officials, although they were subjected to the practice more often. Seth Koven's *The Match Girl and the Heiress* documents the memories of Nellie Dowell (1876–1923), recorded by her loving friend Muriel Lester, of being admitted in 1883 to Forest Gate Industrial School—not a workhouse, but a similar Poor Law institution for Poor Law orphans. Nellie recalls her futile resistance to the cutting of her hair with visceral, present memory:

> Nellie caused some trouble among the attendants and had even to be taken to the matron during the first month of her stay. [...] This was because she had passionately resisted the hair cutter when it came to her turn to be cropped on the first Saturday after her arrival. She had been terrified by the big scissors wielded over her head by a strange person. A strange sense of outrage filled her as she saw herself shorn of her curls.[13]

As Koven says of the passage: "Lice flourished in locks of hair: to control the former required shearing the latter," but such "decisions about the management of pauper children's bodies could and did erode the fragile boundaries of the child's individuality."[14]

Dowell's traumatic childhood memory and keen sense of injustice cast an illuminating light on the fictional experiences of Jane Eyre, an orphan in a charity school (an institution funded by private subscription rather than the state) who witnesses her fellow students lose their hair in an act of humiliation not even papered over as hygienic in rationale. A literary account such as we find in *Jane Eyre* (1847) suggests how widely understood it was in the nineteenth century that ostensibly benevolent hair shearing was an assault on more than just lice—it was an attack on expressions of individuality within the context of an institution, and one that was particularly sexualized in the case of women and girls. Charlotte Brontë presents Mr. Brocklehurst as "dazzled or shocked" by the sight of orphan student Julia Severn's "curled hair [...] red hair [...] curled all over," and he thunders, "I have again and again intimated that I desire the hair to be arranged closely, modestly, plainly. [...] that girl's hair must be cut off entirely; I will send a barber tomorrow: and I see others who have far too much of the excrescence." Scrutinizing the other girls, he declares: "All those top-knots must be cut off [...] each of the young persons before us has a string of hair twisted in plaits which vanity itself might have woven; these, I repeat, must be cut off."[15] If biopolitics and state-sponsored hygiene were the motivating forces behind the shearing of Nellie Dowell's curls, Mr. Brocklehurst's stern evangelicalism engenders his anti-hair tirade. Jane would grow up to embody, in many respects, the style of "modest, plain" womanhood that Brocklehurst promotes, but she maintained a fierce hatred for Brocklehurst deeply entwined with his attacks on the girls' hair. Describing him to Mr. Rochester years later, Jane instantly recalls the episode: "I disliked Mr. Brocklehurst; and I was not alone in the feeling. He is a harsh man; at once pompous and meddling: he cut off our hair."[16] Here Jane merges herself with her fellow students, saying "he cut off our hair" despite the fact that her own hair was not cut. This suggests how deindividualization could cut both ways for state and religious authorities: such deindividualization may seem to facilitate control over groups of unruly

CLASS AND SOCIAL STATUS

bodies, but the experience of merging into a collective may also stir feelings of rebellion all the more strong and powerful for being shared rather than individual.

THE TRADE IN HAIR

Close-cropped hair, then, could mark its wearer as abject but could also stir feelings of injustice, and this was equally true in cases where the hair was sold as in cases where it was shorn without consent. Whether subject to the direct authority of the Poor Law or the indirect coercion of the market, poor women who lost their hair—even if they sold it for profit—were often represented as subjects of pity. A trade in human hair was present throughout the period, but the market became particularly hot around 1870, when women's hairstyles changed to emphasize volume and lushness in the extreme: "The bigger the hair, the better: huge, coiling tresses wrapped loosely round and round, held with decorative combs and stuck with flowers."[17] As the *Punch* cartoon in Figure 8.2 demonstrates, the popular style among fashionable women at this time was the chignon, a top-heavy protuberance that could add significantly to the head's dimensions such that the Venus de Milo herself appears in contrast to have "a ridiculous little head." The statue's relative paucity of hair is actually a class marker in this satirical cartoon: "*no chignon! She's no lady!*" the other women declare. As the classed language of "lady" suggests, this moment in the history of hairstyles was an inauspicious one for working-class women, since the preferred style was "a difficult look to maintain while doing any sort of useful work."[18] Such "expensive and elaborate hair fashions" for women, Galia Ofek argues, were means of conveying "conspicuous leisure and consumption."[19] But many wealthy women did not have thick enough hair to wear this style without help, and thus, Ofek states, "sales of false hair went up by 400 percent from 1855 to 1868."[20] In

FIGURE 8.2: *Punch* cartoon with chignon, 1870.

this market, poorer women who chose to sell their hair could get a good price for it, but representations of such transactions often depict them as an act of class pillaging against working-class women.

Thomas Hardy's novel *The Woodlanders* (1887), to take one example, opens with Barber Percomb on the track of Marty South, a young countrywoman whose father has taken ill, whom he hopes to convince to sell her hair. Percomb, the neighbors say: "is not a journeyman hair-cutter, but a master-barber that's left off his pole because 'tis not genteel."[21] He seeks out South at the secret behest of one of his wealthy clients, a woman named Mrs. Charmond who caught sight of South's hair at church, "noticed how exactly [South's] hair matches her own," and decided she wanted it "to help out hers."[22] The class differential between South and Charmond is here also inflected by a rural–urban hierarchy. Marty South is a woman with "little pretension to beauty; save in one prominent particular, her hair," which was abundant in volume and "rare and beautiful" in its chestnut hue.[23] In response to Barber Percomb's cajoling, South at first insists "I can*not* part with it: so there!," but eventually she gives in after he offers her two shillings—as much remuneration as she would earn in three weeks of her usual labors.[24] Although South cuts off her hair herself instead of letting the barber cut it, her lack of full consent in the context of the situation is nonetheless clear: "with tears in her eyes, she got a pair of scissors and began mercilessly cutting off the long locks of her hair." Afterward, she refuses to look in the mirror, "knowing what a deflowered visage would look back at her."[25] For South, the selling of her hair is likened to both a rape and a desexualization. In giving up her hair, she understands herself to be passing on what sexuality she has to the immoral widow, Mrs. Charmond: "She wants my curls to get another lover with; though if stories are true she's broke the heart of many a noble gentleman already."[26]

Poor Englishwomen were not the only ones supplying the wealthy women of Britain with their hirsute powers of sexual attraction. An international market was established in the nineteenth century, since the poorer women of Britain "supplied a section of the hair market" but "did not meet demand," and the hair that made up the wigs and hairpieces worn by the upper crust came from the continent as well as the colony.[27] According to Charles Richard Weld's 1856 book of travel writing, *A Vacation in Brittany*, "many London and Paris ladies are indebted for the magnificent hair which adorns their heads" to hair that "was grown in the wilds of Brittany."[28] In contrast to a poor Englishwoman like Marty South, the close-cropped women of Brittany, in Weld's estimation, are less victims than entrepreneurs: "when the girl was liberated [from the barber], her head assumed the appearance of having been shaved. [...] This terrible mutilation of one of woman's most beautiful gifts, distressed me considerably at first; but when I beheld the indifference of the girls to the loss of their hair [...] my feelings underwent a change."[29] According to Ofek, 6,200 pounds of hair were imported from France to England as early as 1849.[30] Ruth Goodman writes of hair sourced from even further afield: "there was a strong trade in human hair across the empire, especially in hair from India, which was thought to be a closer match to European varieties than that from other countries." Brought back to England, the hair was "bleached and sorted" and "sold on to a host of hair workers in small workshops" before finally appearing "on the head of a society lady."[31]

The international, sometimes interracial market for hair was an uncomfortable subject for the hair industry. Unwin and Albert, a "hair cutting saloon" in Piccadilly that used a good deal of false hair in fulfilling its promise to "imitat[e] nature so correctly [...] as to defy detection" (see Figure 8.3), denied in a letter to *The Times* that they used Chinese hair, which they described as "harsh and stiff." They claimed that most of the "hair of commerce" came from neighboring lands: Brittany, Auvergne, and Germany.³² The cross-class, cross-cultural market in hair also led to frequent speculation about false hair as a transporter of disease, a conduit of impurity from the lower orders of Britain and the world to the upper. As Ofek notes, the periodical press often "referred to hair additions, which were highly popular from the 50s to the 90s, as a bodily corruption or infection."³³ A report in *The Times* from March 9, 1867 titled "False Hair As a Cause of Disease" describes a meeting of the Harveian Society of London to discuss "the scientific points involved in the 'chignon question'"—that is, the question of whether parasites can be communicated through false hair. While the speaker suggests that parasites do not travel in this way, he "described a real source of danger" in "some of the light brown or reddish false hair, of German origin," in which "he had found a species of 'mildew' fungus" that could cause ringworm.³⁴ He recommends cleaning false hair before wearing it.

Attention to the traffic in hair between poor women and rich shows up across Victorian literature, and such traffic was an especially rich cultural undercurrent in novels concerned with class boundaries, such as *Lady Audley's Secret* (1862). In this novel, the transposition of a poor woman's hair for a rich woman's emerges as a class issue, symptomatic of a capitalist and imperial economy in which the natural resources of one group are harvested for the benefit of another. Here, the duplicitous Lady Audley, formerly Helen Talboys, pays off the mother of a young, poor, ill woman named Matilda who is in the final stages of consumption: "I bought the mother, who was poor and greedy, and who for a gift of money, more money than she had ever before received, consented to submit to anything I wished."³⁵ The agreement is that Matilda will pass for Helen Talboys upon her deathbed,

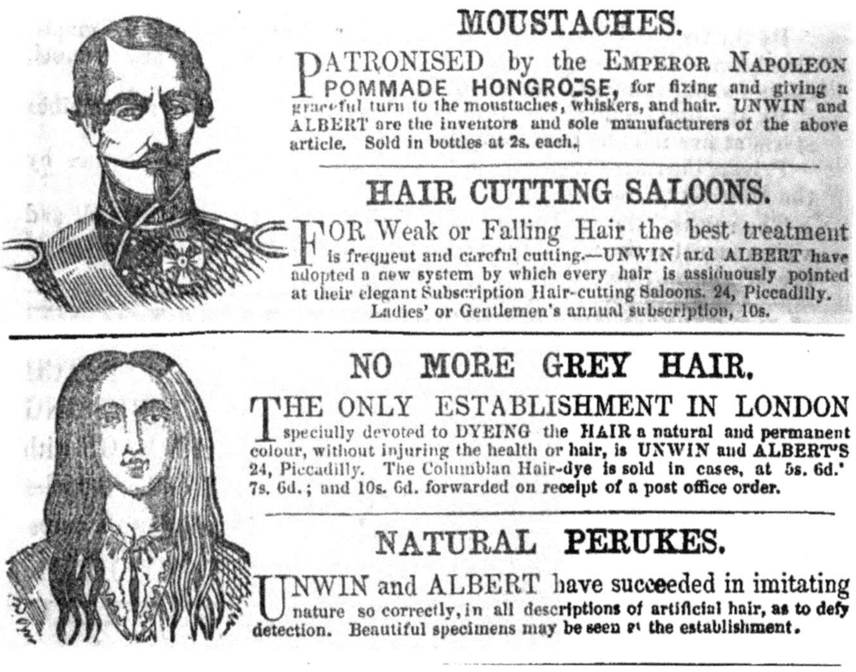

FIGURE 8.3: Advertisement for Unwin and Albert, from the opening pages of *The Great Eastern Steam Ship* (London: H.G. Clarke, n.d. [ca. 1857]).

so that Helen may fake her own death to her estranged husband, and a lock of Matilda's hair will provide "proof" of Helen's passing. When George Talboys returns, looking for his wife, Matilda's mother gives him "a long tress of hair wrapped in silver paper" and "he pressed the soft lock to his lips."[36] Here, the avaricious and social-climbing motives of Lady Audley, who makes use of the poor woman's hair to pass as her own, recast the drama of cross-class hair exchange in terms of the commodification of lower-class women's bodies and bodily resources.

COMMERCIALIZATION OF HAIR CARE

Matilda is not the only lower-class woman in *Lady Audley's Secret* whose hair is represented as a potential stand-in for Lady Audley's: the lady's maid Phoebe Marks is another hair-double for the upper-class villain, albeit one who will require a little help from the bottle to make a convincing substitute. Looking closely at her maid one evening, Lady Audley remarks:

> Do you know, Phoebe, I have heard some people say that you and I are alike? ... it is only colour that you want. My hair is pale yellow shot with gold, and yours is drab; my eyebrows and eyelashes are dark brown, and yours are almost—I scarcely like to say it, but they're almost white [...] Why, with a bottle of hair-dye, such as we see advertised in the papers, and a pot of rouge, you'd be as good-looking as I, any day, Phoebe.[37]

The passage hints at some use that Lady Audley will make of her maid's resemblance, suggesting again a prominent cultural undercurrent in which lower-class women's hair is understood to be a resource available to be exploited to meet the desires of upper-class women. On the other hand, the passage also suggests that there is no essential difference between lower- and upper-class hair, and it points to the commercialized haircare products that had emerged in the course of the nineteenth century, including commercially available hair dyes, as means of annihilating the appearance of class difference. Certainly, this is how such products were marketed to the Victorian middle classes.

Advertisements such as those referred to by Lady Audley appear with growing frequency throughout the nineteenth century, not only for dye, but for all manner of hair products which went from being "generally produced at home" in the early part of the century to being more and more commercially available as the century wore on.[38] As with so many features of nineteenth-century life and culture, the advertising, marketing, and commercialization of hair products were heavily overladen with class markers and class aspirations. In the early part of the century, prepared hair products were reserved mainly for elite customers, but usage trickled down into the middle and lower classes as the century went on. Eventually such products came to be represented most often as a species of middle-class veneer that was intended to make a Helen Talboys appear, falsely, as a Lady Audley.

Commercialization affected men's hair products first, such that one finds references to commercial hair products for well-heeled men in early-nineteenth-century novels such as Jane Austen's *Persuasion* (1818). By the 1870s, "most pharmacists stocked a wide range of male hair products [...] carefully packaged to differentiate them from female varieties and varying in price for the rich and the poor."[39] Bear's grease was a popular product for men, whether made from real bear fat or not. In Charles Dickens's *David Copperfield* (1850), David's awkward transition to manhood—and more specifically, to the classed position of gentleman—is marked by an embarrassingly liberal application of the stuff: "What other changes have come upon me, besides the changes in my growth and looks, and in the knowledge I have garnered all this while? I wear a gold watch and chain, a ring upon my little finger, and a long-tailed coat; and I use a great deal of bear's grease—which, taken in conjunction with the ring, looks bad."[40] It was widely understood that when it came to such products as bear's grease, not all of them were made of what they claimed to be made of, nor did they always do what they claimed to do. In the correspondence column of London's *Magazine of Domestic Economy*, a reader's letter dated July 4, 1838, requests from the editor a recipe for bear's grease, since "that it is composed of bear's fat is all nonsense, and the price of that sold as such, is enormous."[41] The editor explained that the preparation was "sometimes made from the fat of the bear," but could be just as effectively produced by mixing hog's lard, almond oil, spermaceti, and perfume. This was a middle-class version of what had originally been a luxury product.[42]

Adulteration and puffery were common problems in the manufacture and marketing of nineteenth-century haircare products, and the products became, by extension, overlaid with an aura of middle-class pretension. The hyperbolic language of the advertisements was alone enough to raise suspicion, as in an advertisement for "The Atrapilatory, or Liquid Hair Dye" in *The Times* in 1841, which presented "the above dye as infallible."[43] Allegations and investigations of toxic hair dyes regularly surfaced throughout the century, and one 1869 dust-up drew letters from chemistry professors as well as haircare firms in the correspondence section of *The Times*.[44] By the early twentieth century, a degree of skepticism had entered the advertisements for these overmarketed products, as is evident in the advertisement for Kosmeo Hair Tonic pictured in Figure 8.4. This particular advertisement appeared, ironically enough, in the socialist journal the *New Age*, and the publication's manager even stooped to provide a somewhat sheepish testimonial: "I must own that I have always been greatly prejudiced against advertised Hair Tonics, and therefore hesitated a long time before using your preparation. The results have been a most agreeable surprise." Readers of the *New Age* were promised a discount and urged, in best capitalist fashion, "DON'T MISS THIS OPPORTUNITY."

The class vulgarity of hair dye and other commercial hair products was most prominently staged, perhaps, in the 1868 trial of Madame Rachel, the criminal cosmetologist who ran a beauty shop on Bond Street and was indicted for fraud three times, most famously in 1868. Among other products, Madame Rachel sold hair dyes that were named in such a way as to deny that they were dyes at all. Figure 8.5 shows an excerpt from her price list, which includes the "Circassian Golden Hair Wash," a "Medicated Cream for rendering the hair black or chesnut [sic] brown," as well as "Astringents and stimulants for rendering the hair Italian brown," all on offer for two pounds and two shillings.[45] The product names disingenuously suggest that the products do not so much "dye" the hair as simply "wash," "medicate," or "stimulate" it, in the process, of course, turning it to a different color.

Madame Rachel's 1868 trial, as I discuss elsewhere, occasioned a media frenzy and was widely reported across the Victorian press.[46] Readers following the coverage knew that Madame Rachel was really Sarah Rachel Leverson, an illiterate Jewish entrepreneur who was charged with swindling money and goods from a wealthy lady customer of her Bond Street shop. Such readers would have also learned about Rachel's home in the suburbs, her box at the opera, and her Paris-educated children. Even if there had not already been, prior to Rachel's trial, an association between the commercialization of haircare products and middle-class arrivisme, there would have been after 1868. Such an association did a

DON'T MISS THIS OPPORTUNITY.

In order to introduce our celebrated **KOSMEO HAIR TONIC** to readers of "The New Age," we have decided to offer a large 5/10 bottle for 4/10 (a month's supply), together with our unique system of Hair Culture.

POINTS TO REMEMBER.

A written guarantee is given **to return the money in full** in any case where improvement is not shown in one month.

This offer has never before appeared, and only one bottle can be supplied to each applicant at this rate, and the offer is limited to 10,000 bottles. State whether scalp is dry or greasy.

MR. FRANK PALMER,

The Manager of THE NEW AGE, writes:—"I must own that I have always been greatly prejudiced against advertised Hair Tonics, and therefore hesitated for a long time before using your preparation. The results have been a most agreeable surprise, and fully carried out all your claims for the Tonic. The hair is thickening splendidly and growing stronger, and this is especially noticeable where it had a tendency to be flat and lifeless. All scurf has entirely disappeared."

OUR METHOD OF BUSINESS—
MONEY BACK UNLESS SATISFIED.

THE KOSMEO CO.,
80, DUKE STREET, GROSVENOR SQUARE, LONDON, W.

FIGURE 8.4: Advertisement for Kosmeo Hair Tonic. *New Age* (January 25, 1908): 258.

HAIR PREPARATION.

Circassian Golden Hair Wash	2	2	0
Madagascar, Arabian, Circassian, and Armenian Oils ...	2	2	0
Preservative Cream	2	2	0
Medicated Cream for rendering the hair black or chesnut brown	2	2	0
Astringents and stimulents for rendering the hair Italian brown	2	2	0

FIGURE 8.5: Excerpt from Madame Rachel's price list for hair products. *The Extraordinary Life & Trial of Madame Rachel at the Central Criminal Court* (vii).

great deal of work to characterize grasping and ambitious women throughout Victorian fiction. To take one example, Lizzie Greystock in Anthony Trollope's *The Eustace Diamonds* (1873), who uses her beauty to inveigle the wealthy, aristocratic Sir Florian Eustace into marrying her, raises Lady Fawn's suspicions in part because she uses scent in her hair: "A peculiar perfume came up from Lizzie's hair which Lady Fawn did not like. Her own girls, perhaps, were not given to the use of much perfumery."[47] The use of such products signifies the immutable class difference between a vulgar Lizzie and the aristocratic Miss Fawns.

Much further down the social ranks, Arabella Donn in Thomas Hardy's *Jude the Obscure* (1895) uses false hair, itself a widely used commercial hair product in the nineteenth century, to convey an exaggerated social position. On the night of their marriage, Jude sees her undress for the first time and is disturbed to watch as the "long tail of hair, which Arabella wore twisted up in an enormous knob at the back of her head, was deliberately unfastened, stroked out, and hung upon the looking-glass which he had bought her."

> "What—it wasn't your own?" he said, with a sudden distaste for her.
> Oh no—it never is nowadays with the better class.
> Nonsense! Perhaps not in towns. But in the country it is supposed to be different. Besides, you've enough of your own, surely?
> "Yes, enough as country notions go. But in town the men expect more, and when I was barmaid at Aldbrickham—"
> Barmaid at Aldbrickham?
> Well, not exactly barmaid—I used to draw the drink at a public-house there—just for a little time; that was all. Some people put me up to getting this, and I bought it just for a fancy. The more you have the better in Aldbrickham, which is a finer town than all your Christminsters. Every lady of position wears false hair—the barber's assistant told me so.[48]

Arabella's naïve reliance on the barber's assistant, supplier of false hair, as a reliable informant on hair fashions for "the better class" demonstrates, most obviously, her own rustic uncouthness, but it is also symptomatic of the broader shift toward the commercialization of hair care and hair styling throughout the period. Such commercialization often presented itself as having the power to democratize hair, such that a barmaid could now imagine herself to appear as a "lady of position" through proper hair styling, but in fact it simply changed the terms by which class was designated by hair rather than obliterating such distinctions altogether.

HAIR IN SERVICE

Arabella Donn's assertion to Jude, whether true or not, that she needed to wear false hair to meet the standards of appearance expected of a woman working as barmaid in town suggests the extent to which social designations regarding the wearing of the hair were related to occupational status. Domestic servants were one section of the working classes whose hair attracted much discussion throughout the period; based on the amount of attention given to the subject in the periodical press, hair seems to have been the cause of many a dispute between mistress and maid. The nineteenth century saw a huge rise in the number of domestic servants, mostly women, who were cheaper to employ than male servants. According to Vivien Richmond, domestic service "was the largest single female occupation throughout the period until at least the end of World War Two. In England and Wales, the number of female domestic servants rose from just over three-quarters of a million in 1851 to nearly 1.4 million in 1891." Many were quite young—"in 1880, 42 percent of female domestic servants were under the age of twenty"—and the dress and appearance of these young women were a subject of public conversation throughout the era.[49] Uniforms had become relatively standardized by 1860, and the typical hairstyle for servants, as described in the article "Household Reform" from the ladies' column of the *Penny Illustrated Paper*, was simple and neat: "Let the hair be worn off the face, in the fashionable style, and neatly braided close to the head behind. A small round, white cap, without ribbons or trimming. No pads or frizettes, no chignons, no hair ribbons or velvet."[50] Figure 8.6 shows a cartoon from the May 23, 1874 issue of *Punch*, with three female servants in typical morning attire (light dresses were worn in the morning, dark in the afternoon) and the requisite white cap. In Figure 8.7, a photograph from a 1903 soap advertisement shows a servant in essentially the same hairstyle almost thirty years later, albeit a little fuller in the front.

Publications aimed at servants had much to say about the wearing of the hair. Often these were philanthropic organs more focused on "improvement" than entertainment, and their thinly veiled belittlement of working women is now only too apparent. In a piece called "A Word to My Servant," for example, by an anonymous author identified only as "A Pastor" in *The Servants' Magazine, or Female Domestics Instructor* of 1842, the author warns young women in service that: "An undue fondness for the outward adorning of plaiting the hair, and wearing apparel to the neglect of the inward adorning of a meek and quiet spirit, may be *the* snare by which you may be entangled and ruined."[51] *The Servants' Magazine* was sponsored by the London Female Mission, an organization that sought to help friendless servants and reform fallen women.[52] The fire-and-brimstone tone employed here evokes Wilkie Collins's dead-on satire of evangelical tracts in his 1860 novel *The Moonstone*. In one passage, the busybody Miss Clack leaves a tract for a young servant, Penelope, who is wearing ribbons in her cap:

> The person who answered the door, took my message in insolent silence, and left me standing in the hall. [...] I sat down in the hall to wait for my answer—and, having always a few tracts in my bag, I selected one which proved to be quite providentially applicable to the person who answered the door. The hall was dirty, and the chair was hard; but the blessed consciousness of returning good for evil raised me quite above

FIGURE 8.6: Cartoon featuring servants from the May 23, 1874 issue of *Punch* magazine.

FIGURE 8.7: Advertisement for Pearline soap. *Christian Work and Evangelist* (April 11, 1903): 549.

any trifling considerations of that kind. The tract was one of a series addressed to young women on the sinfulness of dress. In style it was devoutly familiar. Its title was, "A Word With You On Your Cap-Ribbons."[53]

A similar note was struck, absent the humorous intention, in an 1855 article titled "The Dress of Female Servants" from the *Family Economist*, a publication that, like many of its ilk, "aimed to instil middle-class ideals of domesticity in the working classes while keeping them firmly in their place."[54] Interestingly, this article discusses the different styles of appearance that may be appropriate for female servants at varying ranks of the stratified world of service: "*The housekeeper and lady's maid* may, with propriety, approach nearer to the style of dress of their employer than the *house-maid, laundry-maid* or *under servants*."[55] In terms of hair, however, the article offers general advice for all servants, and the emphasis is again on plainness, simplicity, and a lack of ornamentation. If Miss Clack was perhaps unduly perturbed by cap ribbons, this author is similarly distressed by curls and curl papers:

> Will it be considered as entering too much into particulars to mention with censure the common mode with which maid servants dress their hair? In the morning they are disfigured with tiers of curls in paper; in the afternoon sometimes decorated with long pendant ringlets, to induce which much time is bestowed at night, when, if rest be not needful to them, they might be better engaged in repairing clothes. A servant of correct taste in dress would never appear in curl papers, nor keep her hair of such a length as to require more than very simple curling.[56]

For middle-class "improvers" like Miss Clack and the author of "The Dress of Female Servants," fiction that masked itself as entertainment proved yet another means by which to regulate the hair of women and girls in service. A work of short fiction titled *Myra's Pink Dress* by Emma Leslie, published in pamphlet form by the Sunday School Union in 1873, provides a melodramatic example of how such fiction warned serving girls against the dangers of aspiring to dress and appear "better" than they were. In the story, the mistress of the house, Lady Hayward, and her housekeeper, Mrs. Parkins, enforce rules regarding neatness, plainness, and simplicity of appearance for their female servants, including the young servant Myra. But vain Myra, in a fit of hair hubris, decides to dress her hair in the same style as her mistress, "for Lady Hayward had only just come from London, and therefore [Myra] thought that the style she wore her hair must be the newest and most fashionable."

Readers are never left to wonder what to make of Myra's hair styling choices, as Leslie reinforces the story's moral at every turn: "Thus was this foolish girl's mind running upon how she could make herself of more importance in the eyes of others by a vain display, instead of trying to win the esteem of the wise and good by a faithful discharge of her duties."[57] As Lady Hayward's nursemaid, Myra is supposed to mind the children, but instead she plops them on the floor and sits down before a mirror to experiment with her hair and attempt to mimic the style worn by her mistress. Meanwhile, the children are left unattended on the nursery floor: "an hour or two passed, and Willie had sucked the paint off his horse, and made himself sick, and Marian had been trying to clean the fender with her white diaper pinafore." Another servant enters upon this shocking scene just in time to see Myra "adjusting one of the plaits across her head in the form of a coronet."[58] The servant decides not to report Myra, who promises never to do it again, but soon after, baby Willie drowns when she again leaves him unattended. The rumor in town following this tragic accident is that "Myra was engaged in braiding and plaiting her hair instead of minding the child." Her hairstyle had already attracted notice and comment, since "she had succeeded in copying Lady Hayward's style of doing her hair, and had appeared in church several times with her bonnet pushed far back and her hair plaited in a coronet across her head, to the great astonishment of the villagers. [...] These, and many other little things, were all remembered against her now."[59] Myra was actually crocheting an ornamental collar, not plaiting her hair, when the child drowned, but the fact that the townspeople blame the event on her penchant for aristocratic hairstyles demonstrates the vivid power of hair as a signifier of class. The style Myra was emulating, after all, was a "coronet," and this crown of hair could not make her improper class ambitions more obvious.

One wonders if stories like this were part of the reason that there never seemed to be enough nineteenth-century girls willing to go into service. Indeed, Herbert P. Miller's *The Scarcity of Domestic Servants: The Cause and Remedy* (1876) "placed freedom of dress above the issues of time off and references" when formulating a list of servants' demands.[60] To illustrate how key of an issue such freedom was, particularly for young female servants, Miller describes how "A likely-looking factory girl was asked why she did not try to improve her position by taking a situation as kitchenmaid or nurse. 'Because,' replied the earner of tenpence a day, 'because I'm above that poor scum that mustn't wear a feather or a ribbon [...] because I likes my liberty.'"[61] Self-presentation, including the presentation of one's hair, emerges here as a primary means by which a sense of individuation is achieved in liberal societies.

MEN'S HAIR AND FACIAL HAIR

Although the previous sections have discussed men's hair care in various social strata from the workhouse to the club, most of this chapter has focused on women's hair, which unquestionably offered a more visible staging of class throughout the nineteenth century. Yet men's hair also expressed a potent, if subtler, class politics. This is evident, for example, in Frank Churchill's sudden trip to London for a hair cut in Jane Austen's *Emma* (1815), a trip that turns out later to have been a deception on Frank's part, but which is interpreted at the time by Emma and those around her as a decidedly ungentlemanly act:

> Emma's very good opinion of Frank Churchill was a little shaken the following day, by hearing that he was gone off to London, merely to have his hair cut. A sudden freak seemed to have seized him at breakfast, and he had sent for a chaise and set off [...] with no more important view that appeared than having his hair cut. There was certainly no harm in his travelling sixteen miles twice over on such an errand; but there was an air of foppery and nonsense in it which she could not approve. It did not accord with the rationality of plan, the moderation in expense, or even the unselfish warmth of heart, which she had believed herself to discern in him yesterday. Vanity, extravagance, love of change, restlessness of temper [...] he became liable to all these charges. His father only called him a coxcomb and thought it a very good story; but that Mrs. Weston did not like it, was clear enough, by her passing it over as quickly as possible.[62]

The class politics of the passage are complex, for clearly "extravagance" and a lack of "moderation in expense" are themselves déclassé, in Emma's estimation, pointing to an older notion of class, rooted in aristocratic notions of good breeding, that would proscribe certain forms of overindulgence as vulgar. Conceptions of masculinity and gender are also crucial here: "foppery" and "coxcomb" both suggest dandyism, and no one in the novel seems to consider it extravagant, by contrast, that Emma herself keeps a maid, in part to style her hair. (Austen, with her typical lack of interest in the lower orders, makes deft use of passive voice to discourage readers from considering who does the work of caring for Emma's hair: "The hair was curled, and the maid sent away, and Emma sat down to think.")[63]

The idea that active interest in one's hair is in some crucial way feminine, an idea that generally persists today, perhaps explains why the class distinctions among nineteenth-century hairstyles appear to have been less pronounced for men than for women. Long hair, for example, was "never fashionable for Victorian men," and "throughout the period, men's hair stopped at the collar."[64] Some men of a more Bohemian persuasion did violate this dictum—a piece in the 1842 *London Saturday Journal*, for example, describes the type of the "long-haired musician," whose hair is "his bank, his revenue, his family, his idol, his second self. Cut off his hair, and you cut off his entail of genius"—but for the most part, men of all classes kept their hair short.[65] Fashions in facial hair, too, tended to cut across classes in a general way. Writing of the sudden popularity of beards in the mid-Victorian period, Christopher Oldstone-Moore writes: "it is a remarkable feature of the Victorian era that beards were just as popular with working-class men as they were with middle-class men or aristocratic men."[66] Ruth Goodman likewise writes that the rim beard, a style of male facial hair that preceded the full bushy beard of the 1870s, was popular among men "from all classes" in the 1850s.[67]

Just because such fashions had cross-class appeal, however, does not mean that there was no class signification at work in the style. As Oldstone-Moore notes: "in the early nineteenth century beards indicated particular radical political affiliations, including socialism or Chartism, and were generally unfashionable"—unfashionable among non-radicals at least, one is tempted to add.[68] It was not until after 1848 that beards came into general fashion, and Oldstone-Moore argues that above all it was "the passing of the revolutionary era that triggered the rise of beards."[69] This suggests that the style of the beard was actually an appropriation of the edginess of radical class politics, an appropriation of Bohemian radicalism by mainstream culture. The general popularity of this style also represented a cooptation of the kind of virile masculinity associated with the working-class Chartist movement. As Oldstone-Moore notes, Feargus O'Connor, leader of the physical force Chartists who were willing to consider violence as a possible means to social equality, was known for his beard. James Gregory writes that O'Connor's beard was "symbolic of real plebeian status when contrasted with the smooth-faced labour aristocracy of his critics," this despite the fact that O'Connor himself was not plebeian.[70] Over a hundred years before Che Guevara T-shirts could be purchased at the mall, Victorian men's beards provided an early example of class cooptation and the appropriation of a style that was originally sported by a politically and economically marginalized group.

CONCLUSION

A consideration of nineteenth-century class and social status in relation to hair turns up many of the themes that scholars have found to be most historically significant about the era: social welfare policy, liberalism, evangelicalism, commercialism, capitalism and its discontents, the rise of advertising, changing gender roles, democratization, and threats to aristocratic rule play out in the field of hair as they do in other forums of culture. As Alexander Rowland, magnate of nineteenth-century hair products, put it in his *A Practical and Philosophical Treatise on the Human Hair*, "In every age and country A FINE HEAD OF HAIR, has always been viewed as the most distinguished ornament of the human frame."[71] Like all ornaments, hair proves to have a social value that far exceeds the decorative and, indeed, the social value of hair is so potent that it effectively erases the line between the useful and the decorative.

CHAPTER NINE

Cultural Representations: Hair as the Abundant Signifier

SALLY WEST

The Great Exhibition of 1851, held in the new Crystal Palace in Hyde Park, London, was the first of a series of exhibitions designed to display the best of the world's culture and industry. One commentator in the British periodical *John Bull* described the event as a unique educational opportunity: "All nature and art are brought under our survey, and an area of twenty acres is made, as it were, an epitome of the whole world."[1] In addition to displaying a wide variety of technology, art, and culture from around the world, the Great Exhibition also contained some rather more curious exhibits. Alexander Rowland observed that it boasted a wide variety of "lighter ornamental works" of which "few were finer or more curious than those executed in human hair."[2] The items which particularly struck Rowland were part of a collection by the French exhibitors, containing:

> A portrait of her Majesty, Queen Victoria, worked in hair, being so chaste and delicate, and at the same time so truthful, that it was difficult to believe that it was not a sepia drawing. There was also shown in an ornamental frame in the south gallery an interesting collection of likenesses, correct and pleasing, worked in hair, of her Majesty, Prince Albert, and all the royal children. Beneath these were emblems of church and state, the army and navy, arts and sciences, commerce and industry, &c., beautifully executed in hair and gold, and exceedingly minute and perfect.[3]

As part of an exhibition which aimed to display the cultural artifacts and technological advances of nations, these portraits of the royal family and of the workings of the British state stand as symbolic representations of how hair was woven through the culture of the nineteenth century. Hair not only appeared *in* art, it *was* art. It was not only styled on the head, it was fashioned into jewelry and other products. Hair was an indicator of sexuality and potency, of propriety or voluptuousness. It could be read as a means of gauging the character of its owner, or, severed from the body, become a commodity to be bought and sold, to adorn, enrich, and recreate identity. As Janice Miller has argued, "hair itself is clearly loaded with meanings that are both part of and contribute to our understanding of the social body and the culture in which it is formed."[4] Throughout the nineteenth century, hair's rich array of significations can be discerned in the cultural products of the era which reflect and comment on the social, ideological, and cultural importance of hair.

THE LOCK: A TOKEN GESTURE

The British periodical press of the nineteenth century abounds with trite verses eulogizing—and satirizing—the lock of hair as a synecdoche for its owner, an "Unfading emblem of my heart's true love; / Memento sacred!"[5] Such verses emphasize the intimate connection between the severed hair and the body of its owner: "Aye, a lock of hair is far better than any picture—it is part of the beloved object herself."[6] Elizabeth G. Gitter observes the fascination with the creation and exchange of hair tokens in the mid-nineteenth century: "the ubiquitous lock of hair, encased in a locket or ring or framed on the wall, became, through a Midas touch of imagination, something treasured, a totem, a token of attachment, intrinsically valuable, as precious as gold."[7] Gitter's point about the "Midas touch of the imagination" suggests that the romantic investment in such ornaments could, however, be delusory, and it is true that the bestowal of a lock of hair as a token of love and fidelity is a ritual which comes under scrutiny in nineteenth-century literature. Far from the sentimental gesture indicated in the doggerel of the periodicals, nineteenth-century writers frequently use the lock of hair as a means of indicating hidden passions, expedient gestures, and downright deceit.

Heathcliff's final gesture as he rants and raves over Cathy's deathbed in Emily Brontë's *Wuthering Heights* (1846) is to remove from her locket a lock of hair belonging to her husband, Edgar, and replace it with his own. Finding the discarded hair, Cathy's former nurse, Nellie Dean, takes it upon herself to "twist the two and enclose them together" in the locket around Cathy's neck, thus confirming symbolically the continuance of the strange ménage of Cathy, Edgar, and Heathcliff.[8] Nellie's gesture may be read as reconciliatory or interfering, depending on one's viewpoint, but the intertwining of hair here indicates the complex network of passions which informs the text and which will continue after Cathy's death, blighting the next generation in the second half of the novel.

That the symbolic and romantic connotations of bestowing of a lock of hair may be no more than superficial can be seen in Jane Austen's *Sense and Sensibility* (1811). The youngest Dashwood daughter, Margaret, is in no doubt that her sister, Marianne, will marry Willoughby, "'for he has got a lock of her hair'."[9] When the sensible Elinor expresses skepticism, Margaret informs her:

> 'But, indeed, Elinor, it is Marianne's. I am almost sure it is, for I saw him cut it off. Last night after tea, when you and mama went out of the room, they were whispering and talking together as fast as could be, and he seemed to be begging for something of her, and presently he took up her scissors and cut off a long lock of her hair, for it was all tumbled down her back; and he kissed it, and folded it up in a piece of white paper; and put it into his pocket-book'.[10]

That it is the naïve Margaret who is so sure of the symbolic currency of the lock suggests that Austen intends to undercut the romantic assumption that such a bestowal is a certain preface to marriage. Austen's symbolism in this passage is more complex than Margaret can understand and alerts us to the danger that Marianne is in. That her hair is "all tumbled down her back" is doubly suggestive. Firstly, it reminds us how very young Marianne is; as Galia Ofek points out, hair etiquette in the nineteenth century dictated that while a young girl's locks could be worn loose and free, on maturity, those same locks should be contained and worn "up."[11] Marianne's loose hair is thus indicative of her physical immaturity, of being on the borderline between girlhood and adulthood. She is old enough to attract the attentions of Willoughby but lacks the maturity to read him successfully. In this context, her tumbling locks are suggestive of inappropriate emotional and sexual openness: loose hair may lead to loose morals. Thus Marianne's liminal position is a vulnerable one. As a mature child without agency she is prey to sexual advances; as an immature adult allowed to make her own decisions regarding a lover, she risks a sexual fall. Here, Austen embodies Marianne's character—her youth, her excess of sensibility, her naïvety—in the condition of her hair.

The cutting of the lock is also revelatory of Willoughby's character. That he takes the hair, rather than having it bestowed upon him, suggests a desire for instant gratification and the potential for sexual rapaciousness.[12] Both of these characteristics are demonstrated, as we later discover, in his prior treatment of Colonel Brandon's ward, whom he had abandoned, pregnant. Marianne is to suffer because of his impatience for financial gain, when she is discarded in favor of a wealthier rival better able to supply Willoughby's material needs, but, Austen suggests here through the hair symbolism, the outcome could have been much worse. When the affair breaks down, Marianne demands, and receives back, the lock of hair, restoring the lost part of herself.[13]

The latent associations between the lock of hair and sexual ownership observable in Austen are developed more explicitly in later literature of the nineteenth century. In Christina Rossetti's "Goblin Market," "sweet-tooth" Laura's decision to pay for the fruits of the Goblin Men with "a precious golden lock" of her hair leads to a physical decline which has been interpreted as allegorical of a sexual fall.[14] As Jill Rappoport comments, "Laura trades a lock that ultimately surrenders her body" because the Goblins "want the real thing, the material object backing Laura's symbolic currency."[15] However, beneath this surface allegory of the lock being representative of Laura's body and potentially her virginity, lies a more complex connection between women's lack of economic control and lack of sexual control. Lacking financial agency—"'I have no coin'"—Laura pays for her pleasures with her body, and her pleasures make her body pay in turn.[16]

The image from the frontispiece of the 1865 edition of "Goblin Market," by Dante Gabriel Rossetti, illustrates the moment when Laura cuts the golden curl with which she will pay for her fruit—and pay dearly. Laura is positioned centrally, her fair hair loose, the scissors in her hand poised to cut. Her expression is one of concentration, but in its direction her gaze encounters that of one of the Goblin Men who appears to be staring at her longingly. This figure appears to be a conflation of Christina Rossetti's description of two of the Goblin Men: "One had a cat's face / One whisked a tail," for a long tail coils around his leg, pointing upwards.[17] The tail is unmistakably serpentine, recalling biblical connotations of temptation and a fall from grace, and potentially phallic, inflecting the nature of the transaction in which Laura is engaged, where her currency is part of her body. As in *Sense and Sensibility*, the lock is invested with symbolic meanings to do with intimacy, the body, and sexuality, and the nature of the transaction which it enables is inherently ambiguous, and not to the giver's advantage.

ORDERED AND DISORDERLY HAIR

The connection between loose hair and (potentially) loose morals in women was inscribed, according to Ofek, as "a common cultural code which was legible to all" in the nineteenth century.[18] This cultural code can be observed in a number of publications designed to teach women and young girls the practical aspects of womanhood: clothing, behavior, appearance, and demeanor, frequently implying the connection between the surface which a woman presents to the world and the presumed morality of what lies beneath. In *On Womankind* (1877) Charlotte Yonge is inflexible in her advice about the arranging of hair. Loose, untamed locks were acceptable in girlhood, but on reaching maturity a woman must "reduce the hair to well-ordered obedience," for "tumbledown hair, falling dishevelled on the shoulders, sounds grand in fiction but it is disgusting in real life."[19] Yonge's aversion to untamed female tresses in adulthood speaks of a connection between physical and moral disorder; uncontrolled hair becomes a visible symbol of similarly uncontrolled conduct. This symbolism finds expression in the art and literature of the period. In an 1867 review of Rhoda Broughton's *Cometh Up as a Flower*, Margaret Oliphant commented on the proliferation of golden locks in novels of the period and asked: "What need has a woman for a soul when she has upon her head a mass of wavy gold?"[20]

However, despite the connotations of innocence denoted by long, loose hair in girlhood, there is evidence in the literature of the period that even in youth, where loose locks denoted "innocence and virginity,"[21] a girl's hair was already beginning to acquire an array of symbolic meanings foreshadowing those of the hair of the mature woman. "Self-willed Jessie: Or, the Girl with the Golden Hair," serialized in the children's periodical *Little Folks* toward the end of the century, tells the story of an unhappy, orphaned young girl, living with her aunt and bullying cousins, who resents being put to work around the house.[22] Jessie snaps up a chance to perform with a visiting circus, where she was accepted at least in part because of her beautiful hair, but, seconds before she is due on stage, her cousin informs her that her aunt is dangerously ill. Jessie chooses to continue with her performance, but her moral "fall" in neglecting her aunt precipitates a literal fall onstage, with the result that she becomes dangerously ill. When she regains consciousness some days later, she realizes that her beautiful golden hair has been cut off. Jessie's initial reaction of horror and anger gives way to acceptance and thankfulness for the care that has been taken of her during her illness. While the story presents Jessie sympathetically, the conclusion, which sees her reconciled to her aunt and promising to do her domestic duties and trust in God, carries the heavy-handed moral that girls should be selfless. This moral is crystalized in the loss of her golden hair; the implication is that vanity led Jessie to neglect her duty and that her illness and subsequent loss of this external manifestation of beauty are a punishment—a lesson from which she duly learns.

In George Eliot's *The Mill on the Floss* (1860), Maggie Tulliver is repeatedly berated for the state of her thick, dark hair which "'won't curl'" and compared unfavorably with her blonde cousin Lucy who has "'a row o' curls round her head, an' not a hair out o' place'."[23] When, frustrated with such criticism, Maggie cuts off her hair, she initially feels "a sense of clearness and freedom, as if she had emerged from a wood into the open plain."[24] However, this is followed by regret in the face of the rebukes and amusement of her family. Aunt Glegg opines "'Little gells as cut their own hair should be whipped and fed on bread and water'."[25] Maggie's act of hair cutting constitutes a defiance of appropriate feminine order and propriety, as the comparisons with neat and tidy Lucy demonstrate. As Ofek comments, Maggie's hair is "the site where her identity is formed through a struggle between natural urges to resist external dictations and restrictive social regulations."[26] This struggle, epitomized by Maggie's relationship to her hair in childhood, also foreshadows the future trajectory of the novel where her natural instincts repeatedly come into conflict with social expectations of female behavior, firstly in her forced renunciation of education and culture in order to support her mother, and secondly in her conflicted and socially unacceptable attraction toward Stephen Guest, suitor to cousin Lucy.

As a liminal space, both of the individual body and outside it, it is fitting that hair should become a site of conflict between the individual and society. The contrast that Eliot draws between perceptions of Maggie as unruly and disordered and those of Lucy as demure and controlled registers that there is a connection not only between blonde hair and beauty, but also between blonde hair and goodness and order. This dichotomy is in evidence in the work of a number of nineteenth-century writers. In Thomas Hardy's novels, for instance, which are peppered with references to hair, morally ambiguous female characters are often dark-haired. In *The Return of the Native*, Hardy's opening description of Eustacia Vye's hair establishes her character: "To see her hair, was to fancy that a whole winter did not contain darkness enough to form its shadow."[27] The intense blackness of Eustacia's hair proves portentous of the darkness at the heart of her character; she is a siren figure, manipulating those around her and is indirectly responsible for the death of Clym's mother. In *Jane Eyre*, madwoman in the attic Bertha Mason has "thick and dark hair hanging long down her back," and is compared to "the foul German spectre, the Vampyre."[28] Bertha's appearance, epitomized by her dark, uncontrolled hair, functions as a physical signifier of her similarly uncontrolled psychological state. A particularly striking example of the moral connotations of hair color occurs in Bram Stoker's *Dracula*. Here, the much admired, much courted Lucy Westenra has blonde hair prior to falling victim to a vampiric attack. When ill, but still human, Lucy's hair is described as lying in "its usual sunny ripples" on her pillow.[29] Once she has become undead, however, she is described as "a dark-haired woman," predating on a "fair-haired child."[30] The juxtaposition of deviancy and innocence, dark and light, embodied in Lucy's nocturnal hunting is further connected to ideas of deviant sexuality in the repeated use of the adjective "voluptuous" to describe her expression and gestures. Victim of a penetration and infection from the Count, Lucy has fallen morally and, it is implied through Stoker's descriptions of her, sexually; this fall is registered in her changing hair color.

DEVIANT HAIR

The good blonde/evil dark dichotomy, is, however, open to challenge. Ofek identifies a mid-century shift in attitudes to hair color, with the advent of the sensation novel. Here, she argues, novelists like Mary Elizabeth Braddon in *Lady Audley's Secret*, exploit the association of blondeness with goodness and innocence in characters like Lady Audley herself, who is both blonde and a murderer.[31] Like their owner, Lady Audley's golden curls perform conventionality rather than being the real thing, allowing her to capture a rich husband and lead the sort of privileged lifestyle that was denied her in her former life as Helen Talboys. Throughout the novel, Braddon shows subtly how hair encodes character. For the sensible Alicia, Lady Audley's golden curls are an outward manifestation of what she deems her stepmother's silliness. For her indulgent husband, the same curls function as an indicator of innocence and fragility, appealing to his protective instincts. It is only Robert Audley who struggles to marry the surface of his aunt with what he fears lies beneath. In the earliest serialized edition of the novel, as Robert's uneasiness grows, he dreams that Lady Audley's "face had grown ghastly white, and that her beautiful golden ringlets were changing into serpents and slowly creeping down her fair neck."[32] This transformation of beautiful Lucy Audley into the threatening Medusa, capable of turning men to stone, registers not only Robert's fears of her involvement in his friend's disappearance, but a wider societal fear of what may lie beneath the surface of conventional femininity. As Ofek argues, "Sensational hair […] introduces the concept of unknown and unmappable femaleness," where what is on the outside may not be truly representative of what lies beneath.[33] The anti-heroine of the sensation novel can exploit societal constructions of acceptable female behavior to her own ends. In the case of Lucy Audley, one of her weapons is the childish innocence embodied in her golden hair.

As Ofek observes, the awareness of both Lady Audley and Braddon of the currency of external signs enables them to "manipulate the signifying system and sell their products."[34] Such knowingness about the power of hair to signify character is also observable in Henrik Ibsen's *Hedda Gabler* (1891) in the relationship between Hedda and Thea Elvsted. Referred to by Hedda as "The woman with the provoking hair," Thea's tresses become a point of focus for Hedda's anxiety, jealousy, and personal ennui.[35] When Thea enters the room in Act One, Ibsen's stage direction describing her appearance is typically detailed: *"Her hair is strikingly fair, almost whitish-yellow, and unusually rich and wavy. She is a couple of years younger than Hedda."*[36] While it would be in keeping with Hedda's character for her to be jealous of the striking appearance of Thea's hair, simple cosmetic envy does not tell the whole story. We learn that when at school, Hedda pulled Thea's hair and threatened to "burn it off," a threat which Hedda repeats at the end of Act Two of the play.[37] This threat is carried out by proxy when, at the end of Act Three, Hedda burns Lövborg's manuscript: "Now I'm burning your child, Thea! With your curly hair! [...] Your child and Ejlert Lövborg's. [...] I'm burning ... burning your child."[38] It is arguable that Hedda's act of wanton destruction is an outward projection of the suicidal impulse which is at her heart; she identifies the manuscript as a symbolic "child," representing something fruitful, a product of the efforts of Lövborg and Thea. To destroy a child is to destroy potential, to destroy the future, and this gesture thus accords with Hedda's nihilism and foreshadows her suicide at the end of the play. That she should again reference Thea's "curly" hair at this moment allows us to make sense of Ibsen's focus on it earlier in the play. Thea's hair is unusual, rich, and, in its waves, suggests life and movement. These are elements that Hedda feels have been denied to her, trapped, as she always has been, by social constraints. Despite her apparent strength of character and willfulness, her susceptibility to conformity is revealed when Brack attempts to blackmail her over her role in Lövborg's death. This, along with the prospect of another productive working relationship developing between her husband and Thea, and another potential "child," leads Hedda to her inevitable "beautiful" end.[39] Ibsen uses hair in *Hedda Gabler* to express the warped psychology of his protagonist by making Thea's tresses represent everything that Hedda believes is denied to her.

At the very dawn of the century, in 1798, Coleridge's poem "The Rime of the Ancient Mariner" was first published in the jointly authored volume with Wordsworth, *Lyrical Ballads*. Perhaps his most well-known poem, telling a tale of crime, punishment, and (partial) redemption, it was one to which Coleridge would return repeatedly throughout his life, editing and adjusting, and it was republished in its evolving forms throughout the nineteenth century. One detail, however, which remains relatively consistent in all of the versions of the poem, is the physical description of the woman whom the Mariner sees on the specter ship, later identified, in Coleridge's 1817 revisions, as "Life-in-Death":

> Her lips were red, her looks were free,
> Her locks were yellow as gold:
> Her skin was as white as leprosy
> The Night-mare Life-in-Death was she
> Who thicks man's blood with cold.[40]

Here, the white skin, the red lips and "yellow" hair seem a grotesque parody of conventional feminine beauty. Coleridge might use the simile "yellow *as* gold" (my emphasis), yet the literary device does as much to hold apart the image from its comparison as it does to bring them together; her hair may be "as" gold, but it is not golden. Instead, in the context of the uncannily sickly "white" skin and exaggerated "red" lips, her "yellow" hair is suggestive of disease and decay, while her "free" looks imply a potential sexual abandon. As in Robert Audley's nightmare of his aunt's hair transforming into snakes, the myth of the Medusa appears here in the fear of petrification; she "thicks man's blood with cold." In both examples, the power of untamed, oddly sentient hair is seen as a threat, specifically a threat to a man from a woman.

Coleridge was not alone in associating illness, death, and decay with yellow hair. Robert Browning's poem "Porphyria's Lover," first published in 1836, dramatizes the murder of Porphyria by the unnamed speaker of the poem, who uses her "yellow hair" as the murder weapon:

That moment she was mine, mine, fair,
Perfectly pure and good: I found
A thing to do, and all her hair
In one long yellow string I wound
Three times her little throat around,
And strangled her.[41]

While it is dangerous to ascribe certain motivation to Browning's notoriously unreliable narrators, there is a sense here that the speaker is capturing and preserving Porphyria at the moment when she is, to him, "Perfectly pure and good." The need to preserve her at this moment speaks of a fear that she will fall, that this perfection will prove to be transitory. This is borne out by his description of her behavior earlier in the poem:

She put my arm about her waist,
And made her smooth white shoulder bare,
And all her yellow hair displaced,
And, stooping, made my cheek lie there,
And spread, o'er all, her yellow hair,
Murmuring how she loved me.[42]

This description cannot be taken at face value, but rather demonstrates the speaker's own psychological state and how he interprets that of Porphyria. This is an eroticized moment, centered on her use of her hair to connect her body to his. The repetition of "yellow hair" here marks his growing obsession with this aspect of her, something which is both of her and separate from her and which can be used to tempt and overwhelm. Browning's speaker focuses his fear of Porphyria—of losing her, of her changing—in her hair. As such, it is perfectly apt that he should take control of that uncontrollable not-body part and use it to preserve her alongside him: "And thus we sit together now, / And all night long we have not stirred."[43]

As with Coleridge and Browning, Christina Rossetti also aligns yellow hair with sexual impropriety, but actual rather than potential, in "A Triad." "Three sang of love together," Rossetti writes, "one with lips / Crimson, with cheeks and bosom in a glow, / Flushed to the yellow hair and finger-tips."[44] In the sestet of the sonnet, we learn that this was one who "shamed herself in love."[45] While she carries the blush of shame, the "crimson" lips and "yellow" hair recall the "free" looks of Coleridge's spectral figure in "The Rime of the

Ancient Mariner." Thus yellow hair in the literature of the period is treated distinctly differently to its golden counterpart, carrying with it the suggestion of disease and decay and the threat of sexual impropriety.

UNCANNY HAIR

Coleridge's Life-in-Death, Browning's Porphyria, and Stoker's Lucy are examples of cultural representations of hair in the nineteenth century which emphasize its uncanny qualities. Janice Miller discusses hair's "troubled relationship to the rest of the human body" in terms of its liminality; it is both of the living body and yet dead matter.[46] In this context, it is unsurprising that hair should be a focal point in registering a figure's uncanny nature. Edvard Munch's painting *Vampire* (1893) depicts what first appears to be a couple embracing. The woman faces toward us, but her head is angled downwards, half buried in the back of the neck of a man whose head is against her breast. The most striking feature of the painting is how her abundant red hair spreads out like a curtain over both of them, the color of its tendrils suggesting flowing blood. Jacky Colliss Harvey cites a Romanian belief that when a red-head died, they would return in the form of one of the lesser animals and suck the blood of young women. She comments, "Vampires, so the thinking goes, are bloody; red is the color of blood, therefore redness must predispose one to vampirism."[47] While in Munch's painting the depiction of the red hair as flowing blood accords with this aspect of folklore, it is perhaps also the liminality of hair, existing, like the vampire, somewhere between life and death, which imparts an uncanny ambience to the painting.

Hair's uncanny qualities also derive from the belief that it continues to grow after death. A short note in *Cleve's Gazette of Variety* from 1838 asserts: "It sometimes happens that the hair and nails continue to grow after death notwithstanding the decomposition of the body. The *Journal des Savons* mentions a female whose hair was found, forty-three years after the internment of the body, to have forced itself through the chinks of the coffin. This hair crumbled on being touched."[48] This myth contains a paradox: hair, which is dead, gains its life force from the body, yet, on the death of that body, continues to grow, taking on a life of its own and breaking the bounds of the body's internment. It is hair's complex and paradoxical relationship with the body that produced it from which its uncanny properties derive.[49]

This idea lies behind a story about Elizabeth Siddal—artist, poet, and famous model and muse to the Pre-Raphaelite painters. On her death in 1862, from an overdose of laudanum, her grieving lover Dante Gabriel Rossetti buried her with a collection of his poems, placed "between her cheek and beautiful hair."[50] Some years later, thinking better of his romantic gesture, and wanting to publish the poetry, he called for her to be exhumed. According to the account of Charles Augustus Howell, on opening the coffin, "Elizabeth remained as beautiful as she had ever been in life and her hair, which had kept growing after death, now filled the coffin and was as brilliantly copper-coloured as it had been in life."[51]

Ofek argues persuasively that Howell's account was the inspiration for Bram Stoker's short story "The Secret of the Growing Gold" (1897).[52] Here, the dissolute Geoffrey Brent spurns and attempts to kill his equally mercurial lover, Margaret Delandre. Unbeknown to him, she survives his attempt, returning, and vowing revenge. Although hideously changed by her experience, one feature remains: her beautiful golden hair. In the ensuing confrontation with Brent, who is now married and expecting a child, he succeeds this time in killing her, burying her beneath the slabs of the hall of his mansion. Yet her hair survives, growing profusely between the slabs, functioning as a visual embodiment of both Brent's guilt and Margaret's vengeance. Brent's new wife develops a fascination with the "growing gold" and the story concludes with the Brents discovered, dead, in the room full of growing golden hair:

> "Sit here," said his wife as she put out the light. "Sit here by the hearth and watch the gold growing. The silver moonlight is jealous! See, it steals along the floor towards the gold—our gold!" Geoffrey looked with growing horror, and saw that during the hours that had passed the golden hair had protruded further through the broken hearth-stone.[53]

Abigail Heiniger has investigated the debts that Stoker's narrative owes to Hungarian folk stories where a woman's hair is uncannily animated. She argues "the undead blond hair is an active character that speaks for the woman whose voice has been violently silenced."[54] Once again, hair's liminal position in being both of the body and external to it, both dead and alive, imbues it with a curious autonomy once its owner has ceased to be. In the case of Margaret Delandre, and that of Lizzie Siddal, the feature which was a focal point during life takes on a life of its own in death. As Heiniger comments, "the identity of the woman is synonymous with her hair. It may be argued that the undead blond hair is transformed into the active heroine of the tale by revealing hidden transgressions."[55] This is clearly the case for the fictional Margaret Delandre, where the hair reveals her place of internment and, by extension, the crime of her lover. How, though, to account for the story spread about the uncanny state of Lizzie Siddal's hair? According to Louise Tondeur, Siddal's "ghostly presence" was established before her death in the multiple paintings by the Pre-Raphaelites in which she featured as model, "her vibrant hair being one of the most striking things about the paintings."[56] Yet if we inflect the story with Stoker's fictional retelling of it in "The Secret of the Growing Gold," we can read Lizzie Siddal's abundant, uncanny hair as "a refusal to be buried, a refusal of the woman poet to be covered up."[57] In this context it is perhaps pertinent that many of Rossetti's poems collected from Siddal's coffin had disintegrated, and those he reconstructed and published received bad reviews.[58] The text which endures most memorably from Siddal's exhumation is the story of the hair that survived death.

Siddal's hair makes another appearance in Rossetti's portrait *Beata Beatrix*, completed in 1870, eight years after Siddal's death. Siddal, as Beatrice, sits with her eyes closed, head tilted slightly back, her hands loosely clasped in her lap. Behind her head is a bright golden light, which illuminates her copper-colored hair, giving the effect of an aureole, so that the light seems to emanate from Beatrice, specifically from her hair. On the right-hand side of the painting, a red dove with a halo above its head delivers a white flower.[59] Casting Siddal as Beatrice can be read as Rossetti confirming his love for her, likening it to Dante's faithful, unexpressed passion for Beatrice, which survived her early death and was immortalized in his works *Vita Nuova* and *The Divine Comedy*. As Lucinda Hawksley notes, "from the time he met Lizzie, [Rossetti] identified her strongly with Beatrice. After Lizzie's death, she was no longer his troublesome, flawed wife. Instead she would become a beatified beauty, who would never grow old."[60] However, there is also something disturbing in Rossetti casting his dead wife as the dying love object. While it can be interpreted as a Dante-esque statement of devotion, it is arguable that it does little to honor or immortalize Siddal herself. The loose white-green clothing she wears is uncomfortably reminiscent of a shroud, giving the effect, as Elizabeth K. Helsinger observes, of "flesh and garments [...] gradually assuming the dead color of the stone wall against which she is posed."⁶¹ Furthermore, the shadows on her clasped hands, when inflected by knowledge of Siddal's exhumation, recall smears of earth. Angela Dunstan points to evidence from Rossetti's letters which suggests that his motivation in completing *Beata Beatrix* was less devotional than pecuniary. His original conception of the work predated Siddal's death, and he had begun work on sketches of his wife. Returning to the work subsequent to her death, he dropped it again when the proposed buyer backed out. After finding an alternative patron, Rossetti completed the painting, and, in subsequent years, produced copies of it for other parties.⁶² References to *Beata Beatrix* in his letters are uniformly disparaging, citing the money he will receive as the only motivation to continue. In a letter to his brother of 1871 he writes: "I have been doing a replica here (of that *Beatrice*—a beastly job, but lucre was the lure …)."⁶³ Dunstan argues that Rossetti's decision to paint and repaint Siddal as Beatrice after her death represents less a repeated act of memorial than "a continuation of his commodification of her image undertaken in life."⁶⁴ In this context, Siddal's uncanny hair, like that of the fictional Margaret Delandre, is suggestive of a repressed voice finding an outlet. It is perhaps fitting that hair, the dead appendage of the living body, should be the medium of expression, of resistance, from beyond the grave. As Gilbert and Gubar comment: "As if symbolising the indomitable earthliness that no woman, however angelic, could entirely renounce, Lizzie Siddal Rossetti's hair leaps like a metaphor for monstrous female sexual energies from the literal and figurative coffins in which her artist-husband enclosed her."⁶⁵

TRADING HAIR

This commodification of Siddal's image, encapsulated so memorably in the repeated appearances of her striking hair in Rossetti's paintings, raises the broader issue of hair as a commodity in the nineteenth century. The British periodicals of the time provide copious examples of the extent to which hair had become an industry: advice for arranging it, advertisements for products to improve its abundance and appearance, and, in the more satirical examples of the genre, a considerable amount of mockery of the latest fashions and trends. For instance, the chignon, which gained popularity in the 1850s, gradually increased in size and complexity in the following decades, requiring women to supplement their own head hair with swathes of artificial hair.⁶⁶ This trend spawned many magazine articles advising on the handling and arrangement of this new accessory. *The Englishwoman's Domestic Magazine* noted: "Such a large quantity of false hair is necessary to the formation of modern coiffures that we think it well to initiate our female readers into the secrets of the fictitious curls, bows, plaits and chignons to be used for each of them."⁶⁷ The article is accompanied by illustrations of these hairpieces both on and off the models in order to illustrate the variety of styles achievable. The styles have names such as "La Capricieuse" and "La Duchesse," suggesting that different styles of hair can impose different characteristics and even identities on the wearer.

This question of constructing identity through the wearing of false hair led to some concerns about the provenance of the new tresses on sale. One unnamed contributor to *Fun* in 1867 upbraids "Lady Chignon Hair of Hair," stating "I stole the plaits from off your head, / Not many months have come and gone / Since they adorned a Kalmuck dead." The writer concludes: "Ask Paris for another freak / But let this nasty fashion go!"⁶⁸ An article in the *Ladies' Treasury* in 1868 claimed that the demand for false hair had caused its price to rise 400 percent in the last dozen years. Examining tresses of false hair, the writer comments, "the various circumstances under which it had been parted with, the poverty, the sickness, the sorrow, the ignorance, and the vice, forcibly suggested themselves."[69]

The ambivalence felt by many Victorians toward the provenance of false hair is apparent in the story "Hair Ghosts," published in *The Treasury of Literature and the Ladies' Treasury* in 1870. This tells the tale of Aunt Patty, who is persuaded by her niece, Emily, to purchase some artificial hair, as she "'would look so much better, so much more like other people, if [she] would only wear a chignon'."[70] To please her niece, Patty agrees and she, Emily and Emily's mother purchase false hair from a hair seller, but it is clear that there is something mysterious about these particular tresses, which are fetched from well-hidden boxes and cause alarm in the shop assistant. Accordingly, on the stroke of midnight, the three women transform into the original owners of their false hair. It is clear that at least two of these are poor girls, forced to sell their hair from financial necessity, recalling the concerns of the anonymous writer in the *Ladies' Treasury*. Each woman can only speak in the language of the hair donor; Patty reflects "I tried hard to prevent my individuality from slipping away from me," surely a satirical reminder of Emily's reasoning for Patty purchasing the hair: to look "so much more like other people."[71] Patty manages to remove the false hair from their heads and they return to themselves. Subsequent to this ordeal, they are visited by a (male) friend who counsels: "'If the ladies only knew [...] where the false tresses with which they adorn themselves come from, or what strange vitality and subtle influences lie in human hair, and how long it retains these qualities, I think they would hesitate before wearing any hair but their own'."[72] Once again, we can see the uncanny nature of hair registered here, its "strange vitality and subtle influences" which survive its severance from the body. The story is, on the one hand, a fairly simplistic morality tale about vanity, yet in Emily's desire to be "like other people" it also registers the social pressures of fashion conformity among middle- and upper-class women. Furthermore, in the uncanny transformations that the women undergo, we gain a glimpse of the class-based nature of the trade in false hair, where the poor give up a part of themselves to assuage the vanity of the rich. This manifests itself in the story as a fear of racial and cultural miscegenation; one of the middle-class Englishwomen transforms into a poor Irish girl, another into a "swarthy" woman "of Mongolian blood."[73] It is perhaps not coincidental, either, that the seller of the hair is a German Jew (portrayed in traditional nineteenth-century anti-Semitic style as cruel and avaricious). Once again, the liminal nature of hair finds expression in its cultural manifestations; the severed hair retains the essence of she who grew it and maintains an ability to alter the cultural, racial, and social identity of the wearer.

This connection between severed hair, economics, and identity is observable in Thomas Hardy's *The Woodlanders* where the innocent Marty South sells her hair in an effort to provide for her family. Predated on by the avaricious Percombe to sell her hair to the upper-class Felice Charmond, because it is "'the exact shade of her own, and 'tis a shade you can't match by dyeing'," Marty accepts two sovereigns and cuts her locks.[74] Unlike in "Hair Ghosts," however, Marty's severed locks do not impart something of her own innocence to their recipient. As Gitter notes, "once sold, the hair becomes false, and Marty, out of her inarticulate despair, becomes a participant in the commercialization of human relationships that pervades *The Woodlanders*."[75]

If we turn to American fiction of the same period, we can observe, on the surface at least, a greater sense of agency in the young woman who cuts her hair. In *Little Women* (1868–1869), Jo March's decision to sell her hair is based, like that of Marty South, on a desire to aid her family at a time of financial hardship. However, Jo's relationship to her hair is already a vexed one. A committed tomboy, Jo rails against cultural constructions of femininity, especially those concerning personal appearance. In the opening chapter of the novel, Jo rejects the notion that to "turn up" her hair makes her "a young lady" and swears that she will "wear it in two tails till I'm twenty!"[76] Unlike her more demure sister, Meg, who is turned "into a fine lady" by her friends, the Moffats, who "crimp" her hair, Jo steadfastly rejects the cultural construction of gender via the arrangement of her hair.[77] Nonetheless, despite her insistence that "it will do my brains good to have that mop taken off," Jo does cry in private for her lost hair. She says "It almost seemed as if I'd an arm or leg off," registering once again hair's intermediate position of being both of and separate from the body.[78] In her refusal to style her hair in the fashion of the demure young lady, Jo, like Maggie Tulliver in *The Mill on the Floss*, articulates a rejection of the impulse to conform to the restrictions imposed on her gender. However, in her genuine distress in the face of the loss of her "mop," Alcott registers the extent of the indoctrination of young women and the cultural pressures of performing femininity encoded in hair.

CONCLUSION

Cultural representations of hair in the nineteenth century exhibit a complex array of significations, moral judgments, and anxieties which cast a slightly ironic light on the hair portraits of Queen Victoria displayed at the Great Exhibition of 1851. The monarch, a symbol of stability, tradition, and hegemony, is constructed in a material which is deeply unstable and potentially subversive in its meanings. Hair, as we have seen, can be read as a reflection of the moral robustness of its owner; it can become a site where the individual's relationship to her society is played out; it can be deceptive, deathly, monstrous, and threatening. While hair, especially when severed from the head of its owner and transformed into a commodity, can participate in the capitalist transactions of the age, it also possesses an uncanny agency which undermines various manifestations of conventional social ideology. As the knowledgeable counsellor of "Hair Ghosts" observes, hair possesses "strange vitality and subtle influences" making it an eloquent medium for the representation of the era's social and cultural anxieties.[79]

NOTES

Introduction

1. See "History", *Cefn Park*. Available online: http://www.cefnpark.co.uk (accessed 31 May 2017).
2. Gillian Wagner, *Miss Palmer's Diary: The Secret Journals of a Victorian Lady* (London: I.B.Tauris, 2017).
3. Eric Hobsbawm, *The Age of Empire* (London: Abacus, 1988), 9.
4. Ibid., 57.
5. "Lock of Napoleon's Hair Found in Surrey House about to Be Demolished", *Ewbank's*. Available online: https://www.ewbankauctions.co.uk/News-Blog/lock-of-napoleon-s-hair-found-in-surrey-house-about-to-be-demolished (accessed 20 October 2016).
6. Russell Martin, *Beethoven's Hair: An Extraordinary Historical Odyssey and a Scientific Mystery Solved* (New York: Broadway Books, 2000).
7. Dante Gabriel Rossetti, "Life-in-Love," Sonnet xxxvi, in *Collected Poetry and Prose*, ed. Jerome McGann (New York: Vail-Ballou Press, 2000), 15, 143.
8. Galia Ofek, *Representations of Hair in Victorian Literature and Culture* (Farnham: Ashgate, 2009), 81.
9. Sadie Whitelock, "The Real-life Rapunzels: How Seven Sisters with Tresses Measuring 37 Feet between Them Tantalized Their Audiences to Make Their Fortune... And Patented a 'Miracle' Hair Tonic," *Daily Mail*, September 10, 2013. Available online: http://www.dailymail.co.uk/femail/article-2416873/The-real-life-Rapunzels-How-seven-sisters-37-feet-hair-fame-fortune-19th-century.html (accessed 20 October 2016).
10. See Leslie A. Marchand, *Byron: A Portrait* (London: John Murray, 1971), 130. James Soderholm, *Fantasy, Forgery and the Byron Legend* (Lexington: University of Kentucky Press, 1996), 58.
11. Tim Hilton, *John Ruskin* (New Haven, CT: Yale University Press, 2002), 118.
12. Ibid., 197.
13. Abigail Solomon-Godeau, "The Legs of the Countess," *October* 39 (1986): 97.
14. Richard Oram, "The Locks of Ages: The Leigh Hunt Hair Collection," *The Harry Ransom Center Magazine*, January 13, 2011. Available online: http://sites.utexas.edu/ransomcentermagazine/2011/01/13/locks-of-ages-the-leigh-hunt-hair-collection/.
15. Leigh Hunt, "Pocketbook and Keepsakes," in *The Essays of Leigh Hunt*, ed. Arthur Symons (London: Walter Scott, 1888), 17–18. Available online: https://archive.org/details/essaysofleighhun00huntuoft (accessed 4 November 2016).
16. William L. Bird, *Souvenir Nation: Relics, Keepsakes, and Curios from the Smithsonian's National Museum of American History* (New York: Princeton Architectural Press, 2013), 130.
17. Ibid. 130.
18. George Virtue, *The Art Journal Illustrated Catalogue: The Industry of all Nations* (London: Bradbury and Evans Printers, 1851), 159.
19. Robert Ellis, *The Official Catalogue of the Great Exhibition of the Works of Industry of All Nations, 1851* (London: Spicer, 1851), 113.

20. Ibid., 122.
21. Robert Ellis, *The Official Descriptive and Illustrated Catalogue of the Great Exhibition of the Works of Industry of all Nations, 1851*, Vol. 2 (London: Spicer, 1851), 682.
22. Ibid., 690.
23. Ibid., 690.
24. Ibid., 137 and 8.
25. Ibid., 165.
26. Ibid., 199.
27. Ibid., 273.
28. Ibid., 258.
29. Ibid., 253.
30. Ibid., 309.
31. See Jeffrey Auerbach, *The Great Exhibition of 1851: A Nation on Display* (Yale, CT: University of Yale Press, 1999) and Geoffry Cantor, "Emotional Reactions to the Great Exhibition," *Journal of Victorian Culture* 20 (2015): 230–45.
32. Ibid., 159.
33. "Hair Jewelry Exhibit at the Bangsbo Museum," *Atlas Obscura*. https://www.atlasobscura.com/places/hair-jewelry-exhibit-bangsbo-museum (accessed 4 November 2016).
34. Anne Louise Luthi, *Sentimental Jewellery* (Buckinghamshire: Shire Publishing, 2001), 29.
35. Joanne Entwistle, "The Dressed Body," in *Body Dressing*, eds. J. Entwistle and E. Wilson (Oxford: Berg, 2001), 45–6.
36. Alexander Warwick and Dani Cavallaro, *Fashioning the Frame: Boundaries, Dress and the Body* (Oxford: Berg, 1998), 15.
37. Deborah Lutz, *The Brontë Cabinet: Three Lives in Nine Objects* (London: Norton, 2016), 199.
38. Ibid., xvii.
39. Geraldine Biddle-Perry and Sarah Cheung, "Thinking about Hair," in *Hair: Styling, Culture and Fashion* (Oxford: Berg, 2008), 3.
40. Royce Mahawatte, "Hair and Fashioned Femininity in Two Nineteenth-Century Novels," in *Hair: Styling, Culture and Fashion* (Oxford: Berg, 2008), 193.
41. Doreen Yarwood, *European Costume: 4000 Years of Fashion* (London: B.T. Batsford, 1975), 215.
42. James Laver, *A Concise History of Costume* (London: Thames and Hudson, 1969), 191.
43. Laver, *A Concise History of Costume*, 168.
44. Ibid., 241.
45. Ofek, *Representations of Victorian Hair*, 169.
46. Bram Stoker, *Dracula* (Hertfordshire: Broadview, 2000), 197 and 249.
47. Stoker, *Dracula*, 69.
48. Allison Lowry, *Historical Wig Styling: Victorian to the Present* (New York: Focal Press, 2013), 82.
49. Edith Wharton, *The Mother's Recompense* (Gloucester: Dodo Press, 1925), 12.
50. Laver, *A Concise History of Costume*, 161.
51. Joan Nunn, *Fashion in Costume, 1200–2000* (Chicago: New Amsterdam books, 2000), 143.
52. Jessica P. Clark, "Grooming Men: The Material World of the Nineteenth-Century Barbershop," in *Gender and Material Culture in Britain since 1600*, eds. Hannah Grieg, Jane Hamlett, and Leonie Hannan (London: Palgrave, 2016), 108 and 104.

53. Jane Plitt, "Martha Matilda Harper: How one Woman Changed the Face of Modern Business" (Blog). Available online: http://www.marthamatildaharper.org/ (accessed 4 November 2016).
54. Clark, "Grooming Men," 104–5.
55. Jessica Gross "Who Made That Hair Dryer," *New York Times Magazine*, July 19, 2013. Available online: http://www.nytimes.com/2013/07/21/magazine/who-made-that-hair-dryer.html.
56. Lou Taylor, *Mourning Dress: A Costume and Social History* (Abingdon: Routledge, 2009), (accessed 4 November 2016), 241.
57. Lutz, *The Brontë Cabinet*, 198–9.
58. Hobsbawm, *The Age of Empire*, 9.

Chapter One

1. Emma Wilby, *Cunning Folk and Familiar Spirits: Shamanistic Visionary Traditions in Early Modern British Witchcraft and Magic* (Brighton: Sussex Academic Press), 36.
2. David Pickering, *Cassell's Dictionary of Witchcraft* (London: Orion, 2002), 122.
3. Richard Noakes, "Spiritualism, Science, and the Supernatural," in *The Victorian Supernatural*, eds. Nicola Bown, Carolyn Burdett, and Pamela Thurschwell (Cambridge: Cambridge University Press, 2004), 23.
4. Janet Oppenheim, *The Other World: Spiritualism and Psychical Research in England, 1850–1914* (Cambridge: Cambridge University Press, 1985), 199.
5. Thomas Carlyle, *Sartor Resartus* (Boston, MA: James Munroe and Company, 1837), 263.
6. Cesare Lombroso, *Criminal Man*, trans. Mary Gibson and Nicole Hahn Rafter (Durham, NC: Duke University Press, 2006), 51–3.
7. Cesare Lombroso, *After Death – What?* (Boston, MA: Small, Maynard and Company, 1909), 264.
8. Carolyn L. White, "The Fall of Big Hair," in *The Importance of British Material Culture to Historical Archaeologies of the Nineteenth Century*, ed. Alisdair Brooks (Lincoln: University of Nebraska Press, 2015), 175.
9. Jill Galvan, "The Victorian Post-Human: Transmission, Information, and the Séance," in *The Ashgate Companion to Nineteenth-Century Spiritualism and the Occult*, ed. Tatiana Kontou (London: Routledge, 2016), 92.
10. Pickering, *Cassell's Dictionary of Witchcraft*, 122.
11. William and Henry James, *Selected Letters*, eds. Ignas K. Skrupskelis and Elizabeth M. Berkeley (Charlottesville: University Press of Virginia, 1997), 244–5.
12. Thomas Hardy, *Return of the Native* (New York: Charles Scribner's Sons, 1909), 66.
13. Deborah Lutz, *The Brontë Cabinet* (New York: Norton & Company, 2015), 202.
14. Walter Scott, *Letters on Demonology and Witchcraft* (London: William Tegg, 1868), 166.
15. Abigail Bardi, "The Gypsy as Trope in Victorian and Modern Literature" (PhD thesis, University of Maryland, 2007), 118.
16. William Michael Rossetti, *Dante Gabriel Rossetti: His Family Letters With a Memoir*, Vol. 1 (London: Ellis, 1895), 5.
17. William Bell Scott, "Letter to Alice Boyd, 1866," in *The Correspondence of Dante Gabriel Rossetti: The Chelsea Years*, Vol. 5, ed. William E. Fredeman (Cambridge: D.S. Brewer, 2005), 402.
18. Caroline Franklin and Michael J. Franklin, "Victorian Gothic Poetry: The Corpse's [a] text," in *Victorian Gothic*, ed. Andrew Smith (Edinburgh: Edinburgh University Press, 2012), 72.

19. Joanna Pitman, *On Blondes* (London: Bloomsbury, 2003), 143.
20. Pitman, *On Blondes*, 143.
21. Christina Rossetti, *The Face of the Deep: A Devotional Commentary on the Apocalypse* (Bristol: Thoemmes Press, 2003), 271.
22. Kathy Psomiades, *Beauty's Body: Femininity and Representation in British Aestheticism* (Stanford, CA: Stanford University Press, 1997), 68.
23. William Hendry Stowell, *Eclectic Review*, Vol. 2 (London: Ward & Co., 1862), 496.
24. Christina Rossetti, "Goblin Market," in *The Norton Anthology of English Literature: The Victorian Age*, Vol. E, 9th edn., ed. Stephen Greenblatt (London: W.W. Norton & Company, 2012), 1496–508; line numbers given in main body of chapter.
25. Danu Forest, *Celtic Tree Magic: Ogham Lore and Druid Mysteries* (Woodbury: Llewellyn Publications, 2014), n.n.
26. Psomiades, *Beauty's Body*, 128.
27. Pickering, *Cassell's Dictionary of Witchcraft*, 122.
28. Galia Ofek, *Representations of Hair in Victorian Literature and Culture* (Aldershot: Ashgate, 2009), 7.
29. Dante Gabriel Rossetti, "Body's Beauty," in *The Norton Anthology of English Literature*, ed. Greenblatt, 1488, lines 1–4.
30. Dante Gabriel Rossetti, "Faust." Translation inscribed on frame of *Lady Lilith* taken from Met Museum Archive. Available online: http://www.metmuseum.org/art/collection/search/337500 (accessed February 27, 2017).
31. Christina Rossetti, "In An Artist's Studio," in *The Norton Anthology of English Literature*, ed. Greenblatt, 1493, l. 1.
32. Rossetti, *Dante Gabriel Rossetti*, 95.
33. Suzanne Maureen Waldman, *The Demon and the Damozel: Dynamics of Desire in the Works of Christina Rossetti and Dante Gabriel Rossetti* (Athens: Ohio University Press, 2008), 89.
34. Serena Trowbridge, *Christina Rossetti's Gothic* (London: Bloomsbury, 2013), 120.
35. Christina Rossetti, "The World," in *Christina Rossetti: Selected Poems*, ed. Dinah Roe (London: Penguin, 2008), 26, lines 1–4.
36. Anne DeLong, *Mesmerism, Medusa, and the Muse: The Romantic Discourse of Spontaneous Creativity* (Lanham, MD: Lexington Books, 2012), 102.
37. Silvana Coella, "Olfactory Ghosts: Michael Faber's *The Crimson Petal and the White*," in *Haunting and Spectrality in Neo-Victorian Fiction: Possessing the Past*, eds. Rosario Arias and Patricia Pulham (Basingstoke: Palgrave Macmillan, 2010), 85.
38. Mark Llewellyn, "Spectrality, S(p)ecularity, and Textuality: Or, Some Reflections in the Glass," in *Haunting and Spectrality in Neo-Victorian Fiction*, eds. Arias and Pulham, 30.
39. Paul Koudounaris, *Heavenly Bodies: Cult Treasures and Spectacular Saints from the Catacombs* (London: Thames and Hudson, 2013).
40. Laura Kilbride, "Byatt: Victorian Poets in Possession," *Cambridge Authors*. Available online: http://www.english.cam.ac.uk/cambridgeauthors/byatt-victorian-poets/ (accessed February 28, 2017).
41. A.S. Byatt, "In the Grip of Possession," *Independent*, February 2, 1995. Available online: http://www.independent.co.uk/arts-entertainment/in-the-grip-of-possession-1571141.html (accessed February 28, 2017).
42. A.S. Byatt, *Possession* (London: Vintage, 1991), 7.
43. DeLong, *Mesmerism, Medusa, and the Muse*, 102.
44. Byatt, *Possession*, 153.
45. Ibid., 63.

NOTES 173

46. Ibid., 258.
47. Ibid., 93.
48. Ibid., 333.
49. Ibid., 272.
50. *Rules and Regulations of the General Penitentiary Millbank* (London: The Philanthropic Society, 1825), 72.
51. Henry Mayhew and John Binny, *Criminal Prisons of London and Scenes of Prison Life* (London: Griffin, Bohn and Company, 1862), 273.
52. Sarah Waters, *Affinity* (London: Virago Press, 2007), 239.
53. Waters, *Affinity*, 239.
54. Ibid., 240.
55. Ibid., 258.
56. Ibid., 317.
57. Ibid., 275.
58. Ibid., 336.

Chapter Two

1. Elizabeth Cook (ed.), *John Keats* (Oxford: Oxford University Press, 1990).
2. Mary Shelley, *Frankenstein*, ed. Maurice Hindle (Harmondsworth: Penguin, 1985), 209.
3. Galia Ofek, *Representations of Hair in Victorian Literature and Culture* (Aldershot: Ashgate, 2009), 9.
4. Charles Dickens, *David Copperfield*, ed. Jerome H. Buckley (1850; New York: Norton, 1990), 12.
5. Susan P. Casteras, *Images of Victorian Womanhood in English Art* (Rutherford, NJ: Fairleigh Dickinson University Press, 1987), 136.
6. Charlotte Brontë, *Shirley* (1849; Ware: Wordsworth, 1993), 65.
7. Celia Brayfield, "A Lifetime Haircut," *The Times*, July 20, 2004, 11.
8. Ofek, *Representations of Hair*, 70–7.
9. Ibid., 63, 89.
10. The pattern is visible everywhere we look in Victorian fiction. To be dark or fair, or to make finer distinctions between terms such as sandy, auburn, and red, meant something about character and temperament. To take just the example of red hair, we find it is typically the mark of villainy, aggression, but also of sexual threat or deviance in both males and females. Figures such as Fagin, Uriah Heep, Lizzie Siddal, and Swinburne come to mind. In *Barchester Towers* (1857) the ambitious and unscrupulous low-churchman Obadiah Slope has hair which "is lank and of a dull pale reddish hue. It is always formed into three straight, lumpy masses, each brushed with admirable precision and cemented with much grease" (Anthony Trollope, *Barchester Towers* [1857; Ware: Wordsworth, 1994], 24). The grease adds to his general oiliness. Famously in James's *The Turn of the Screw* (1898), which I also discuss toward the end of this chapter, Peter Quint's threatening masculinity is encoded through his "red hair, very red, close-curling, and [...] rather queer whiskers that are as red as his hair" (Henry James, *The Turn of the Screw and the Aspern Papers*, ed. Anthony Curtis [1907–1909; Harmondsworth: Penguin, 1986], 173). The governess tells Mrs. Grose "he's like nobody"—the irony being that Quint is exactly like any other supposedly aggressive red-haired male in fiction.
11. Alexander Rowland, *A Practical and Philosophical Treatise on the Human Hair* (London: J. Evans & Son, 1814), 5.

12. Ibid., 7.
13. Ibid., 8.
14. Leonard De Vries, *Victorian Advertisements* (London: John Murray, 1968), 34.
15. Ibid., 52.
16. Victoria Sherrow, *Encyclopedia of Hair: A Cultural History* (Westport, CT: Greenwood Press, 2006), 387.
17. Ofek notes that "the prospering hair trade included the following articles in 1867: hair jewellery, hair-made jewellery, wigs and toupees, braids, curls, frizettes, bows, false chignons, fronts, nets, ornamental hair partings, curling sticks, crimping irons, creams, soaps, oils, combs, brushes, pins, silver and gold powders and diadems" (Ofek, *Representations of Hair*, 22).
18. Louisa May Alcott, *Little Women*, ed. Valerie Alderson (1869; Oxford: Oxford University Press, 2008), 7.
19. Ibid., 159.
20. Ibid., 160.
21. De Vries, *Victorian Advertisements*, 53.
22. Charles Dickens, *Dombey and Son* (1848; Harmondsworth: Penguin, 2010), 71.
23. Ofek, *Representations of Hair*, 105.
24. See Judith Butler, "Performative Acts and Gender Constitution," *Theatre Journal* 40, no. 4 (December 1988): 519–31.
25. William Makepeace Thackeray, *Vanity Fair*, ed. Peter Shillingsburg (1848; New York: Norton, 1994), 508.
26. Ibid., 618. In the manuscript Thackeray had originally referred to Lady and Lord Carabas—in reference to the aristocrat in Perrault's *Puss in Boots* (1816)—which a compositor, unaware of the allusion, of the revised edition corrected to Bareacres. I have also made the change here for the sake of intelligibility.
27. "The Fool's Head of Hair," *Punch*, July 25, 1857, 40.
28. Ibid.
29. Mark Twain, *A Connecticut Yankee in King Arthur's Court*, ed. M. Thomas Inge (1889; Oxford: Oxford University Press, 2008), 133.
30. Thackeray, *Vanity Fair*, 279.
31. Charles Dickens, *Little Dorrit* (1857; Harmondsworth: Penguin, 1994), 238.
32. Dickens, *David Copperfield*, 68–9.
33. See John Strachan, *Advertising and Satirical Culture in the Romantic Period* (Cambridge: Cambridge University Press, 2007), 204–25.
34. Elizabeth Gaskell, *Cranford/Cousin Phillis*, ed. Peter Keating (1853; Harmondsworth: Penguin, 1986), 164.
35. Ibid., 174, 55.
36. Charles Dickens, *Our Mutual Friend*, ed. Stephen Gill (1865; Harmondsworth: Penguin, 1977), 315.
37. Ibid., 475.
38. Ibid., 625.
39. Ibid., 485. A cartoon from *Punch* of September 19, 1857, made the same comic point about the amusement to be found in the adolescent mustache.
40. Charles Dickens, *Nicholas Nickleby*, intro. Tim Cook (1839; Ware: Wordsworth, 1995), 122–3.
41. Ibid., 758.

42. William Makepeace Thackeray, *The Newcomes* (1855; London: Macmillan and Co., 1901), 80.
43. Ibid., 442.
44. Sherrow, *Encyclopedia of Hair*, 279.
45. *The Favorite* (London: Partridge, Oakey, and Co., 1854), 44.
46. See *Punch*, April 2, 1851, 185.
47. Thomas S. Gowing, *The Philosophy of Beards* (1854; London: The British Library, 2014), 14, 26.
48. Ibid., 25. The opposite was true of earlier periods, as Rebecca M. Herzig notes, "an 'unblemished' face was a primary standard of physical beauty in the eighteenth century, an achievement distinguished, in part, by upper lips and temples free of visible fuzz." Herzig, *Plucked: A History of Hair Removal* (New York: New York University Press, 2015), 35.
49. Gowing, *The Philosophy of Beards*, 16–17. A similar argument was advanced by Henry Morley in *Household Words* in August 1853: "A protection of considerable importance is provided in the same way by the hair of the face to a large and important knot of nerves that lies under the skin near the angle of the lower jaw, somewhere about the point of junction between the whiskers and the beard. Man is born to work out of doors and in all weathers, for his bread; woman was created for duties of another kind, which do not involve constant exposure to sun, wind, and rain. Therefore man only goes abroad whiskered and bearded, with his face muffled by nature in a way that shields every sensitive part alike from wind, rain, heat, or frost, with a perfection that could be equaled by no muffler of his own devising" (Henry Morley, "Why Shave?" *Household Words* 7, no. 177 [August 13, 1853]: 560–3, 561).
50. See also Gowing, who cites a letter from the men working on the Scottish Central Railway who have been encouraged "to cultivate the growth of their beards" (*The Philosophy of Beards*, 18).
51. Ibid., 24.
52. H. Rider Haggard, *She*, ed. Daniel Karlin (1887; Oxford: Oxford University Press, 2008), 11.
53. Ibid., 70.
54. Thackeray, *Vanity Fair*, 316–18.
55. Ofek, *Representations of Hair*, 34.
56. Andrew H. Miller, *Novels Behind Glass: Commodity Culture and Victorian Narrative* (Cambridge: Cambridge University Press, 1995), 17.
57. Richard Corson, *Fashions in Hair: The First Five Thousand Years* (London: Peter Owen, 1965), 474.
58. Mary Elizabeth Braddon, *Lady Audley's Secret*, ed. David Skilton (1867; Oxford: Oxford University Press, 1998), 336.
59. Ibid., 58.
60. Orson Squire Fowler, *The Practical Phrenologist* (New York: Mrs. O.S. Fowler, 1869), 56. Fowler notes, for example, that "straight, even, smooth, and glossy hair indicates strength, harmony, and evenness of character, and hearty, whole-souled affections, as well as a clear head and superior talents; while stiff, straight, black hair and beard indicate a coarse, strong, rigid, straightforward character" (56). He even goes so far as to suggest the types of employment best suited to people of different hair types. See also Henry Frith, *How to Read Character in Features, Forms, and Faces: Outlines of Physiognomy* (London: Ward, Lock and Co., 1891), 5.

61. Elizabeth Gaskell, *North and South* (1855; Ware: Wordsworth, 1994), 157.
62. Ibid., 31, 48.
63. Ibid., 147.
64. Ofek, *Representations of Hair*, 180.

Chapter Three

1. Geitel Winakor, "Economics and Clothing," in *The Berg Companion to Fashion*, ed. Valerie Steele (New York: Berg, 2010), 243.
2. Penny Storm, *Functions of Dress: Tool of Culture and the Individual* (Englewood Cliffs, NJ: Prentice-Hall, 1987), 38.
3. Women, men, and children enslaved in the United States lived in cruelty, were mistreated on a daily basis, and worked dangerous jobs with poor medical care. Conditions were not much better in the early years of the twentieth century and even for those African Americans who gained financial freedom living conditions were harsh under Jim Crow laws.
4. Steven Watson, *The Harlem Renaissance: Hub of African-American Culture, 1920–1930* (New York: Pantheon Books, 1995).
5. Patricia Warner and Debra Parker, "Slave Clothing and Textiles in North Carolina, 1775–1830," in *African American Dress and Adornment: A Cultural Perspective*, eds. B.M. Starke, L.O. Holoman, and B.K. Nordquist (Dubuque, IA: Kendall/Hunt Publishing, Co., 1990), 84.
6. Patricia Hunt-Hurst, "'Round Homespun Coat & Pantaloons of the Same': Slave Clothing as Reflected in Fugitive Slave Advertisements in Antebellum Georgia," *The Georgia Historical Quarterly* 83, no. 4 (Winter 1999): 727–40.
7. Quoted in Patricia K. Hunt, "The Struggle to Achieve Individual Expression through Clothing and Adornment: African American Women Under and After Slavery," in *Discovering the Women in Slavery: Emancipating Perspectives on the American Past*, ed. Patricia Morton (Athens: University of Georgia Press, 1996), 227–40.
8. Ibid.
9. Joan L. Severa, *Dressed for the Photographer: Ordinary Americans and Fashion, 1840–1900* (Kent, OH: Kent State University Press, 1995), 10.
10. Shane White and Graham White, "Slave Hair and African American Culture in the Eighteenth and Nineteenth Centuries," *The Journal of Southern History* 61, no. 1 (February 1995): 70.
11. Shane White and Graham White, *Stylin': African American Expressive Culture from Its Beginnings to the Zoot Suit* (London: Cornell University Press, 1998), 38.
12. Severa, *Dressed for the Photographer*, 61, 218, 281.
13. Ibid., 69.
14. Gerilyn Tandberg, "Decoration and Decorum: Accessories of Nineteenth Century Louisiana Women," *Southern Historical Quarterly: A Journal of the Arts in the South* 27, no. 1 (Fall 1998): 8–31. Tandberg, "Decoration and Decorum," 14.
15. "Fashions for May," *Lady's National Magazine*, May 1844, 179.
16. "Fashions for March," *Peterson's Magazine*, March 1851, 168.
17. Linda Baumgarten, "'Clothes for the People' Slave Clothing in Early Virginia," *Journal of Early Southern Decorative Arts* 14, no. 2 (November 1988): 38.
18. Tandberg, "Decoration and Decorum," 14.
19. "Turbans and Head-dresses," *The Lady's*, March 1846, 66.

20. Helen Bradley Greibel, "The African American Woman's Headwrap: Unwinding the Symbols," in *Dress and Identity*, eds. Mary Ellen Roach-Higgins, Joanne B. Eicher, and Kim K.P. Johnson (New York: Fairchild Publications, 1995), 450.
21. Dominique Cocuzza, "The Dress of Free Women of Color in New Orleans: 1780–1840," *Dress* 27 (2000): 81.
22. Ibid.
23. Ibid.
24. Ibid.
25. Greibel, "The African American Woman's Headwrap," 445.
26. Quoted in Patricia Hunt, "Swathed in Cloth: The Headwraps of Some African American Women in Georgia and South Carolina During the Late Nineteenth and Early Twentieth Centuries," *Dress* 25 (1994): 30; Annie Harper, *Annie Harper's Journal: A Southern Mother's Legacy* (Denton, TX: Flower Mound Writing Company, 1983): 33.
27. Nehemiah D.D. Adams, *A South-side View of Slavery: Or, Three Months at the South in 1854* (Boston, MA: T.R. Marvin, Sanborn, Carter and Bazin, 1855), 32.
28. Hunt, "Swathed in Cloth."
29. Quoted in Charles Joyner, *Down by the Riverside: A South Carolina Slave Community* (Chicago: University of Illinois Press, 1984), 107–8.
30. Quoted in Leon Stone Bryan, Jr., "Slavery on a PeeDee River Rice Plantation, 1825–1865" (MA thesis, Johns Hopkins University, 1963).
31. Warner and Parker, "Slave Clothing and Textiles," 86.
32. Hunt-Hurst, "'Round Homespun Coat & Pantaloons of the Same'".
33. For the most part clothing between 1800 and 1865 was stitched by hand. Some plantations had sewing machines in the 1850s but, typically, purchased ready-made clothing was stitched by hand and made in general sizes meant to be loose-fitting rather than fitted.
34. Baumgarten, "Clothes for the People," 39.
35. Gerilyn Tandberg, "Field Hand Clothing in Louisiana and Mississippi During the Ante-Bellum Period," *Dress* 6 (1980): 90.
36. On some plantations cloth was provided instead of clothing. In that case, enslaved women often did sewing after work in the fields. See Hunt-Hurst, "'Round Homespun Coat & Pantaloons of the Same'."
37. *Winyaw Intelligencer*, January 30, 1819. Fugitive slave notices also known as runaway slave advertisements were posted in newspapers to find runaway slaves. The ads included the name, age, sex, and occupation of the enslaved person as well as their clothing.
38. Severa, *Dressed for the Photographer*, 61.
39. Ibid.
40. Ibid., 281.
41. Ibid., 125.
42. Ibid.
43. Ibid., 61.
44. Ibid., 123.
45. Tandberg, "Field Hand Clothing," 92.
46. Ibid., 98.
47. Ibid.
48. Helen Bradley Foster, "African American Jewellery Before the Civil War," in *Beads and Bead Makers: Gender, Material Culture and Meaning*, eds. Lidia D. Sciama and Joanne B. Eicher (New York: Berg, 1998): 177–92.

49. Tandberg, "Decoration and Decorum," 24.
50. Foster, "African American Jewellery," 180.
51. Eugene D. Genovese, *Roll Jordon Roll* (New York: Pantheon Books, 1972).
52. White and White, *Stylin*, 10.
53. Ibid., 21.
54. Joyner, *Down by the Riverside*, 107.
55. White and White, *Stylin*, 23.
56. Ibid.
57. Ibid.
58. Charlotte Forten, "Life on the Sea Islands, Part I," *The Atlantic Monthly: A Magazine of Literature, Art, and Politics* 13 (May 1864): 588. Port Royal was one of the South Carolina Sea Islands. The US Navy occupied Port Royal after its victory at the Battle of Port Royal on November 7, 1861. The islands remained in Union hands until the end of the war. The enslaved people on the island were not "legally considered free" so they were considered abandoned and "contraband of war." On January 1, 1863, President Abraham Lincoln's Emancipation Proclamation went into effect for the contrabands of the Sea Islands; thereafter they were "freedmen." Available online: http://sc150civilwar.palmettohistory.org (accessed November 6, 2015).
59. Forten, "Life on the Sea Islands," 589.
60. Ibid., 590.
61. John Hope Franklin, *From Slavery to Freedom: A History of Negro Americans* (New York: Alfred A. Knopf, 1980).
62. Sara Beth Brubacher, "African American Working Class Clothing as Photographed by William E. Wilson and Robert E. Williams 1872 to 1898" (MS thesis, University of Georgia, 2002), 38.
63. Tandberg, "Decoration and Decorum," 29.
64. Severa, *Dressed for the Photographer*, 333; Brubacher, "African American Working Class," 40.
65. Quoted in Hunt, "Swathed in Cloth," 30.
66. Ibid.
67. Ibid.
68. Ibid., 31.
69. Quoted in Hunt, "The Struggle to Achieve Individual Expression through Clothing and Adornment," 233.
70. Griebel, "The African American Woman's Headwrap," 445.
71. Brubacher, "African American Working Class," 41.
72. Ibid., 58.
73. *The Afro-American*, May 13, 1896, no pagination.
74. *The Afro American*, May 16, 1896, no pagination.
75. "Brilliantine," in *American Fabrics Encyclopedia of Textiles* (Englewood Cliffs, NJ: Prentice Hall, 1972), 523.
76. *The Atlanta Independent*, July 6, 1907.
77. *The Afro-American*, May 16, 1896, no pagination.
78. *The Afro-American*, November 2, 1895, no pagination.
79. Ibid., 184.
80. Ibid., 185.
81. Ibid., 171.
82. Jane Farrell-Beck and Jean Parsons, *20th Century Dress in the United States* (New York: Fairchild, 2007), 21.

83. Ibid., 22.
84. White and White, *Stylin*, 188.
85. Ibid.
86. Ibid., 174.
87. *The Atlanta Independent*, October 12, 1907. Auburn Ave was a major retailing and business center for the African American community living in Atlanta, Georgia, in the early twentieth century.
88. *The Atlanta Independent*, May 4, 1904.
89. *The Afro-American*, October 1896.
90. Mme. Rumford, "The Prevailing Styles for Summer," *The Coloured American Magazine*, June 1901.
91. Patricia K. Hunt and Lucy R. Sibley, "African American Women's Dress in Georgia, 1890–1914: A Photographic Examination," *Clothing and Textiles Research Journal* (Winter 1994): 20–6.
92. Quoted in Hunt and Sibley, *African American Women's Dress*, 25.

Chapter Four

1. Maria Josepha, Lady Stanley, cited in Richard Corson, *Fashions in Hair: The First Five Thousand Years* (London: Peter Owen, 1965), 463.
2. Ibid.
3. (1) A head band of any suitable material used for keeping the headdress in position, binding the hair, or as an ornament. (2) In the eighteenth century, a hair net to cover the head at night. (3) An artificial front of hair. (4) A fringe of hair.
4. Eric Hobsbawm, *Industry and Empire from 1750 to the Present Day* (London: Penguin Books, 1999), 11.
5. Victoria Sherrow, *Encyclopedia of Hair: A Cultural History* (Westport, CT: Greenwood Press, 2006), 89–90.
6. Paul Du Gay, ed., *Doing Cultural Studies: The Story of the Sony Walkman* (London: Sage, 1997).
7. Stuart Hall, "The West and the Rest: Discourse and Power," in *Formations of Modernity*, eds. Stuart Hall and Bram Gieben (Cambridge: Polity, 1992), 277.
8. Hall, "The West and the Rest," 277.
9. Galia Ofek, *Representations of Hair in Victorian Literature and Culture* (Farnham: Ashgate, 2009); Helen Sheumaker, *Love Entwined: the Curious History of Hairwork in America* (Philadelphia: University of Pennsylvania Press, 2007).
10. Corson, *Fashions in Hair*, 480.
11. Louisa May Alcott, *Little Women* (1868; London: Vintage, 2008); Thomas Hardy, *The Woodlanders* (1886–1887; London: Penguin Classics, 1998).
12. Hardy, *The Woodlanders*, 12–13.
13. Alcott, *Little Women*, 181.
14. Caroline Cox, *Good Hair Days: A History of British Hairstyling* (London: Quartet Books, 1999), 24.
15. Alexander Rowland, *The Human Hair, Popularly and Physiologically Considered with Special Reference to its Preservation, Improvement and Adornment, and the Various Modes of its Decoration in All Countries* (London: Piper, Brothers & Co., 1853), 157.
16. Adolphus T. Trollope, *A Summer In Brittany*, ed. Frances Trollope (London: Henry Colburn, 1840), 323.

17. Corson, *Fashions in Hair*, 478.
18. Rowland, *The Human Hair*, 159.
19. Trollope, *A Summer In* Brittany, 323.
20. Corson, *Fashions in Hair*, 477.
21. Ibid., 485.
22. Ibid., 477.
23. Rowland, *The Human Hair*, 161.
24. Ibid., 159.
25. Ofek, *Representations of Hair in Victorian Literature and Culture*, 22.
26. Anon., *The Art of Beauty* (London: D.S. Maurice, 1824), 309.
27. Georgine de Courtais, *Women's Hats, Headdresses and Hairstyles* (Mineola, NY: Dover Publications, 1973), 124.
28. Leonore Davidoff, *Worlds Between: Historical Perspectives on Gender and Class* (Cambridge: Cambridge University Press, 1995).
29. Sarah Cheang, "Roots: Hair and Race," in *Hair: Styling, Culture and Fashion*, eds. Geraldine Biddle-Perry and Sarah Cheang (London: Bloomsbury, 2013), 28.
30. *Hairdressers' Weekly Journal*, July 8, 1882, 151.
31. Robert Tomes, *The Bazar Book of Decorum* (New York: Harper & Brothers, 1870), 32–3.
32. Sheumaker, *Love Entwined*, 156.
33. Cox, *Good Hair Days*, 24.
34. "Artificial Hair," *The Ladies' Treasury*, October 1, 1868, 53–4.
35. "Hair," *The Ladies' Gazette of Fashion*, February 1875, 22.
36. Hall, "The West and the Rest."
37. Ofek, *Representations of Hair in Victorian Literature and Culture*, 9.
38. Corson, *Fashions in Hair*; de Courtais, *Women's Hats, Headdresses and Hairstyles*.
39. Margaret Beetham, *A Magazine of Her Own? Domesticity and Desire in the Woman's Magazine, 1800–1914* (London: Routledge, 1996).
40. *Young Ladies' Journal*, 1873, n.p.
41. *Godey's Lady's Book*, cited in de Courtais, *Women's Hats, Headdresses and Hairstyles*, 104.
42. Alexander Rowland, *An Essay on the Cultivation and Improvement of the Human Hair with Remarks on the Virtues of the Macassar Oil* (London: J. Stratford, 1809), 25.
43. Tomes, *The Bazar Book of Decorum*, 33.
44. Isabel Mallon, *Ladies' Home Journal*, July, 1892, 32.
45. "A Chat About Hair and Hair Dyeing," in *Leisure Hour: A Family Journal of Instruction and Recreation* 1 (March 1867): 142.
46. Ibid., 142.
47. Ibid.
48. Corson, *Fashions in Hair*, 467.
49. "Isobel," in *The Art of Beauty: A Book for Women and Girls* (London: C.A. Parson, 1899), 24.
50. Lori Anne Loeb, *Consuming Angels: Advertising and Victorian Women* (Oxford: Oxford University Press, 1994), 5.
51. These included London 1851; New York 1853; Paris 1855; London 1862; Paris 1867; Vienna 1873; Philadelphia 1876; Paris 1876; Paris 1878; Paris 1889; Chicago 1893; Paris 1900. Judith Flanders, *Consuming Passions: Leisure and Pleasure in Victorian Britain* (London: Harper Press, 2006).

NOTES

52. *Official and Descriptive Catalogue of the Great Exhibition of the Works of Industry of All Nations 1851*, Vol. 2, 122.
53. Ibid., 113.
54. Corson, *Fashions in Hair*, 472.
55. Sherrow, *Encyclopaedia of Hair*, 147.
56. *Gleason's Pictorial Drawing-Room Companion*, October 8, 1853, 233.
57. *Official Catalogue of the New York Exhibition of the Industry of all Nations*, 1853, 79.
58. *Gleason's Pictorial Drawing-Room Companion*, 233.
59. Paris Universal Exhibition, 1855. Catalogue of the works exhibited in the British section of the exhibition, in French and English, together with exhibitors' prospectuses, prices, etc., n.p.
60. Ibid., 65.
61. Ibid., n.p.
62. Ibid., 58.
63. Ofek, *Representations of Hair in Victorian Literature and Culture*, 41.
64. Loeb, *Consuming Angels*, 121.
65. Penny Howell Jolly, "The Ideal Woman," in *Hair: Untangling a Social History*, ed. Penny Howell Jolly (Saratoga Springs, NY: The Frances Young Tang Teaching Museum and Art Gallery at Skidmore College, 2004), 51.
66. Howell Jolly, "The Ideal Woman," 51–2.
67. *The Art of Beauty*, 1825, 315.
68. Rowland, *An Essay on the Cultivation and Improvement of the Human Hair with Remarks on the Virtues of Macassar Oil*, 23.
69. Ibid., 24.
70. Ibid., 25–6.
71. Ibid., 27–8.
72. Ibid., 26.
73. Ibid.
74. Ibid., 23.
75. Ibid., 25.
76. General De Marbot, *The Memoirs of the General de Marbot* (1892), trans. Oliver C. Colt (2000), n.p. Available online: https://archive.org/details/thememoirsofgene02401gut (accessed 11 November 2015).
77. Ibid., n.p.
78. Ibid., n.p.
79. Christopher Oldstone-Moore, "The Beard Movement in Victorian Britain," *Victorian Studies* 48, no. 1 (2005): 12.
80. Ibid., 7.
81. Ibid., 8.
82. Rowland, *The Human Hair*, 124.
83. Sherrow, *Encyclopaedia of Hair*, 59
84. Robert Southey, *The Doctor* (London: Longman 1834/47), 275. Available online: https://archive.org/details/doctorc01soutgoog (accessed 14 December 2015).
85. Oldstone-Moore, "The Beard Movement in Victorian Britain," 29.
86. Ibid., 29.
87. Corson, *Fashions in Hair*, 567.
88. Oldstone-Moore, "The Beard Movement in Victorian Britain," 9–10.
89. King Camp Gillette, in Gordon McKibben, *Cutting Edge: Gillette's Journey to Global Leadership* (Boston, MA: Harvard Business School Press, 1998), 5.

90. McKibben, *Cutting Edge*.
91. Sheumaker, *Love Entwined*, 33.
92. Beetham, *A Magazine of Her Own?*, 32.
93. Ibid., 34.
94. Thorstein Veblen, *The Theory of the Leisure Class: An Economic Study* (1899; Amherst, NY: Prometheus Books, 1998).
95. Sheumaker, *Love Entwined*, 31.
96. Ibid., 59.
97. Sonia Solicari, "Selling Sentiment: The Commodification of Emotion in Victorian Visual Culture," *19: Interdisciplinary Studies in the Long Nineteenth Century* 4 (2007): 1.
98. Sheumaker, *Love Entwined*, 31–2.
99. Alexanna Speight, *The Lock of Hair: Its History, Ancient and Modern, Natural and Artistic, With the Art of Working in Hair* (London: A. Goubard, 1871), n.p.
100. Ibid., 88.
101. A.P.P., "Hairwork as a Highly Remunerative Employment for Girls," *The Girl's Own Paper*, 1890, 70. Available online: http://www.victorianvoices.net/ARTICLES/GOP/Work/1900-Hairwork.pdf (accessed 23 October 2015).
102. Ibid., 70.
103. Ibid., 141.
104. Ibid.
105. Ibid., 151.
106. Sheumaker, *Love Entwined*, 88.
107. Ibid., 89.
108. Ibid., 156.
109. Ibid., 156–7.
110. Elaine Showalter, *Sexual Anarchy: Gender and Culture at the Fin del Siècle* (London: Bloomsbury, 1991), 38–9.
111. Eric Hobsbawm, *The Age of Empire 1875–1914* (London: Abacus, 2007), 204–5.
112. Hobsbawm, *The Age of Empire*, 217.
113. Corson, *Fashions in Hair*, 605.
114. Ibid., 485–7.
115. Ibid., 605–6.
116. Steven Zdatny, ed., *Hairstyles and Fashion: A Hairdresser's History of Paris, 1910–1920* (Oxford: Berg, 1999), 42.
117. Mary Trasko, *Daring Do's: A History of Extraordinary Hair* (Paris: Flammarion, 1994), 107.
118. Charles Panati, *Extraordinary Origins of Everyday Things* (New York: Harper & Row, 1987), 235–6.
119. Ingrid Banks, *Hair Matters: Beauty, Power and Black Women's Consciousness* (London: New York University Press, 2000); Noliwe M. Rooks, *Hair Raising: Beauty, Culture and African American Women* (London: Rutgers University Press, 2000); Juliette Harris and Pamela Johnson, eds., *Tenderheaded: A Comb-Bending Collection of Hair Stories* (London: Washington Square Press, 2001).
120. Kobena Mercer, "Black Hair/Style Politics," *New Formations*, 3 (1987): 37.
121. Hall, "The West and the Rest"; Cheang, "Roots: Hair and Race."
122. Sherrow, *Encyclopaedia of Hair*, 17.
123. Willie Morrow, "A Short History of Early Hair Straightening," in Harris and Johnson, *Tenderheaded*, 125.

124. Morrow, "A Short History," 125.
125. Rooks, *Hair Raising*, 25. The different meanings associated with head coverings are discussed by Harris and Johnson, *Tenderheaded*, 133–52.
126. Ibid., 25.
127. Sherrow, *Encyclopaedia of Hair*, 17.
128. Ibid., 126.
129. Rooks, *Hair Raising*, 31.
130. Ibid., 42.
131. Ibid., 43.
132. Ibid., 51.
133. Ibid., 56.
134. Ibid., 65.
135. Juliet E.K. Walker, *The History of Black Business in America: To 1865*. Vol. 1: *Capitalism, Race, Entrepreneurship* (Chapel Hill: University of North Carolina Press, 2010), 183.
136. Walker, *The History of Black Business in America*, 183.
137. Harris and Johnson, *Tenderheaded*, 143–4.
138. Ibid., 144.
139. Rooks, *Hair Raising*, 25.

Chapter Five

1. "False Hair: Where it Comes From," *The London Review* (September 23, 1863): 328–30, 330.
2. "Human Hair Supplies," *The Examiner*, November 28, 1874, 1295–6, 1295.
3. Katharina Boehm, *Bodies and Things in Nineteenth-Century Literature and Culture* (Basingstoke: Palgrave Macmillan, 2012), 4.
4. Mary Douglas, *Purity and Danger: An Analysis of Concept of Pollution and Taboo* (London: Routledge, 2002), xiv, 2.
5. Ibid., 44.
6. Sabine Schulting, *Dirt in Victorian Literature and Culture: Writing Materiality* (London: Routledge, 2016), 6.
7. Douglas, *Purity and Danger*, 44.
8. Schulting, *Dirt in Victorian Literature and Culture*, 6.
9. Ian Hodder, *Entangled: An Archaeology of the Relationships between Humans and Things* (Chichester: Wiley-Blackwell, 2012), 17, 33.
10. See book 1, chapter 7 of George Eliot's *The Mill on the Floss*, ed. Oliver Lovesey (1860; Peterborough: Broadview Press, 2007) and vol. 1, chapter 2 of Mary Braddon's *Aurora Floyd*, eds. Richard Nemesvari and Lisa Surridge (1863; Peterborough: Broadview Press, 1998).
11. Galia Ofek, *Representations of Hair in Victorian Literature and Culture* (Farnham: Ashgate Publishing, 2009), 34.
12. H.V., "The Trade in Locks," *London Society* (June 1869): 547–52, 550.
13. Bill Brown, *A Sense of Things: the Object Matter of American Literature* (Chicago: University of Chicago Press, 2003), 78.
14. Hodder, *Entangled*, 3, 6.
15. Ibid., 51.
16. "False Hair," *The Hairdresser's Journal*, April 1863, 21–3, 22.

17. Ibid., 22–3.
18. "False Hair," *The Hairdresser's Journal*, May 1863, 32–4, 33.
19. "Several Heads of Hair," *Household Words* 9 (March 4, 1854): 61–4, 62.
20. Andrew Wynter, "Ladies' Tresses," *Peeps into the Human Hive*. 2 vols. (London: Chapman and Hall, 1874, Vol. 2, 116–23, 116.
21. "The Commerce in Human Hair," *The Times*, October 10, 1868, 4.
22. "False Hair," *Hairdressers' Journal*, June 1863, 43–5, 45.
23. "Something New," *All the Year Round* 19 (October 27, 1877): 277–9, 278.
24. "Human Hair," *The London Reader*, October 6, 1877, 549.
25. "Artificial Hair," *Penny Illustrated Paper*, August 15, 1868, 103, rpt. from *Daily News*.
26. G. Vigier La Fosse, untitled article, rpt. in *Hairdressers' Journal*, December 1863, 120.
27. Ibid.
28. "Coiffure by M. Alexandre Charèntre," *Hairdressers' Journal*, June 1863, 43.
29. "Description of the English Plate," *Hairdressers' Journal*, April 1863, 19–20, 20.
30. The term "on foot" designates that the hair was purchased from a living source and cut from the head.
31. "Artificial Hair," 103.
32. "Domestic Philosophy: Servants and Mistresses," *London Society* 3, no. 2 (February 1863): 120–7, 127.
33. "Miscellaneous," *The London Reader*, May 28, 1887, 119.
34. "High Art in Hair," *The Examiner*, February 21, 1880, 232.
35. "The False Hair: A Tale," *Chambers's Edinburgh Journal* 450 (August 14, 1852): 98–102, 99.
36. "The Lock of Hair," rev. of *The Lock of Hair* by A. Speight. *The Saturday Review*, June 17, 1871, 782–2, 782.
37. Thomas Adolphus Trollope, *A Summer in Britany*, ed. France Trollope (London: Henry Colburn, Publisher, 1840), 323.
38. "False Hair," *Hairdressers' Journal*, May 1863, 32–4, 32. Emphasis in original. A similar view is offered by Andrew Wynter: "So distinct are the various nations of the earth, that even the hair of the inhabitants of different countries can be easily distinguished by the manufacturer. Where the heads of hair are made to resemble each other externally, the workmen can, by the odour, detect the products of each country" (Wynter, "Chignons and Hair Fashions," *Curiosities of Toil and Other Papers* [London: Chapman and Hall, 1870], 202–8, 203).
39. Frederick Marshall, "False Hair," *Bentley's Miscellany* 53 (January 1863): 537–41, 538.
40. Trollope, *Summer in Brittany*, 307, 310.
41. Ofek, *Representations of Hair*, 3.
42. See Ariel Beaujot, *Victorian Fashion Accessories* (London: Bloomsbury, 2012), 139; and Carol Rifelj, *Coiffures: Hair in Nineteenth-Century French Literature and Culture* (Newark: University of Delaware Press, 2010), 83–118.
43. Ofek, *Representations of Hair*, 27.
44. Ibid., 44.
45. "A Hair-Dressing Contest," *Penny Illustrated Paper*, July 13, 1867, 31.
46. "Only a Woman's Hair," *The Speaker*, July 31, 1897, 128–9, 129.
47. Tammy Whitlock, *Crime, Gender and Consumer Culture in Nineteenth-Century England* (Farnham: Ashgate Publishing, 2005), 72.

NOTES

185

48. Andrew Wynter, "Diseases of the Human Hair," *Quarterly Review*, March 1853, 305–28, 310.
49. Marshall, "False Hair," 538.
50. Ofek, *Representations of Hair*, 130.
51. "Extraordinary Robbery of Human Hair," *Birmingham Daily Post*, November 29, 1882, 5.
52. "The False Hair: A Tale," 99.
53. Ibid.
54. Babette Bärbel Tischleder, *The Literary Life of Things: Case Studies in American Fiction* (Frankfurt: Campus Verlag, 2014), 23–4.
55. "Fashions in Hair and Head-Dresses," *Fraser's Magazine*, September 1870, 322–31, 331.
56. "News of the Day," *Birmingham Daily Post*, January 17, 1872, 4.
57. "Chignonlogy," *The London Review* (February 23, 1867): 227–8, 227.
58. "Fashions in Hair and Head-Dresses," 329.
59. "The First Coiffure of His Age," *Chambers's Journal* (March 27, 1869): 193–8, 195.
60. Ibid., 196.
61. Ibid.
62. Ibid., 197.
63. "False Hair," *Hairdressers' Journal*, June 1863, 43–5, 44.
64. "False Hair: Where it Comes From," 329.
65. Paul Knepper, *The Invention of International Crime: A Global Issue in the Making, 1881–1914* (Basingstoke: Palgrave Macmillan, 2010), 64.
66. Elizabeth Fry, *Observations on the Visiting, Superintendence, and Government, of Female Prisoners* (London: John and Arthur Arch, 1827), 61.
67. Frederick William Robinson, *Female Life in Prison. By a Prison Matron*. 2 vols. (London: Hurst and Blackett, 1862), Vol. 1, 12–13, 16–17.
68. "False Hair: Where it Comes From," 329.
69. Lucia Zedner, *Women, Crime and Custody in Victorian England* (Oxford: Clarendon Press, 1991), 169.
70. In 1868 a correspondent for *The Times* acknowledged that "Inasmuch as human hair of any fine quality is worth four or five times as much per ounce as silver, the temptation to rob the dead of this particular ornament is sufficient to make us uneasy on this score" ("The Commerce in Human Hair," 4).
71. "Human Hair," 549.
72. "Human Hair Supplies," 1925.
73. "Something New," 278.
74. "Dangers of 'Chignons'," *The Lancet*, rpt. in *Littell's Living Age* 93 (April 6, 1867): 64.
75. "[Untitled]," *Daily Telegraph*, rpt. in *Littell's Living Age* 93 (April 6, 1867): 64.
76. Ibid.
77. Ibid. The gregarine thesis was debunked by Dr. Tilbury Fox who demonstrated that the parasites were actually a form of vegetable fungus, thus giving rise to the term "chignon fungus." See Tilbury Fox, "The Chignon Fungus," *The American Naturalist*, September 1867, 379–86.
78. "Artificial Hair," 103.
79. Ibid.
80. H.V., "The Trade in Locks," 551.
81. Ibid.

82. "[Untitled]," *Daily Telegraph*, 64.
83. Ofek, *Representations of Hair*, 35.
84. "Peeps into the Human Hive," rev. of *Peeps into the Human Hive* by Andrew Wynter. *The Saturday Review*, January 31, 1874, 151–2, 152.
85. Alison Bashford, *Purity and Pollution: Gender, Embodiment and Victorian Medicine* (Basingstoke: Macmillan Press, 2000), xii.

Chapter Six

1. Brothers Grimm, "Rapunzel," in *The Complete First Edition: The Original Folk and Fairy Tales of The Brothers Grimm*, ed. Jack Zipes (Princeton: Princeton University Press, 2016), 38.
2. Ibid., 39.
3. Sigmund Freud, "Totem and Taboo," in *The Standard Edition of the Complete Works of Sigmund Freud*, trans. and ed. James Strachey, Vol. 13 (London: Routledge, 1950), 27.
4. Galia Ofek, *Representations of Hair in Victorian Literature and Culture* (Farnham: Ashgate, 2009), 3.
5. Sinead Furlong-Clancy, "Fashion and the Painting of Parisian Modernity: New Academic and Curatorial Perspectives," *The DS Project: Image, Text, Space/Place*, (accessed 20 May 2015) *1830–2015*. Available online: http://thedsproject.com/.
6. Jan Marsh, *The Pre-Raphaelite Women: Images of Femininity in Pre-Raphaelite Art* (London: Nicholson & Weidenfeld, 1987), 48.
7. Ofek, *Representations of Hair*, 3.
8. Louisa May Alcott, *Little Women* (1868; London: Penguin, 1989), 25.
9. Ibid., 203.
10. Ibid., 152.
11. Ibid., 164.
12. Ibid., 90, 93.
13. Nathaniel Hawthorne, *The Scarlet Letter* (1850; Oxford: Oxford University Press, 2008), 129.
14. Ibid., 158.
15. Elizabeth Barrett Browning, *Aurora Leigh* (1856; Oxford: Oxford University Press, 2008), sec. III, lines 813–16, p. 98.
16. Ibid., sec. III, l. 817, p. 98.
17. Ibid., sec. III, l. 1049, p. 105.
18. Ibid., sec. V, lines 614–17, p. 164.
19. Ibid., sec. V, lines 1126–34, p. 180.
20. Ibid., sec. I, lines 272–6, p. 12.
21. Freud, "Totem and Taboo," 27.
22. Thomas Hardy, *Far from the Madding Crowd* (1874; Hertfordshire: Wordsworth, 2000), 260.
23. Ibid., 5.
24. Elizabeth Gaskell, *Ruth* (1853; Oxford: Oxford University Press, 1985), 6.
25. Ibid., 74–5.
26. Gaskell, *Ruth*, 145.
27. Christina Rossetti, "Goblin Market," in *The Complete Poems* (London: Penguin, 2001), 12–8, 8.

NOTES 187

28. Sandra M. Gilbert and Susan Gubar, *The Madwoman in the Attic: The Woman Writer and the Nineteenth-Century Literary Imagination* (New Haven, CT: Yale University Press, 2000), 566.
29. Ibid., 471, 17.
30. Ibid., 510, 18.
31. Ibid., 496, 500, 505, 18.
32. Ibid., 514–17, 521–3, 18–19.
33. Ibid., 184, 197, 10.
34. Ibid., 552, 19.
35. Ofek, *Representations of Hair*, 166.
36. George Eliot, *Silas Marner* (1861; London: Penguin, 1996), 121.
37. Ibid., 138.
38. Ibid.
39. Rodney Engen, *Kate Greenaway: A Biography* (London: Macdonald Futura, 1981), 148.
40. Hawthorne, *The Scarlet Letter*, 71.
41. Ibid., 80.
42. Ibid.
43. Ibid., 73, 78, 140.
44. Zane Grey, *Riders of the Purple Sage* (1912; Oxford: Oxford University Press, 1998), 75.
45. Ibid., 117.
46. Mary Elizabeth Braddon, *Lady Audley's Secret* (1862; London: Wordsworth, 2007), 43.
47. Ibid., 171.
48. Ibid., 126.
49. Ibid., 235.
50. Ibid., 277.
51. Ibid., 311.
52. Ibid., 57–8.
53. Ofek, *Representations of Hair*, 3.
54. Braddon, *Lady Audley's Secret*, 267.
55. Ibid., 57.
56. Ofek, *Representations of Hair*, 191.
57. Émile Zola, *Nana* (1880; London: Penguin, 1972), 33.
58. Ibid., 44.
59. Ibid., 223.
60. Ibid., 222–3.
61. Émile Zola, *The Kill* (1871–1872; Oxford: Oxford University Press, 2008), 5.
62. Ibid., 131.
63. Ibid., 125.
64. Ibid., 133.
65. Ibid., 134–5.
66. Charlotte Brontë, *Jane Eyre* (1847; London: Penguin, 2006), 75.
67. Ibid., 76.
68. Christine Bayles Kortsch, *Dress Culture in Late Victorian Women's Fiction: Literacy, Textiles and Activism* (Farnham: Ashgate, 2009), 81.
69. Richard Altick, *The Presence of the Present: Topics of the Day in the Victorian Novel* (Columbus: Ohio State University Press, 1991), 321–2 and 322–3.
70. Jessica Lenihan, "Shades of Meaning: The Significance of Hair Colour in Braddon's Lady Audley's Secret (1862) and Rossetti's Lady Lilith (1866–68, Altered 1872–73)," *Vides* 2 (2014): 104.

71. Dante Gabriel Rossetti, "Life-in-Love," Sonnet XXXVI, *Collected Poetry and Prose*, ed. Jerome McGann (New York: Vail-Ballou Press, 2000), 15, 143.
72. Ofek, *Representations of Hair*, 81
73. Ibid., 78.
74. Lenihan, "Shades of Meaning," 106.
75. Dante Gabriel Rossetti, "Body's Beauty," Sonnet LXXVIII, *Collected Poetry and Prose*, ed. McGann, 6–7, 161.
76. Sharyn R. Udall, "Between Dream and Shadow: William Holman Hunt's 'Lady of Shalott'," *Woman's Art Journal* 11, no. 1 (1990): 34–8. 34.
77. W.H. Holman, *The Pre-Raphaelites and the Pre-Raphaelite Brotherhood* (London: Macmillan & co., 1905), 124. The 1857 edition of Tennyson's poem by the publisher Moxon included fifty-four wood engraved illustrations by eight artists, including John Everett Millais, William Holman Hunt, and Dante Gabriel Rosetti.
78. Braddon, *Lady Audley's Secret*, 57.
79. Charles Baudelaire, "La Chevelure," in *Selected Poems* (London: Penguin, 1995), 21.
80. Ibid., 20.
81. Ibid., 20–1.
82. Edgar Allan Poe, "For Annie," in *The Fall of the House of Usher and Other Writings* (London: Penguin, 1987), 86.
83. Elisabeth G. Gitter, "The Power of Women's Hair in the Victorian Imagination," *PMLA* 99, no. 5 (1984): 942.
84. Robert Browning, "Pauline," in *The Poems of Browning Vol. 1 1826–1840*, eds. John Woolford and Daniel Karlin (London: Longman, 1991), 3–7, 29.
85. Dante Gabriel Rossetti, "The Stream's Secret," *Collected Poetry and Prose*, ed. McGann, lines 79–84, 56.
86. Dante Gabriel Rossetti, "The Blessed Damozel," *Collected Poetry and Prose*, ed. McGann, 21–2.
87. Gitter, "The Power of Women's Hair," 942.
88. Charles Dickens, *Great Expectations* (1861; Hertfordshire: Wordsworth, 1996), 46.
89. Margaret Oliphant, *Hester* (1883; London: Virago, 1984), 23.
90. Edith Wharton, *The Mother's Recompense* (1925; Gloucester: Dodo Press, 230), 49.
91. Ibid., 12
92. Ibid.
93. Ibid., 103.
94. Ibid., 41–2.
95. Ibid., 230.

Chapter Seven

1. Gwendolyn Midlo Hall, *Slavery and African Ethnicities in the Americas* (Chapel Hill: University of North Carolina Press, 2005).
2. Niangi Batulukisi, "Hair in African Art and Cultures," in *Hair in African Art and Cultures*, eds. Roy Sieber and Frank Herreman (New York: Prestel, 2000), 26.
3. Esi Sagay, *African Hairstyles: Styles of Yesterday and Today* (Oxford: Heinemann International, 1983), 20. Note that Sagay is vague on the dating of this traditional wedding hairstyle, depicting it as a photograph, possibly dated as late as the time the book was published in the 1980s, as well as in an illustration captioned as "Ancient Ibo hairstyle." However, it can be assumed that the tradition of a specific wedding hairstyle— if not this particular style—would date back several generations.

NOTES

4. Babatunde Lawal, "Orilonise: The Hermeneutics of the Head and Hairstyles among the Yoruba," in *Hair in African Art and Culture*, eds. Sieber and Herreman, 94.
5. Ibid., 96, 96–8.
6. Ayana D. Byrd and Lori L. Tharps, *Hair Story: Untangling the Roots of Black Hair in America* (New York: St. Martin's Press, 2001), 6.
7. Herbert S. Klein, *The Atlantic Slave Trade* (Cambridge: Cambridge University Press, 2010), 47, 46–7.
8. Byrd and Tharps, *Hair Story*, 10–11.
9. Diane Simon, *Hair: Public Political Extremely Personal* (New York: St. Martin's Press, 2000), 45.
10. Simon, *Hair*, 42–3.
11. Shane White and Graham White, *Stylin': African American Expressive Culture from Its Beginnings to the Zoot Suit* (Ithaca, NY: Cornell University Press, 1998), 54.
12. Kennell Jackson, "What Is Really Happening Here? Black Hair among African-Americans and in American Culture," in *Hair in African Art and Culture*, eds. Sieber and Herreman, 182.
13. White and White, *Stylin'*, 41; Byrd and Tharps, *Hair Story*, 15–16.
14. Ibid., 55.
15. Victoria Sherrow, *Encyclopedia of Hair: A Cultural History* (Westport, CT: Greenwood Press, 2006), 13–14.
16. Byrd and Tharps, *Hair Story*, 17.
17. White and White, *Stylin'*, 57.
18. Gerda Lerner, ed., *Black Women in White America: A Documentary History* (New York: Vintage Books, 1972), 24.
19. Steeve O. Buckridge, *The Language of Dress Resistance and Accommodation in Jamaica 1760–1890* (Kingston: University of the West Indies Press, 2004), 17.
20. Ibid., 86.
21. White and White, *Stylin'*, 37.
22. Ibid., 56.
23. Ibid.
24. James Cowles Prichard, *The Natural History of Man*, Vol. 2 (London: H. Baillière, 1855), 647. Available online: *The Internet Archive*, https://archive.org/details/naturalhistorym00unkngoog (accessed September 7, 2015).
25. Ibid., 656.
26. John Campbell, *Negro-mania: An Examination of the Falsely Assumed Equality of the Various Races of Men* (Philadelphia: Campbell and Power, 1851), 78. Available online: *The Internet Archive*, http://www.niggermania.com/library/Negro-Mania.pdf (accessed September 7, 2015).
27. Ibid., 340.
28. Ibid., 345.
29. Byrd and Tharps, *Hair Story*, 14.
30. White and White, *Stylin'*, 61–2.
31. Buckridge, *The Language of Dress*, 7.
32. Ibid., 140.
33. Ibid., 172.
34. White and White, *Stylin'*, 54.
35. Monica Miller, *Slaves to Fashion: Black Dandyism and the Styling of Black Diasporic Identity* (Durham, NC: Duke University Press, 2009), 92.

36. Ibid., 15.
37. Kelley Mohs Gage, "Forced Crossing: The Dress of African Slave Women in Rio Janeiro, Brazil, 1861," *Dress: The Annual Journal of the Costume Society of America* 39, no. 2 (2013): 111–33, 112, 114.
38. Buckridge, *The Language of Dress*, 60.
39. Ibid., 93.
40. Shirley Anne Tate, *Black Beauty: Aesthetics, Stylization, Politics* (Abingdon: Ashgate Publishing Limited, 2009), 35.
41. Miller, *Slaves to Fashion*, 5.
42. Sherrow, *Encyclopedia of Hair*, 385.
43. John Stauffer, *Giants: The Parallel Lives of Frederick Douglass and Abraham Lincoln* (New York: Grand Central Publishing, 2008), 92.
44. Ibid., 233–4.
45. White and White, *Stylin'*, 47, 45–7.
46. "Did Frederick Douglass wear his hair after Afro-Franco writer Alexandre Dumas?" *Frederick Douglass' Washington: the Lion of Anacostia*, April 24, 2012. Available online: https://thelionofanacostia.wordpress.com/2012/04/24/did-frederick-douglass-wear-his-hair-after-afro-franco-writer-alexandre-dumas/ (accessed September 23, 2015).
47. Kathleen Thompson and Hilary Mac Austin, *The Face of Our Past* (Bloomington: Indiana University Press, 1999), 78.
48. Buckridge, *The Language of Dress*, 27.
49. Byrd and Tharps, *Hair Story*, 20.
50. Ibid., 22.
51. Ibid., 37.
52. Noliwe M. Rooks, *Hair Raising: Beauty, Culture, and African American Women* (New Brunswick, NJ: Rutgers University Press, 1996), 13.
53. Rooks, *Hair Raising*, 13, 27, 31–3.
54. Ibid., 35.
55. White and White, *Stylin'*, 171.
56. Ibid., 172.
57. Byrd and Tharps, *Hair Story*, 70; Rooks, *Hair Raising*, 76–7.
58. Laurie A. Wilkie, *The Archaeology of Mothering: An African-American Midwife's Tale* (New York: Routledge, 2003), 111.
59. Hannah Farnham Sawyer Lee, *Memoir of Pierre Toussaint, Born a Slave in St. Domingo* (Boston, MA: Crosby, Nichols and Company, 1854), 34, 5, 16. Available online: *The Internet Archive*, https://archive.org/details/memoirpierretou00leegoog (accessed September 27, 2015).
60. Juliet E.K. Walker, *The History of Black Business in America* (New York: Macmillan Library Reference, 1998), 44.
61. Ibid., 107.
62. Ibid., 107–8.
63. Adia Harvey Wingfield, *Doing Business With Beauty: Black Women, Hair Salons, and the Racial Enclave Economy* (Lanham, MD: Rowman & Littlefield Publishers, 2008), 31.
64. Walker, *The History of Black Business in America*, 141–2.
65. Wingfield, *Doing Business With Beauty*, 32.
66. Walker, *The History of Black Business in America*, 142; Rooks, *Hair Raising*, 24.
67. Rooks, *Hair Raising*, 47.
68. Ibid., 48.

NOTES

69. Walker, *The History of Black Business in America*, 208–9.
70. Rooks, *Hair Raising*, 51, 56–9.
71. Ibid., 91–2.
72. White and White, *Stylin'*, 188.
73. John McMullin, "A Night in Paris," *Vogue*, June 1, 1927, 51.

Chapter Eight

1. See, for example, Elisabeth G. Gitter, "The Power of Women's Hair in the Victorian Imagination," *PMLA* 99, no. 5 (October 1984): 936–54; Galia Ofek, *Representations of Hair in Victorian Literature and Culture* (Farnham: Ashgate, 2009); and Christopher Oldstone-Moore, "The Beard Movement in Victorian Britain," *Victorian Studies* 48, no. 1 (2005): 7–34.
2. See Goodman for more on hair cleaning and brushing, and on how hair washing came to be promoted as healthful near the middle of the nineteenth century. Ruth Goodman, *How to Be a Victorian: A Dawn-to-Dusk Guide to Victorian Life* (New York: Liveright, 2013), 117.
3. Goodman reports that "a trip to the barber's was still something of a treat for most working-class men," whereas a wealthy gentleman who lived in town might visit the barber twice a day for shaving and grooming (Goodman, *How to Be a Victorian*, 148, 145).
4. *The Times* is full of classified advertisements for ladies' maids throughout the whole of the period under question, 1800 to 1920, and hairdressing is nearly always listed as a requirement for such employees. Page 3 of the March 7, 1800 issue of *The Times*, for example, lists this advertisement at the top of the "Want Places" column: "As Lady's Maid, a young Woman who perfectly understands mantua-making, hair-dressing, clear-starching, and plain work." At the other end of the period, an ad in the July 1, 1919 issue of *The Times* reads: "WANTED, French or French-Swiss Lady's Maid, young, for one lady: knowledge of English not essential: town and country and travelling: no dressmaking, but very good hairdresser."
5. H.J. Bramsbury, *A Working-Class Tragedy*, Pt. 7, *Justice*, July 21, 1888.
6. He adds that some large workhouses employed barbers full-time or on a contract basis. Peter Higginbotham, *The Workhouse Encyclopedia* (Stroud: The History Press, 2012).
7. Margaret Drinkall, *Rotherham Workhouse* (Stroud: The History Press, 2009).
8. "Cropping the Hair of Paupers," *The Times*, November 19, 1841, 5.
9. "Inquests," *The Times*, October 27, 1887, 12.
10. Workhouses did not have an official uniform but they did require inmates to wear provided clothing, which, in practice, usually meant clothing that was uniform.
11. "A Fine Idea," *Punch* 5, 1843, 265.
12. Ibid., 265.
13. Seth Koven, *The Match Girl and the Heiress* (Princeton, NJ: Princeton University Press, 2014), 41–2.
14. Ibid., 42.
15. Charlotte Brontë, *Jane Eyre* (1847; New York: W.W. Norton, 2001), 53–4.
16. Ibid., 105.
17. Goodman, *How to Be a Victorian*, 113.
18. Ibid., 114.
19. Ofek, *Representations of Hair*, 2.

20. Ibid., 37.
21. Thomas Hardy, *The Woodlanders* (1887; Oxford: Oxford University Press, 2009), 7.
22. Ibid., 12.
23. Ibid., 10.
24. Ibid., 11.
25. Ibid., 19.
26. Ibid., 13.
27. Goodman, *How to Be a Victorian*, 116.
28. Charles Richard Weld, *A Vacation in Brittany* (London: Chapman and Hall, 1856), 213.
29. Weld, *A Vacation in Brittany*, 220.
30. Ofek, *Representations of Hair*, 106.
31. Goodman, *How to Be a Victorian*, 116.
32. "Chinese Hair," *The Times*, October 8, 1884, 10.
33. Ofek, *Representations of Hair*, 9.
34. "False Hair as a Cause of Disease," *The Times*, March 9, 1867, 11.
35. Mary Elizabeth Braddon, *Lady Audley's Secret* (1862; Peterborough, ON: Broadview, 2003), 365.
36. Ibid., 80–1.
37. Ibid., 95.
38. Goodman, *How to Be a Victorian*, 119.
39. Ibid., 145.
40. Charles Dickens, *David Copperfield* (1850; London: Penguin, 2004), 278.
41. "Bear's Grease," *The Magazine of Domestic Economy* 4 (1839): 61.
42. As evidence of its dearness in the early part of the century, consider David Copperfield's attempts at economy once he determines to marry Dora: "I put myself on a short allowance of bear's grease … as being too luxurious for my stern career" (Dickens, *David Copperfield*, 532).
43. "The Atrapilatory, or Liquid Hair Dye," *The Times*, August 11, 1841, 7.
44. "Poisonous Hair Dyes," *The Times*, January 8, 1869, 8.
45. *The Extraordinary Life & Trial of Madame Rachel at the Central Criminal Court* (London: Diprose and Bateman, n.d. [1868]), vii.
46. For a longer discussion of Madame Rachel and her depiction in Victorian literature and the Victorian press, see chapter two of Elizabeth Carolyn Miller, *Framed: The New Woman Criminal in British Culture at the Fin de Siècle* (Ann Arbor: University of Michigan Press, 2008).
47. Anthony Trollope, *The Eustace Diamonds* (1873; Oxford: Oxford University Press, 1998), 85.
48. Thomas Hardy, *Jude the Obscure* (1895; Oxford: Oxford University Press, 1996), 57.
49. Vivienne Richmond, ed. and intro., *Clothing, Society, and Culture in Nineteenth-Century England*. Vol. 3: *Working-Class Dress* (London: Pickering & Chatto, 2011), xix.
50. "Household Reform," *Penny Illustrated Paper*, January 18, 1868, rpt. in Richmond, ed. and intro., *Clothing, Society, and Culture*, Vol. 3, 370.
51. "A Word to My Servant," in *The Servants' Magazine, or Female Domestics' Instructor*, Vol. 5 (London: Ward & Co., 1842), 82.
52. The UCL Bloomsbury Project has a website about the Female Aid Society. Available at: http://www.ucl.ac.uk/bloomsbury-project/institutions/female_aid_society.htm (accessed 22 August 2018).
53. Wilkie Collins, *The Moonstone* (1868; Oxford: Oxford University Press, 1999), 193.
54. Richmond, ed. and intro., *Clothing, Society, and Culture*, 361.

55. Ibid., 366. Emphasis in original.
56. Ibid.
57. Emma Leslie, "Myra's Pink Dress" (London: Sunday School Union, 1873), rpt. in Richmond, ed. and intro., *Clothing, Society, and Culture, Clothing*, 329.
58. Leslie, "Myra's Pink Dress," 330.
59. Ibid., 332–3.
60. Herbert P. Miller, *The Scarcity of Domestic Servants: The Cause and Remedy* (1876), rpt. in Richmond, ed. and intro., *Clothing, Society, and Culture*, 362.
61. Ibid., 379.
62. Jane Austen, *Emma* (1815; London: Penguin, 2003), 192.
63. Austen, *Emma*, 127.
64. Goodman, *How to Be a Victorian*, 135.
65. "The Long-Haired Musician," *London Saturday Journal*, May 21, 1842, 243.
66. Oldstone-Moore, "The Beard Movement in Victorian Britain," 10.
67. Goodman, *How to Be a Victorian*, 137.
68. Oldstone-Moore, "The Beard Movement in Victorian Britain," 7.
69. Ibid., 19.
70. James Gregory, *The Poetry and the Politics: Radical Reform in Victorian England* (New York: I.B.Tauris, 2014), 40.
71. Alexander Rowland, *A Practical and Philosophical Treatise on the Human Hair* (London: J. Evans & Son, 1814), 3.

Chapter Nine

1. "The Great Exhibition," *John Bull*, May 3, 1851, 288.
2. Alexander Rowland, *The Human Hair: Popularly and Physiologically Considered with Special Reference to its Preservation, Improvement and Adornment, and the Various Modes of its Decoration in all Countries* (London: Piper Brothers & Co., 1853), 177.
3. Ibid.
4. Janice Miller, "Hair Without a Head: Disembodiment and the Uncanny," in *Hair: Styling, Culture and Fashion*, eds. Geraldine Biddle-Perry and Sarah Cheang (London: Berg, 2008), 184.
5. Carolus, "Stanzas on a Lock of Hair," *The Lady's Monthly Magazine*, January 1, 1804, 64.
6. "A Lock of Hair," *The Penny Satirist*, June 27, 1840.
7. Elizabeth G. Gitter, "The Power of Women's Hair in the Victorian Imagination," *PMLA* 99, no. 5 (1984): 942.
8. Emily Brontë, *Wuthering Heights*, ed. Richard J. Dunn (New York: W.W. Norton & Company, 2003), 131.
9. Jane Austen, *Sense and Sensibility*, ed. Kathleen James-Cavan (Peterborough, ON: Broadview, 2001), 94.
10. Ibid.
11. Galia Ofek, *Representations of Hair in Victorian Literature and Culture* (Farnham: Ashgate, 2009), 7–8.
12. This symbolic connection is most famously manifested in Alexander Pope's satire *The Rape of the Lock* (1717), where the forceful severance of one of Belinda's locks of hair is equated to a sexual assault.
13. Locks of hair cause further confusion in *Sense and Sensibility* when Elinor believes that Edward has taken a lock of her hair and had it placed in a ring. It transpires that the lock belongs, in fact, to the conniving Lucy Steele, who bestowed it on Edward as a

mark of ownership. The lock of hair here again acts as a synecdoche for the woman and her emotional proximity—or lack thereof—to the love object. See Austen, *Sense and Sensibility*, 128, 132, 161.
14. Christina Rossetti, "Goblin Market," in *The Norton Anthology of English Literature*, vol. E: *The Victorian Age*, eds. Catherine Robson and Carol T. Christ (London: W.W. Norton & Company, 2012), 1498, (l. 115, l. 126).
15. Jill Rappoport, "The Price of Redemption in 'Goblin Market'," *Studies in English Literature 1500–1900* 50, 4 (2010): 854.
16. Rossetti, "Goblin Market," l. 116.
17. Ibid., lines 71–2.
18. Ofek, *Representations of Hair*, 66.
19. Charlotte Mary Yonge, *Womankind* (New York: Macmillan and Co., 1877), 112.
20. Margaret Oliphant, "Novels," *Blackwood's Edinburgh Magazine* 102 (1867): 257–80, in Rhoda Broughton, *Cometh Up as a Flower*, ed. Pamela K. Gilbert (Peterborough, ON: Broadview, 2010), 352.
21. Ofek, *Representations of Hair*, 7.
22. "Self-Willed Jessie Or The Girl With the Golden Hair," *Little Folks* (London). *Little Folks* was published by Cassell and Company between 1871 and 1933; editions are not dated.
23. George Eliot, *The Mill on the Floss*, ed. Carol T. Christ (London: W.W. Norton & Company, 1994), 12.
24. Ibid., 55.
25. Ibid., 58.
26. Ofek, *Representations of Hair*, 155.
27. Thomas Hardy, *The Return of the Native*, ed. George Woodcock (London: Penguin, 1985), 118.
28. Charlotte Brontë, *Jane Eyre*, ed. Stevie Davies (London: Penguin, 2006), 326, 327.
29. Bram Stoker, *Dracula*, ed. Maurice Hindle (London: Penguin, 1993), 208.
30. Ibid., 270.
31. Ofek, *Representations of Hair*, 186ff.
32. Mary Elizabeth Braddon, *Lady Audley's Secret*, ed. Natalie M. Houston (Peterborough, ON: Broadview, 2003), 33–4. As Houston points out here, this section of Robert's dream, after appearing in the novel's serialization in *Sixpenny Magazine*, was removed from all subsequent editions of the text, perhaps because it "gives too much away too soon" about Lady Audley's true character, albeit mediated by Robert's subconscious.
33. Ibid., 204.
34. Ofek, *Representations of Hair*, 197.
35. Henrik Ibsen, *Hedda Gabler* in *Four Major Plays*, trans. James McFarlane and Jens Arup, ed. James McFarlane (Oxford: Oxford University Press, 1998), 180.
36. Ibid., 181.
37. Ibid., 186, 227.
38. Ibid., 246.
39. Ibid., 258.
40. Samuel Taylor Coleridge, "The Rime of the Ancient Mariner," in *The Collected Works of Samuel Taylor Coleridge*, Vol. 16: *Poetical Works I*, ed. J.C.C. Mays (Princeton, NJ: Princeton University Press, 2001), 387, lines 190–4.

41. Robert Browning, "Porphyria's Lover," in *The Norton Anthology of English Literature,* Vol. E: *The Victorian Age,* eds. Catherine Robson and Carol T. Christ (London: W.W. Norton & Company, 2012), 1279, lines 36–41.
42. Ibid., lines 16–21.
43. Ibid., lines 58–9.
44. Christina Rossetti, "A Triad," in *The Norton Anthology of English Literature,* Vol. E: *The Victorian Age,* eds. Catherine Robson and Carol T. Christ (London: W. W. Norton & Company, 2012), 1492, lines 1–3.
45. Ibid., l. 9.
46. Miller, "Hair Without a Head," 183.
47. Jacky Collis Harvey, *Red: A Natural History of the Redhead,* Kindle edn. (London: Allen and Unwin, 2015), chap. 3, loc. 912.
48. "Hair and Nails of the Dead," *Cleve's Gazette of Variety,* December 22, 1838, 1.
49. See Miller, "Hair Without a Head" for discussion of hair and the uncanny, particularly in relation to severed hair.
50. Thomas Hall Caine, *Recollections of Dante Gabriel Rossetti* (London: Elliot Stock, 1882), 45.
51. Lucinda Hawksley, *Lizzie Siddal: The Tragedy of a Pre-Raphaelite Supermodel* (London: Carlton, 2004), 211.
52. Ofek, *Representations of Hair,* 82.
53. Bram Stoker, "The Secret of the Growing Gold," in *Dracula's Guest* (Brandon: Dingle, Co. Kerry, 1990), 69.
54. Abigail Heiniger, "Undead Blond Hair in the Victorian Imagination: The Hungarian Roots of Bram Stoker's 'The Secret of the Growing Gold'," *Hungarian Cultural Studies* 4 (2011): 2.
55. Ibid.
56. Louise Tondeur, "Elizabeth Siddal's Hair: A Methodology for Queer Reading," *Women: A Cultural Review* 22, no. 4 (2011): 377.
57. Tondeur, "Elizabeth Siddal's Hair," 379.
58. Ibid., 384.
59. "Dove" was one of Rossetti's nicknames for Siddal. The white flower may represent the opium poppy; Siddal was addicted to opium and died of an overdose of the drug. See Hawksley, *Lizzie Siddal,* chap. 9. Elizabeth K. Helsinger provides a compelling reading of *Beata Beatrix,* focusing on how Rossetti's portrayal of Siddal/Beatrice causes the background details of the painting—the sundial, the figure of Dante, a suggestion of Florence—to "almost dissolve." See Elizabeth K. Helsinger, *Poetry and the Pre-Raphaelite Arts: Dante Gabriel Rossetti and William Morris* (New Haven, CT: Yale University Press, 2008), 142.
60. Hawksley, *Lizzie Siddal,* chap. 3.
61. Helsinger, *Poetry and the Pre-Raphaelite Arts,* 142.
62. *Beata Beatrix* was the work of many years. Rossetti worked with his sketches of Siddal from 1864, two years after her death, but the painting was not completed until 1870, the year following her exhumation. See Angela Dunstan, "The Myth of Dante Gabriel Rossetti's *Beata Beatrix* as a Memorial Painting," *British Art Journal* 10, no. 1 (2010): 89–92.
63. William Michael Rossetti, *Dante Gabriel Rossetti: His Family Letters with a Memoir by William Michael Rossetti,* vol. 2 (London: Ellis and Elvey, 1895), 246.

64. Dunstan, "The Myth of Dante Gabriel Rossetti's *Beata Beatrix*," 92.
65. Sandra M. Gilbert and Susan Gubar, *The Madwoman in the Attic: The Woman Writer and the Nineteenth-Century Literary Imagination*, 2nd edn. (New Haven, CT: Yale University Press, 2000), 27.
66. Georgine de Courtais, *Women's Headdress and Hairstyles in England from AD600 to the Present Day* (London: B.T. Batsford, 1973), 124.
67. "Modern Coiffures, with the Accessories Necessary to them, in False Hair," *The Englishwoman's Domestic Magazine*, no. 78 (n.d.). The magazine ran from 1852 to 1879, was published by Samuel Orchart Beeton, and boasted contributions from his wife, Isabella. This particular edition probably dates from the late 1860s.
68. "Lady Chignon Hair of Hair," *Fun*, March 2, 1867, 249.
69. "Artificial Hair," *The Ladies' Treasury*, October 1, 1868, 53.
70. "Hair Ghosts," *The Treasury of Literature and the Ladies' Treasury*, April 1, 1870, 108.
71. Ibid.
72. Ibid.
73. Ibid.
74. Thomas Hardy, *The Woodlanders*, ed. Dale Kramer (Oxford: Oxford University Press, 2005), 12.
75. Gitter, "The Power of Women's Hair," 945.
76. Louisa May Alcott, *Little Women*, ed. Elaine Showalter (London: Penguin, 1989), 3.
77. Ibid., 90.
78. Ibid., 162, 163.
79. "Hair Ghosts," 108.

BIBLIOGRAPHY

Adams, Nehemiah D.D. *A South-side View of Slavery: Or, Three Months at the South in 1854*. Boston, MA: T.R. Marvin, Sanborn, Carter and Bazin, 1855.
Alcott, Louisa May. *Little Women*, edited by Elaine Showalter. 1868. London: Penguin, 1989.
Alcott, Louisa May. *Little Women*. 1868. London: Vintage, 2008.
Alcott, Louisa May. *Little Women*, edited by Valerie Alderson. 1869. Oxford: Oxford University Press, 2008.
Altick, Richard. *The Presence of the Present: Topics of the Day in the Victorian Novel*. Columbus: Ohio State University Press, 1991.
American Fabrics Encyclopedia of Textiles. Englewood Cliffs, NJ: Prentice Hall, Inc., 1972.
A.P.P. "Hairwork as a Highly Remunerative Employment for Girls." *The Girl's Own Paper*, 1890. Available online: http://www.victorianvoices.net/ARTICLES/GOP/Work/1900-Hairwork.pdf. Accessed August 10, 2015.
The Art of Beauty. London: D.S. Maurice, 1825. Available online: https://archive.org/stream/artbeautyorbest00artgoog#page/n0/mode/2up. Accessed November 10, 2015.
"Artificial Hair." *The Ladies' Treasury*, October 1, 1868, 53–4.
"Artificial Hair." *Penny Illustrated Paper*, August 15, 1868, 103. Reprinted from *The Daily News*.
"The Atrapilatory, or Liquid Hair Dye." *The Times*, August 11, 1841, 7.
Austen, Jane. *Sense and Sensibility*. 1811, edited by Kathleen James-Cavan. Peterborough, ON: Broadview, 2001.
Austen, Jane. *Emma*. 1815. London: Penguin, 2003.
Banks, Ingrid. *Hair Matters: Beauty, Power and Black Women's Consciousness*. London: New York University Press, 2000.
Bardi, Abigail. "The Gypsy as Trope in Victorian and Modern Literature." PhD thesis, University of Maryland, 2007.
Bashford, Alison. *Purity and Pollution: Gender, Embodiment and Victorian Medicine*. Basingstoke: Macmillan Press, 2000.
Batulukisi, Niangi "Hair in African Art and Cultures." In *Hair in African Art and Cultures*, edited by Roy Sieber and Frank Herreman, 25–37. New York: Prestel, 2000.
Baudelaire, Charles. *Selected Poems*. London: Penguin, 1995.
Baumgarten, Linda. "'Clothes for the People' Slave Clothing in Early Virginia." *Journal of Early Southern Decorative Arts* XIV, no. 2 (November 1988): 26–70.
"Bear's Grease." *The Magazine of Domestic Economy* 4 (1839): 61.
Beaujot, Ariel. *Victorian Fashion Accessories*. London: Bloomsbury, 2012.
Beetham, Margaret. *A Magazine of Her Own? Domesticity and Desire in the Woman's Magazine, 1800–1914*. London: Routledge, 1996.
Biddle-Perry, Geraldine, and Sarah Cheung, eds. *Hair: Styling, Culture and Fashion*. Oxford: Berg, 2008.
Bird, William L. *Souvenir Nation: Relics, Keepsakes, and Curios from the Smithsonian's National Museum of American History*. New York: Princeton Architectural Press, 2013.

Boehm, Katharina. *Bodies and Things in Nineteenth-Century Literature and Culture*. Basingstoke: Palgrave Macmillan, 2012.
Braddon, Mary Elizabeth. *Lady Audley's Secret*, edited by David Skilton. 1862. Oxford: Oxford University Press, 1998.
Braddon, Mary Elizabeth. *Aurora Floyd*, edited by Richard Nemesvari and Lisa Surridge. 1863. Peterborough, ON: Broadview Press, 1998.
Braddon, Mary Elizabeth. *Lady Audley's Secret*, edited by Nathalie M. Houston. 1862. Peterborough, ON: Broadview, 2003.
Braddon, Mary Elizabeth. *Lady Audley's Secret*. 1862. Hertfordshire: Wordsworth, 2007.
Bramsbury, H.J. *A Working-Class Tragedy*. *Justice*, June 9, 1888 to April 13, 1889.
Brayfield, Celia. "A Lifetime Haircut." *The Times*, July 20, 2004, 11.
Brontë, Charlotte. *Shirley*. 1849. Ware: Wordsworth, 1993.
Brontë, Charlotte. *Jane Eyre*. 1847. New York: W.W. Norton, 2001.
Brontë, Charlotte. *Jane Eyre*, edited by Steve Davies. 1847. London: Penguin, 2006.
Brontë, Emily. *Wuthering Heights*, edited by Richard J. Dunn. 1847. New York: W.W. Norton & Company, 2003.
Brown, Bill. *A Sense of Things: The Object Matter of American Literature*. Chicago: University of Chicago Press, 2003.
Browning, Elizabeth Barrett. *Aurora Leigh*. 1856. Oxford: Oxford University Press, 2008.
Browning, Robert. *Robert Browning's Poetry*, edited by James F. Loucks. New York: Norton, 1979.
Browning, Robert. *The Poems of Browning*, Vol. 1: *1826-1840*, edited by John Woolford and Daniel Karlin. London: Longman, 1991.
Browning, Robert. "Porphyria's Lover." In *The Norton Anthology of English Literature*, Vol. E: *The Victorian Age*, edited by Catherine Robson and Carol T. Christ, 1278–9. London: W.W. Norton & Company, 2012.
Brubacher, Sara Beth. "African American Working Class Clothing as Photographed by William E. Wilson and Robert E. Williams: 1872 to 1898." MS thesis, University of Georgia, 2002.
Bryan, Leon Stone, Jr. "Slavery on a PeeDee River Rice Plantation, 1825–1865." MA thesis, Johns Hopkins University, 1963.
Buckridge, Steeve O. *The Language of Dress: Resistance and Accommodation in Jamaica 1760-1890*. Kingston: University of the West Indies Press, 2004.
Butler, Judith. "Performative Acts and Gender Constitution." *Theatre Journal* 40, no. 4 (December 1988): 519–31.
Byatt, A.S. *Possession*. London: Vintage, 1991.
Byatt, A.S. "In the Grip of Possession." February 1995. Available online: http://www.independent.co.uk/arts-entertainment/in-the-grip-of-possession-1571141.html. Accessed March 10, 2017.
Byrd, Ayana D., and Lori L. Tharps. *Hair Story: Untangling the Roots of Black Hair in America*. New York: St. Martin's Press, 2001.
Byron, Lord. *The Complete Works of Lord Byron*. Paris: Baudry's European Library, 1835.
Caine, Thomas Hall. *Recollections of Dante Gabriel Rossetti*. London: Elliot Stock, 1882.
Campbell, John. *Negro-mania: An Examination of the Falsely Assumed Equality of the Various Races of Men*. Philadelphia: Campbell and Power, 1851. Available online: *The Internet Archive*, http://www.niggermania.com/library/Negro-Mania.pdf. Accessed September 7, 2015.
Carlyle, Thomas. *Sartor Resartus*. Boston, MA: James Munroe and Company, 1837.
Carolus. "Stanzas on a Lock of Hair." *The Lady's Monthly Magazine*, January 1, 1804, 64.

Casteras, Susan P. *Images of Victorian Womanhood in English Art*. Rutherford, NJ: Fairleigh Dickinson University Press, 1987.

"A Chat About Hair and Hair Dyeing." *Leisure Hour: A Family Journal of Instruction and Recreation*, March 1, 1867, 140–2. Available online: http://babel.hathitrust.org/cgi/pt?id=mdp.39015018039647;view=1up;seq=161. Accessed November 24, 2015.

Cheang, Sarah. "Roots: Hair and Race." In *Hair: Styling, Culture and Fashion*, edited by Geraldine Biddle-Perry and Sarah Cheang, 27–42. London: Bloomsbury, 2013.

"Chignonlogy." *The London Review*, 14 (February 23, 1867): 227–8.

"Chinese Hair." *The Times*, October 8, 1884, 10.

Clark, Jessica P. "Barbershop." In *Gender and Material Culture in Britain since 1600*, edited by Hannah Grieg, Jane Hamlett, and Leonie Hannan. London: Palgrave, 2016.

Cocuzza, Dominique. "The Dress of Free Women of Color in New Orleans, 1780–1840." *Dress* 27 (2000): 78–86.

Coella, Silvana. "Olfactory Ghosts: Michael Faber's *The Crimson Petal and the* White." In *Haunting and Spectrality in Neo-Victorian Fiction: Possessing the Past*, edited by Rosario Arias and Patricia Pulham. Basingstoke: Palgrave Macmillan, 2010.

Coleridge, Samuel Taylor. "The Rime of the Ancient Mariner." In *The Collected Works of Samuel Taylor Coleridge*, Vol. 16: *Poetical Works I*, edited by J.C.C. Mays, 365–419. Princeton, NJ: Princeton University Press, 2001.

Collins, Wilkie. *The Moonstone*. 1868. Oxford: Oxford University Press, 1999.

"The Commerce in Human Hair." *The Times*, October 10, 1868, 4.

Cook, Elizabeth, ed. *John Keats*. Oxford: Oxford University Press, 1990.

Corson, Richard. *Fashions in Hair: The First Five Thousand Years*. London: Peter Owen, 1965.

Cox, Caroline. *Good Hair Days: A History of British Hairstyling*. London: Quartet Books, 1999.

"Cropping the Hair of Paupers." *The Times*, November 19, 1841, 5.

"Dangers of 'Chignons.'" *The Lancet*. Reprinted in *Littell's Living Age* 93 (April 6, 1867): 64.

Davidoff, Leonore. *Worlds Between: Historical Perspectives on Gender and Class*. Cambridge: Cambridge University Press, 1995.

De Courtais, Georgine. *Women's Hats, Headdresses and Hairstyles*. Mineola, NY: Dover Publications, 1973.

De Courtais, Georgine. *Women's Headdress and Hairstyles in England from AD600 to the Present Day*. London: B.T. Batsford Ltd, 1973.

DeLong, Anne. *Mesmerism, Medusa, and the Muse: The Romantic Discourse of Spontaneous Creativity*. Lanham, MD: Lexington Books, 2012.

De Marbot, General. *The Memoirs of the General Baron de Marbot*. 1892, translated by Oliver C. Colt, 2000. Available online: http://www.gutenberg.org/cache/epub/2401/pg2401-images.html. Accessed November 30, 2015.

De Vries, Leonard. *Victorian Advertisements*. London: John Murray, 1968.

Dickens, Charles. *The Favorite*. London: Partridge, Oakey, and Co., 1854.

Dickens, Charles. *Our Mutual Friend*, edited by Stephen Gill. 1865. Harmondsworth: Penguin, 1977.

Dickens, Charles. *David Copperfield*, edited by Jerome H. Buckley. 1850. New York: Norton, 1990.

Dickens, Charles. *Little Dorrit*. 1857. Harmondsworth: Penguin, 1994.

Dickens, Charles. *Nicholas Nickleby*. 1839. Ware: Wordsworth, 1995.

Dickens, Charles. *Sketches by Boz*, edited by Dennis Walder. 1839. Harmondsworth: Penguin, 1995.

Dickens, Charles. *Great Expectations*. 1861. Hertfordshire: Wordsworth, 1996.
Dickens, Charles. *David Copperfield*. 1850. London: Penguin, 2004.
"Did Frederick Douglass wear his hair after Afro-Franco writer Alexandre Dumas?" *Frederick Douglass' Washington: the Lion of Anacostia* [Blog], April 24, 2012. Available online: https://thelionofanacostia.wordpress.com/2012/04/24/did-frederick-douglass-wear-his-hair-after-afro-franco-writer-alexandre-dumas/. Accessed September 23, 2015.
"Domestic Philosophy: Servants and Mistresses." *London Society* 3, no. 2 (February 1863): 120–7.
Douglas, Mary. *Purity and Danger: An Analysis of Concept of Pollution and Taboo*. London: Routledge, 2002.
"The Dress of Female Servants." *Family Economist* 4 (1855). Reprinted in *Clothing, Society, and Culture in Nineteenth-Century England*. Vol. 3: *Working-Class Dress*, edited by Vivienne Richmond. 365–7. London: Pickering & Chatto, 2011.
Drinkall, Margaret. *Rotherham Workhouse*. Stroud: The History Press, 2009.
Du Gay, Paul ed. *Doing Cultural Studies: The Story of the Sony Walkman*. London: Sage, 1997.
Dunstan, Angela. "The Myth of Dante Gabriel Rossetti's *Beata Beatrix* as a Memorial Painting." *British Art Journal* 10, no. 1 (2010): 89–92.
Eliot, George. *The Mill on the Floss*, edited by Carol T. Christ. 1860. London: W.W. Norton & Company, 1994.
Eliot, George. *Silas Marner*. 1861. London: Penguin, 1996.
Eliot, George. *The Mill on the Floss*, edited by Oliver Lovesey. 1860. Peterborough, ON: Broadview Press, 2007.
Ellis, Robert. *The Official Catalogue of the Great Exhibition of the Works of Industry of All Nations, 1851*. London: Spicer, 1851.
Ellis, Robert. *The Official Descriptive and Illustrated Catalogue of the Great Exhibition of the Works of Industry of all Nations, 1851*. Vol. 2. London: Spicer, 1851. Available online: https://archive.org/details/officialcatalog06unkngoog. Accessed October 20, 2015.
Engen, Rodney. *Kate Greenaway: A Biography*. London: Macdonald Futura, 1981.
Entwistle, Joanne. "The Dressed Body." In *Body Dressing*, edited by J. Entwistle and E. Wilson, 33–59. Oxford: Berg, 2001.
The Extraordinary Life & Trial of Madame Rachel at the Central Criminal Court. 1868. London: Diprose and Bateman, n.d.
"Extraordinary Robbery of Human Hair." *Birmingham Daily Post*, November 29, 1882, 5.
"False Hair." *The Hairdresser's Journal* 1, no. 2 (April 1863): 21–3.
"False Hair." *The Hairdresser's Journal* 1, no. 3 (May 1863): 32–4.
"False Hair." *The Hairdressers' Journal* 1, no. 4 (June 1863): 43–5.
"The False Hair: A Tale." *Chambers's Edinburgh Journal* 450 (August 14, 1862): 98–102.
"False Hair: Where it Comes From." *The London Review* (September 23, 1863): 328–30.
"False Hair as a Cause of Disease." *The Times*, March 9, 1867, 11.
Farrell-Beck, Jane, and Jean Parsons. *20th Century Dress in the United States*. New York: Fairchild, 2007.
"Fashions for March." *Peterson's Magazine*, March 1851, 168.
"Fashions for May." *Lady's National Magazine*, May 1844, 179.
"Fashions in Hair and Head-Dresses." *Fraser's Magazine* 2, no. 9 (September 1870): 322–31.
"A Fine Idea." *Punch* 5 (1843): 265. Available online: http://babel.hathitrust.org/cgi/pt?id=uc1.32106019785572;view=1up;seq=267. Accessed August 17, 2015.
"The First Coiffure of His Age." *Chambers's Journal* 274 (March 27, 1869): 193–8.

Flanders, Judith. *Consuming Passions: Leisure and Pleasure in Victorian Britain.* London: Harper Press, 2006.

Forest, Danu. *Celtic Tree Magic: Ogham Lore and Druid Mysteries.* Woodbury: Llewellyn Publications, 2014.

Forten, Charlotte. "Life on the Sea Islands, Part I." *The Atlantic Monthly: A Magazine of Literature, Art, and Politics* 13 (May 1864): 587–96.

Foster, Helen Bradley. "African American Jewellery Before the Civil War." In *Beads and Bead Makers: Gender, Material Culture and Meaning*, edited by Lidia D. Sciama and Joanne B. Eicher, 177–192. New York: Berg, 1998.

Fowler, Orson Squire. *The Practical Phrenologist.* New York: Mrs. O.S. Fowler, 1869.

Fox, Tilbury. "The Chignon Fungus." *The American Naturalist* 1, no. 7 (September 1867): 379–86. Available online: https://www.jstor.org/stable/2447149?seq=1#page_scan_tab_contents (accessed 22 August 2018).

Franklin, Caroline, and J. Michael. "Victorian Gothic Poetry: The Corpse's [a] text." In *Victorian Gothic*, edited by Andrew Smith. Edinburgh: Edinburgh University Press, 2012.

Franklin, John Hope. *From Slavery to Freedom: A History of Negro Americans.* New York: Alfred A. Knopf, 1980.

Freedgood, Elaine. *The Ideas in Things: Fugitive Meaning in the Victorian Novel.* Chicago: Chicago University Press, 2006.

Freud, Sigmund. *Totem and Taboo, The Standard Edition of the Complete Works of Sigmund Freud*, translated and edited by James Strachey, Vol. 13. London: Routledge, 1950.

Frith, Henry. *How to Read Character in Features, Forms, and Faces: Outlines of Physiognomy.* London: Ward, Lock, Bowden & Co., 1891.

Furlong-Clancy, Sinead. "Fashion and the Painting of Parisian Modernity: New academic and curatorial perspectives." *The DSProject: Image, Text, Space/ Place,1830-2015*. Available online: http://thedsproject.com/ (accessed 20 May 2015).

Gage, Kelley Mohs. "Forced Crossing: The Dress of African Slave Women in Rio Janeiro, Brazil, 1861." *Dress: The Annual Journal of the Costume Society of America* 39, no. 2 (2013): 111–33.

Galvan, Jill. "The Victorian Post-Human: Transmission, Information, and the Séance." In *The Ashgate Companion to Nineteenth-Century Spiritualism and the Occult*, edited by Tatiana Kontou. London: Routledge, 2016.

Gaskell, Elizabeth. *Ruth.* 1853. Oxford: Oxford University Press, 1981.

Gaskell, Elizabeth. *Cranford/Cousin Phillis*, edited by Peter Keating. 1853. Harmondsworth: Penguin, 1986.

Gaskell, Elizabeth. *North and South.* 1855. Ware: Wordsworth, 1994.

Genovese, Eugene D. *Roll Jordon Roll.* New York: Pantheon Books, 1972.

Gilbert, Sandra M., and Susan Gubar. *The Madwoman in the Attic: The Woman Writer and the Nineteenth-Century Literary Imagination.* New Haven, CT: Yale University Press, 2000.

Gitter, Elisabeth G. "The Power of Women's Hair in the Victorian Imagination." *PMLA* 99, no. 5 (1984): 936–54.

Gleason's Pictorial Drawing-Room Companion, October 8, 1853: 233. Available online: https://archive.org/stream/gleasonspictoria0506glea#page/n238/mode/1up. Accessed November 4, 2015.

Goodman, Ruth. *How to Be a Victorian: A Dawn-to-Dusk Guide to Victorian Life.* New York: Liveright, 2013.

Gowing, Thomas S. *The Philosophy of Beards.* 1854. London: The British Library, 2014.

"The Great Exhibition." *John Bull*, May 3, 1851, 288.

Gregory, James. *The Poetry and the Politics: Radical Reform in Victorian England.* New York: I.B.Tauris, 2014.

Grey, Zane. *The Riders of the Purple Sage*. 1912. Oxford: Oxford University Press, 1998.

Griebel, Helen Bradley. "The African American Woman's Headwrap: Unwinding the Symbols." In *Dress and Identity*, edited by Mary Ellen Roach-Higgins, Joanne B. Eicher, and Kim K.P. Johnson, 445–60. New York: Fairchild Publications, 1995.

Grimm, Jacob, and Wilhelm Grimm. *The Complete First Edition: The Original Folk and Fairy Tales of the Brothers Grimm*. Translated and edited by Jack Zipes. 1812 and 1815. Princeton, NJ: Princeton University Press, 2016.

Gross, Jessica. "Who Made That Hair Dryer." *New York Times Magazine*, July 19, 2013.

"Hair." *The Ladies' Gazette of Fashion*, February 1875, 22–3.

"Hair and Nails of the Dead." *Cleve's Gazette of Variety*, December 22, 1838.

"A Hair-Dressing Contest." *Penny Illustrated Paper*, July 3, 1867, 31.

"Hair Ghosts." *The Treasury of Literature and the Ladies' Treasury*, April 1, 1870, 108.

Hall, Gwendolyn Midlo. *Slavery and African Ethnicities in the Americas*. Chapel Hill: University of North Carolina Press, 2007.

Hall, Stuart. "The West and the Rest: Discourse and Power." In *Formations of Modernity*, edited by Stuart Hall and Bram Gieben, 275–331. Cambridge: Polity, 1992.

Hardy, Thomas. *The Return of the Native*. 1878. New York: Charles Scribner's Sons, 1909.

Hardy, Thomas. *The Return of the Native*, edited by George Woodcock. 1878. London: Penguin, 1985.

Hardy, Thomas. *Jude the Obscure*. 1895. Oxford: Oxford University Press, 1996.

Hardy, Thomas. *The Woodlanders*. 1886–1887. London: Penguin, 1998.

Hardy, Thomas. *Far from the Madding Crowd*. 1874. Hertfordshire: Wordsworth, 2000.

Hardy, Thomas. *The Woodlanders*, edited by Dale Kramer. 1887. Oxford: Oxford University Press, 2009.

Harper, Annie. *Annie Harper's Journal: A Southern Mother's Legacy*. Denton, TX: Flower Mound Writing Company, 1983.

Harris, Juliette, and Pamela Johnson eds. *Tenderheaded: A Comb-Bending Collection of Hair Stories*. London: Washington Square Press, 2001.

Harvey, Jacky Collis. *Red: A Natural History of the Redhead*. Kindle edn. London: Allen and Unwin, 2015.

Hawksley, Lucinda. *Lizzie Siddal: The Tragedy of a Pre-Raphaelite Supermodel*. London: Carlton, 2004.

Hawthorne, Nathaniel. *The Scarlet Letter*. 1850. Oxford: Oxford University Press, 2008.

Heiniger, Abigail. "Undead Blond Hair in the Victorian Imagination: The Hungarian Roots of Bram Stoker's 'The Secret of the Growing Gold'." *Hungarian Cultural Studies* 4 (2011): 1–11.

Helsinger, Elizabeth K. *Poetry and the Pre-Raphaelite Arts: Dante Gabriel Rossetti and William Morris*. New Haven, CT: Yale University Press, 2008.

Herzig, Rebecca M. *Plucked: A History of Hair Removal*. New York: New York University Press, 2015.

Higginbotham, Peter. *The Workhouse Encyclopedia*. Stroud: The History Press, 2012.

"High Art in Hair." *Examiner*, February 21, 1880, 232.

Hilton, Tim. *John Ruskin*. New Haven, CT: Yale University Press, 2002.

Hobsbawm, Eric. *Industry and Empire From 1750 to the Present Day*. London: Penguin Books, 1999.

Hobsbawm, Eric. *The Age of Empire 1875–1914*. London: Abacus, 2007.

Hodder, Ian. *Entangled: An Archaeology of the Relationships between Humans and Things*. Chichester: Wiley-Blackwell, 2012.

Holman, H.W. *The Pre-Raphaelites and the Pre-Raphaelite Brotherhood*. London: MacMillan, 1905.
"Household Reform." *Penny Illustrated Paper*, January 18, 1868. Reprinted in Richmond, Vol. 3, 369–70.
Howell Jolly, Penny. "The Ideal Woman." In *Hair: Untangling a Social History*, edited by Penny Howell Jolly, 51–4. Saratoga Springs, NY: The Frances Young Tang Teaching Museum and Art Gallery at Skidmore College, 2004.
"Human Hair." *The London Reader*, October 6, 1877, 549.
"Human Hair Supplies." *The Examiner*, November 28, 1874, 1295–6.
Hunt, Leigh. "Pocketbook and Keepsakes." In *The Essays of Leigh Hunt*, edited by Arthur Symons, 8–19. London: Walter Scott, 1888.
Hunt, Patricia. "Swathed in Cloth: The Headwraps of Some African American Women in Georgia and South Carolina During the Late Nineteenth and Early Twentieth Centuries." *Dress* 21 (1994): 30–8.
Hunt, Patricia K. and Lucy R. Sibley. "African American Women's Dress in Georgia, 1890-1914: A Photographic Examination." *Clothing and Textiles Research Journal* 12, no. 2 (Winter 1994): 20–6.
Hunt, Patricia K., "The Struggle to Achieve Individual Expression through Clothing and Adornment: African American Women Under and After Slavery." In *Discovering the Women in Slavery: Emancipating Perspectives on the American Past*, edited by Patricia Morton, 227–40. Athens: University of Georgia Press, 1996.
Hunt-Hurst, Patricia. "'Round Homespun Coat & Pantaloons of the Same:' Slave Clothing as Reflected in Fugitive Slave Advertisements in Antebellum Georgia." *The Georgia Historical Quarterly* 83, no. 4 (Winter 1999): 727–40.
H.V., "The Trade in Locks." *London Society* (June 1869): 547–52.
Ibsen, Henrik. *Hedda Gabler*. In *Four Major Plays*, translated by James McFarlane and Jens Arup, edited by James McFarlane. Oxford: Oxford University Press, 1998.
"Inquests." *The Times*, October 27, 1887, 12.
"Isobel." *The Art of Beauty: A Book for Women and Girls*. London: C.A. Parson, 1899.
Jackson, Kennell. "What Is Really Happening Here? Black Hair among African-Americans and in American Culture." In *Hair in African Art and Culture*, edited by Roy Sieber and Frank Herreman, 175–185. New York: Prestel, 2000.
James, Henry. *The Turn of the Screw and The Aspern Papers*, edited by Anthony Curtis. 1907–9. Harmondsworth: Penguin, 1986.
James, William, and Henry James. *Selected Letters*, edited by Ignas K. Skrupskelis and Elizabeth M. Berkeley. Charlottesville: University Press of Virginia, 1997.
Joyner, Charles. *Down by the Riverside: A South Carolina Slave Community*. Chicago: University of Illinois Press, 1984.
Kilbride, Laura. "Byatt: Victorian Poets in Possession." *Cambridge Authors*. Available online: http://www.english.cam.ac.uk/cambridgeauthors/byatt-victorian-poets/ (accessed 22 August 2018).
Klein, Herbert S. *The Atlantic Slave Trade*. Cambridge: Cambridge University Press, 2010.
Knepper, Paul. *The Invention of International Crime: A Global Issue in the Making, 1881–1914*. Basingstoke: Palgrave Macmillan, 2010.
Koudounaris, Paul. *Heavenly Bodies: Cult Treasures and Spectacular Saints from the Catacombs*. London: Thames and Hudson, 2013.
Koven, Seth. *The Match Girl and the Heiress*. Princeton, NJ: Princeton University Press, 2014.
La Fosse, G. Vigier. [Untitled]. Reprinted in *The Hairdressers' Journal* 1, no. 10 (December 1863): 120.

"Lady Chignon Hair of Hair." *Fun*, March 2, 1867, 249.

Laver, James. *A Concise History of Costume*. London: Thames and Hudson, 1969.

Lawal, Babatunde. "Orilonise: The Hermeneutics of the Head and Hairstyles among the Yoruba." In *Hair in African Art and Cultures*, edited by Roy Sieber and Frank Herreman, 93–109. New York: Prestel, 2000.

Lee, Hannah Farnham Sawyer. *Memoir of Pierre Toussaint, Born a Slave in St. Domingo*. Boston, MA: Crosby, Nichols and Company, 1854. Available online: https://archive.org/details/memoirpierretou00leegoog. Accessed September 27, 2015.

Lenihan, Jessica. "Shades of Meaning: The Significance of Hair Colour in Braddon's Lady Audley's Secret (1862) and Rossetti's Lady Lilith (1866–68, Altered 1872–73)." *Vides* 2 (2014): 101-109.

Lerner, Gerda, ed. *Black Women in White America: A Documentary History*. New York: Vintage Books, 1972.

Leslie, Emma. "Myra's Pink Dress." London: Sunday School Union, 1873. Reprinted in *Clothing, Society, and Culture in Nineteenth-Century England*. Vol. 3: *Working-Class Dress*, edited by Vivienne Richmond, 323–43. London: Pickering & Chatto, 2011.

Llewellyn, Mark. "Spectrality, S(p)ecularity, and Textuality: Or, Some Reflections in the Glass." In *Haunting and Spectrality in Neo-Victorian Fiction: Possessing the Past*, edited by Rosario Arias and Patricia Pulham. Basingstoke: Palgrave Macmillan, 2010.

"A Lock of Hair." *The Penny Satirist*, June 27, 1840.

Loeb, Lori Anne. *Consuming Angels: Advertising and Victorian Women*. Oxford: Oxford University Press, 1994.

Lombroso, Cesare. *After Death – What?* Boston, MA: Small, Maynard and Company, 1909.

Lombroso, Cesare. *Criminal Man*, translated by Mary Gibson and Nicole Hahn Rafter. Durham, NC: Duke University Press, 2006.

"The Long-Haired Musician." *London Saturday Journal*, May 21, 1842, 243.

Lowry, Allison. *Historical Wig Styling: Victorian to the Present*. New York: Focal Press, 2013.

Luthi, Anne Louise. *Sentimental Jewellery*. Buckinghamshire: Shire Publishing, 2001.

Lutz, Deborah. *The Brontë Cabinet: Three Lives in Nine Objects*. New York: Norton & Company, 2016.

Mahawatte, Royce. "Hair and Fashioned Femininity in Two Nineteenth-Century Novels." In *Hair: Styling, Culture and Fashion*, edited by Geraldine Biddle-Perry and Sarah Cheang, 193–203. Oxford: Berg, 2008.

Mallon, Isabel. *Ladies Home Journal*, July 1892.

Marchand, Leslie A. *Byron: A Portrait*. London: John Murray, 1971.

Martin, Russell. *Beethoven's Hair: An Extraordinary Historical Odyssey and a Scientific Mystery Solved*. New York: Broadway Books, 2000.

Marsh, Jan. *The Pre-Raphaelite Women: Images of Femininity in Pre-Raphaelite Art*. London: Weidenfeld & Nicholson, 1987.

Marshall, Frederick. "False Hair." *Bentley's Miscellany* 53 (January 1863): 537–41.

Mayhew, Henry, and John Binny. *Criminal Prisons of London and Scenes of Prison Life*. London: Griffin, Bohn and Company, 1862.

McKibben, Gordon. *Cutting Edge: Gillette's Journey to Global Leadership*. Boston, MA: Harvard Business School Press, 1998.

McMullin, John. "A Night in Paris." *Vogue*, June 1, 1927, 49–52.

Mercer, Kobena. "Black Hair/Style Politics." *New Formations* 3 (1987): 33–54.

Miller, Andrew H. *Novels Behind Glass: Commodity Culture and Victorian Narrative*. Cambridge: Cambridge University Press, 1995.

Miller, Elizabeth Carolyn. *Framed: The New Woman Criminal in British Culture at the Fin de Siècle*. Ann Arbor: University of Michigan Press, 2008.

Miller, Herbert P. *The Scarcity of Domestic Servants: The Cause and Remedy*. 1876. Reprinted in *Clothing, Society, and Culture in Nineteenth-Century England*. Vol. 3: *Working-Class Dress*, edited by Vivienne Richmond, 377–84. London: Pickering & Chatto, 2011.

Miller, Janice. "Hair Without a Head: Disembodiment and the Uncanny." In *Hair: Styling, Culture and Fashion*, edited by Geraldine Biddle-Perry and Sarah Cheang, 183–92. London: Berg, 2008.

Miller, Monica. *Slaves to Fashion: Black Dandyism and the Styling of Black Diasporic Identity*. Durham, NC: Duke University Press, 2009.

"Modern Coiffures, with the Accessories Necessary to them, in False Hair." *The Englishwoman's Domestic Magazine*, no. 78 (n.d.).

Morley, Henry. "Why Shave?" *Household Words* 7, no. 177 (August 13, 1853): 560–3.

Morrow, Willie. "A Short History of Early Hair Straightening." In *Tenderheaded: A Comb-Bending Collection of Hair Stories*, edited by Juliette Harris and Pamela Johnson, 125–8. London: Washington Square Press, 2001.

"News of the Day." *Birmingham Daily Post*, January 17, 1872, 4.

Noakes, Richard. "Spiritualism, Science, and the SupernaturalI." In *The Victorian Supernatural*, edited by Nicola Bown, Carolyn Burdett, and Pamela Thurschwell. Cambridge: Cambridge University Press, 2004.

Nunn, Joan. *Fashion in Costume, 1200–2000*. Chicago: New Amsterdam Books, 2000.

Ofek, Galia. *Representations of Hair in Victorian Literature and Culture*. Farnham: Ashgate, 2009.

Oldstone-Moore, Christopher. "The Beard Movement in Victorian Britain." *Victorian Studies* 48, no. 1 (2005): 7–34.

Oliphant, Margaret. "Novels." *Blackwood's Edinburgh Magazine* 102 (1867): 257–80. In Rhoda Broughton, *Cometh Up as a Flower*, edited by Pamela K. Gilbert, 350–3. Peterborough, ON: Broadview, 2010.

Oliphant, Mrs. *Hester*. 1883. London: Virago, 1984.

"Only a Woman's Hair." *The Speaker* 16 (July 31, 1897): 128–9.

Oppenheim, Janet. *The Other World: Spiritualism and Psychical Research in England, 1850–1914*. Cambridge: Cambridge University Press, 1985.

Oram, Richard. "The Locks of Ages: The Leigh Hunt hair collection." In *Cultural Compass*. The University of Texas at Austin: The Harry Ransom Center, 2015.

Panati, Charles. *Extraordinary Origins of Everyday Things*. New York: Harper & Row, 1987. Available online: http://www.ereading.club/bookreader.php/1025263/Panati_Extraordinary_Origins_ofEveryday_Things.html. Accessed December 1, 2015.

Paris Universal Exhibition, 1855. Catalogue of the works exhibited in the British section of the exhibition, in French and English, together with exhibitors' prospectuses, prices, etc. Available online: https://archive.org/details/parisuniversale01goog. Accessed October 20, 2015.

Pickering, David. *Cassell's Dictionary of Witchcraft*. London: Orion, 2002.

Pitman, Joanna. *On Blondes*. London: Bloomsbury, 2003.

Plotz, John. *Portable Property: Victorian Culture on the Move*. Princeton, NJ: Princeton University Press, 2008.

Poe, Edgar Allan. *The Fall of the House of Usher and Other Writings*. 1839. London: Penguin, 1987.

"Poisonous Hair Dyes." *The Times*, January 8, 1869, 8.

Prichard, James Cowles. *The Natural History of Man*. London: H. Baillière, 1855. *The Internet Archive*. Available online: https://archive.org/details/naturalhistorym00unkngoog. Accessed September 7, 2015.

Psomiades, Kathy. *Beauty's Body: Femininity and Representation in British Aestheticism*. Stanford: Stanford University Press, 1997.

Rappoport, Jill. "The Price of Redemption in 'Goblin Market'." *Studies in English Literature 1500-1900* 50, no.4 (2010): 853–75.

Richmond, Vivienne, ed. *Clothing, Society, and Culture in Nineteenth-Century England*. Vol. 3: *Working-Class Dress*. London: Pickering & Chatto, 2011.

Rider Haggard, H. *She*, edited by Daniel Karlin. 1887. Oxford: Oxford University Press, 2008.

Rifelj, Carol. *Coiffures: Hair in Nineteenth-Century French Literature and Culture*. Newark: University of Delaware Press, 2010.

Robinson, Frederick William. *Female Life in Prison. By a Prison Matron*. Vol. 1. London: Hurst and Blackett, 1862.

Rooks, Noliwe M. *Hair Raising: Beauty, Culture and African American Women*. New Brunswick, NJ: Rutgers University Press, 1996/2000.

Rossetti, Christina. *The Complete Poems*. London: Penguin, 2000.

Rossetti, Christina. *The Face of the Deep: A Devotional Commentary on the Apocalypse*. Bristol: Thoemmes Press, 2003.

Rossetti, Christina. "The World." In *Christina Rossetti: Selected Poems*, edited by Dinah Roe. London: Penguin, 2008.

Rossetti, Christina. "In An Artist's Studio." In *The Norton Anthology of English Literature: The Victorian Age*, Vol. E, 9th edn., edited by Catharine Robson and Carol T. Christ. London: W.W. Norton & Company, 2012.

Rossetti, Christina. "Goblin Market." In *The Norton Anthology of English Literature: The Victorian Age*, Vol. E, 9th edn., edited by Stephen Greenblatt. London: W.W. Norton & Company, 2012.

Rossetti, Christina. "A Triad." In *The Norton Anthology of English Literature, Vol. E: The Victorian Age*, edited by Catherine Robson and Carol T. Christ, 1492. London: W.W. Norton & Company, 2012.

Rossetti, Dante Gabriel. *Collected Poetry and Prose*, edited by Jermone McGann. New York: Vail-Ballou Press, 2000/2003.

Rossetti, Dante Gabriel. "Body's Beauty." In *The Norton Anthology of English Literature: The Victorian Age*, Vol. E, 9th edn., edited by Stephen Greenblatt. London: W.W. Norton & Company, 2012.

Rossetti, Dante Gabriel. "Faust" Translation inscribed on frame of *Lady Lilith* taken from Met Museum Archive. Available online: http://www.metmuseum.org/art/collection/search/337500. Accessed February 27, 2017.

Rossetti, William Michael. *Dante Gabriel Rossetti: His Family Letters With a Memoir*, Vols. 1 and 2. London: Ellis and Elvey, 1895.

Rowland, Alexander. *A Practical and Philosophical Treatise on the Human Hair*. London: J. Evans & Son, 1814.

Rowland, Alexander. *An Essay on the Cultivation and Improvement of the Human Hair with Remarks on the Virtues of the Macassar Oil*. London: J. Stratford, 1809. (Facsimile from Nabu Public Domain Reprints, USA).

Rowland, Alexander. *The Human Hair, Popularly and Physiologically Considered with Special Reference to its Preservation, Improvement and Adornment, and the Various Modes of its Decoration in All Countries*. London: Piper, Brothers & Co., 1853.

Ruskin, John. *Sesame and Lilies*, 1864. Available online: www.philaletheians.co.uk/studynotes/down…/ruskin's-sesame-and-lilies.pdf. Accessed October 22, 2015.

Rules and Regulations of the General Penitentiary Millbank. London: The Philanthropic Society, 1825.

Rumford, Mme. "The Prevailing Styles for Summer." *The Colored American Magazine*, June 1901.

Sagay, Esi. *African Hairstyles: Styles of Yesterday and Today*. Oxford: Heinemann International, 1983.

Schulting, Sabine. *Dirt in Victorian Literature and Culture: Writing Materiality*. London: Routledge, 2016.

Scott, Walter. *Letters on Demonology and Witchcraft*. London: William Tegg, 1868.

Scott, William Bell. "Letter to Alice Boyd, 1866." In *The Correspondence of Dante Gabriel Rossetti: The Chelsea Years*, Vol. 5, edited by William E. Fredeman. Cambridge: D.S. Brewer, 2005.

Anon., 'Self-Willed Jessie Or The Girl With the Golden Hair', *Little Folks* (London, England). *Little Folks* was published by Cassell and Company between 1871 and 1933; editions are not dated.

Severa, Joan L. *Dressed for the Photographer: Ordinary Americans and Fashion, 1840–1900*. Kent, OH: The Kent State University Press, 1995.

"Several Heads of Hair." *Household Words* 9 (March 4, 1854): 61–4.

Shelley, Mary, *Frankenstein*, edited by Maurice Hindle. 1818. Harmondsworth: Penguin, 1985.

Sherrow, Victoria. *Encyclopedia of Hair: A Cultural History*. Westport, CT: Greenwood Press, 2006.

Sheumaker, Helen. *Love Entwined: The Curious History of Hairwork in America*. Philadelphia: University of Pennsylvania Press, 2007.

Showalter, Elaine. *Sexual Anarchy: Gender and Culture at the Fin de Siècle*. London: Bloomsbury, 1991.

Sieber, Roy, and Frank Herreman. *Hair in African Art and Culture*. New York: Prestel, 2000.

Simon, Diane. *Hair: Public Political Extremely Personal*. New York: St. Martin's Press, 2000.

Smith, Harriet Amelia. Diary Entry, September 1, 1963. In *To Pike's Peak by Ox-Wagon: The Harriet A. Smith Day-Book*, edited by Fleming Fraker Jr., 37. Iowa City: State Historical Society of Iowa, 1959.

Soderholm, James. *Fantasy, Forgery and the Byron Legend*. Lexington: University of Kentucky Press, 1996.

Soloman-Godeau, Abigail. "The Legs of the Countess", *October* 39 (1986): 65–108.

Solicari, Sonia. "Selling Sentiment: The Commodification of Emotion in Victorian Visual Culture." *19: Interdisciplinary Studies in the Long Nineteenth Century*, 4 (2007).

"Something New." *All the Year Round* 19 (October 27, 1877): 277–79.

Southey, Robert. *The Doctor*. London: Longman 1834/1847. Available online: https://archive.org/details/doctorc01soutgoog. Accessed November 12, 2015.

Speight, A. "The Lock of Hair." [Review] *The Saturday Review* 31 (June 17, 1871): 782–92.

Speight, Alexanna. *The Lock of Hair: Its History, Ancient and Modern, Natural and Artistic, With the Art of Working in Hair*. London: A. Goubard, 1871.

Stauffer, John. *Giants: The Parallel Lives of Frederick Douglass and Abraham Lincoln*. New York: Grand Central Publishing, 2008.

Stoker, Bram. "The Secret of the Growing Gold." In *Dracula's Guest*, 57–70. Brandon: Dingle, Co. Kerry, 1990.

Stoker, Bram. *Dracula*, edited by Maurice Hindle. 1897. London: Penguin, 1993.

Stoker, Bram. *Dracula*, edited by Glennis Byron. 1897. Hertfordshire: Broadview, 2000.
Storm, Penny. *Functions of Dress and Adornment: Tool of Culture and the Individual.* Englewood Cliffs, NJ: Prentice-Hall, Inc., 1987.
Stowell, William Hendry. *Eclectic Review*, Vol. 2. London: Ward & Co., 1862.
Strachan, John. *Advertising and Satirical Culture in the Romantic Period*. Cambridge: Cambridge University Press, 2007.
Tandberg, Gerilyn. "Decoration and Decorum: Accessories of Nineteenth Century Louisiana Women." *Southern Historical Quarterly: A Journal of the Arts in the South* 27, no. 1 (Fall 1998): 8–31.
Tandberg, Gerilyn. "Field Hand Clothing in Louisiana and Mississippi During the Ante-Bellum Period." *Dress* 6 (1980): 89–102.
Tate, Shirley Anne. *Black Beauty: Aesthetics, Stylization, Politics*. Abingdon: Ashgate, 2009.
Taylor, Lou. *Mourning Dress: A Costume and Social History*. Abingdon: Routledge, 2009.
Tennyson, Alfred. "Merlin and Vivien." In *The Complete Poetical works of Alfred Tennyson*. Boston, MA: James R. Osgold and Company, 1875.
Thackeray, William Makepeace. *Vanity Fair*, edited by Peter Shillingsburg. 1848. New York: Norton, 1994.
Thackeray, William Makepeace. *The Newcomes*. London: Macmillan and Co., 1901.
Thompson, Kathleen, and Hilary Mac Austin. *The Face of Our Past*. Bloomington: Indiana University Press, 1999.
Tischleder, Babette Bärbel. *The Literary Life of Things: Case Studies in American Fiction*. Frankfurt: Campus Verlag, 2014.
Tomes, Robert. *The Bazar Book of Decorum*. New York: Harper & Brothers, 1870. Available online: https://archive.org/details/bazarbookofdecor00tomerich. Accessed October 22, 2015.
Tondeur, Louise. "Elizabeth Siddal's Hair: A Methodology for Queer Reading." *Women: A Cultural Review* 22, no. 4 (2011): 370–86.
Trasko, Mary. *Daring Do's: A History of Extraordinary Hair*. Paris: Flammarion, 1994.
Trollope, Anthony. *Barchester Towers*.1857. Ware: Wordsworth, 1994.
Trollope, Anthony.*The Eustace Diamonds*. 1873. Oxford: Oxford University Press, 1998.
Trollope, T. Adolphus. *A Summer In Brittany*, edited by Frances Trollope. London: Henry Colburn, 1840.
Trowbridge, Serena. *Christina Rossetti's Gothic*. London: Bloomsbury, 2013.
"Turbans and Head-dresses." *The Lady's*, March 1842, 66.
Twain, Mark. *A Connecticut Yankee in King Arthur's Court*, edited by M. Thomas Inge. 1889. Oxford: Oxford University Press, 2008.
Udall, Sharyn R. "Between Dream and Shadow: William Holman Hunt's 'Lady of Shalott'." *Woman's Art Journal* 11, no. 1 (Spring-Summer, 1990): 34–8.
"[Untitled]." From the *Daily Telegraph*, February 20, 1867. Reprinted in *Littell's Living Age* 93 (April 6, 1867): 64.
Veblen, Thorstein. *The Theory of the Leisure Class: An Economic Study of Institutions*. 1899. Amherst, NY: Prometheus Books, 1998.
Virtue, George. *The Art Journal Illustrated Catalogue: The Industry of all Nations*. London: Bradbury and Evans Printers, 1851.
Wagner, Gillian. *Miss Palmer's Diary: The Secret Journals of a Victorian Lady*. London: I.B.Tauris, 2017.
Waldman, Suzanne Maureen. *The Demon and the Damozel: Dynamics of Desire in the works of Christina Rossetti and Dante Gabriel Rossetti*. Athens: Ohio University Press, 2008.

Walker, Juliet E.K. *The History of Black Business in America*. New York: Macmillan Library Reference, 1998.

Walker, Juliet E.K. *The History of Black Business in America: To 1865*. Vol. 1: *Capitalism, Race, Entrepreneurship*. Chapel Hill: University of North Carolina Press, 2010.

Warner, Patricia Campbell, and Deborah Parker. "Slave Clothing and Textiles in North Carolina, 1775 – 1835." In *African American Dress and Adornment: A Cultural Perspective*, edited by B.M. Starke, L.O. Holloman, and B.K. Nordquist, 82–91. Dubuque, IA: Kendall/Hunt, 1990.

Warwick, Alexander, and Dani Cavallaro. *Fashioning the Frame: Boundaries, Dress and the Body*. Oxford: Berg, 1998.

Waters, Sarah. *Affinity*. London: Virago Press, 2007.

Watson, Steven. *The Harlem Renaissance: Hub of African-American Culture, 1920–1930*. New York: Pantheon Books, 1995.

Weld, Charles Richard. *A Vacation in Brittany*. London: Chapman and Hall, 1856.

Wharton, Edith. *The Mother's Recompense*. 1925. Gloucester: Dodo Press.

White, Carolyn L. "The Fall of Big Hair." In *The Importance of British Material Culture to Historical Archaeologies of the Nineteenth Century*, edited by Alisdair Brooks. Lincoln: University of Nebraska Press, 2015.

White, Shane, and Graham White. "Slave Hair and African American Culture in the Eighteenth and Nineteenth Centuries." *The Journal of Southern History* 61, no. 1 (February 1995): 45–76.

White, Shane, and Graham White. *Stylin' African American Expressive Culture from Its Beginnings to the Zoot Suit*. Ithaca, NY: Cornell University Press, 1998.

Whitelock, Sadie. *The Daily Mail*, September 10, 2013.

Whitlock, Tammy. *Crime, Gender and Consumer Culture in Nineteenth-Century England*. Farnham: Ashgate Publishing, 2005.

Wilby, Emma. *Cunning Folk and Familiar Spirits: Shamanistic Visionary Traditions in Early Modern British Witchcraft and Magic*. Brighton: Sussex Academic Press, 2005.

Wilkie, Laurie A. *The Archaeology of Mothering: An African-American Midwife's Tale*. New York: Routledge, 2003.

Winakor, Geitel. "Economics and Clothing." In *The Berg Companion to Fashion*, edited by Valerie Steele. New York: Berg, 2010.

Wingfield, Adia Harvey. *Doing Business With Beauty: Black Women, Hair Salons, and the Racial Enclave Economy*. Lanham: Rowman & Littlefield Publishers, 2008.

Winyaw Intelligencer, January 30, 1819.

"A Word to My Servant." *The Servants' Magazine, or Female Domestics' Instructor*. Vol. 5, 80. London: Ward & Co., 1842.

Wynter, Andrew. "Diseases of the Human Hair." *Quarterly Review* 92 (March 1853): 305–28.

Wynter, Andrew. "Chignons and Hair Fashions." In *Curiosities of Toil and Other Papers*. Vol. 2, 202–8. London: Chapman and Hall, 1870.

Wynter, Andrew. "Ladies' Tresses." In *Peeps into the Human Hive*. Vol. 2, 116–23. London: Chapman and Hall, 1874.

Wynter, Andrew. "Peeps into the Human Hive." Review of *Peeps into the Human Hive*. *The Saturday Review* 37 (January 31, 1874): 151–2.

Yarwood, Doreen. *European Costume: 4000 years of fashion*. London: B.T. Basford Ltd, 1975.

Yonge, Charlotte Mary. *Womankind*. New York: Macmillan and Co., 1877.

Zedner, Lucia. *Women, Crime and Custody in Victorian England*. Oxford: Clarenden Press, 1991.

Zdatny, Steven, ed. *Hairstyles and Fashion: A Hairdresser's History of Paris, 1910–1920*. Oxford: Berg, 1999.
Zola, Émile. *Nana*. 1880. London: Penguin, 1972.
Zola, Émile. *The Kill*. 1871–1872. Oxford: Oxford University Press, 2008.

CONTRIBUTORS

Janice M. Allan is Associate Dean within the School of Arts and Media at the University of Salford, UK. She has published widely on nineteenth-century sensation and crime fiction. She is the Executive Editor of *Clues: a Journal of Detection* and *The Cambridge Companion to Sherlock Holmes* (2018), coedited with Christopher Pittard.

Sarah Heaton is Head of English at the University of Chester, UK. Her interests are fashion and clothing in literature. She is currently working on her monograph *Fashioning the Transatlantic*. She has an edited collection *Fashioning Identities: Cultures of Exchange*, and has published essays in various edited collections and journals including *The Human Vampire; Images of the Modern Vampire: The Hip and the Atavistic; Apocalyptic Chic; Catwalk; Critical Studies in Men's Fashion; Fashioning Horror*; and *Fashion and Contemporaneity*.

Patricia Hunt-Hurst is a dress historian with publications in *Dress, Clothing and Textiles Research Journal; Discovering the Women in Slavery; "We specialize in the Wholly Impossible": A Reader in Black Women's History*; and *Fashioning Identities: Cultures of Exchange*. She currently serves as Associate Dean for Academic Programs, College of Family and Consumer Sciences, University of Georgia, USA.

Richard Leahy teaches English Literature at the University of Chester, UK, where he also completed his PhD on nineteenth-century literature and artificial light in 2016. His first monograph, which is based on this thesis, is entitled *Literary Illumination* and is due for publication in 2018.

Sallie McNamara is Senior Lecturer at Solent University, UK. Her publications include "'We have to keep going, whatever happens': The austerity narratives of *Girls, Breaking Bad*, and *Downton Abbey*" in *Cultural Politics in the Age of Austerity*, ed. David Berry (2017); and "Lady Eleanor Smith and the Society Column, 1927–1930" in *Women and the Media: Feminism and Femininity in Britain, 1900 to the Present*, ed. Maggie Andrews and Sallie McNamara (2014).

Elizabeth Carolyn Miller is Professor of English at the University of California, Davis, USA, and the author of *Framed: The New Woman Criminal in British Culture at the Fin de Siècle* (2008) and *Slow Print: Literary Radicalism and Late Victorian Print Culture* (2013).

Jonathon Shears is Senior Lecturer in English at Keele University, UK. His main areas of interest are Byron and Romantic poetry, and he edits *The Byron Journal*. He has published books on topics including Milton and the Romantics and the Great Exhibition and is completing a book titled *The Hangover: A Cultural History*.

Elizabeth Way is Assistant Curator of Costume at The Museum at the Fashion Institute of Technology. She cocurated the exhibitions *Global Fashion Capitals* and *Black Fashion Designers*. Way earned an MA in Costume Studies from New York University, USA. Her research focuses on the intersection of African American culture and fashion.

Sally West is Senior Lecturer in English at the University of Chester, UK. Her research interests include literature of the long nineteenth century, particularly Romantic poetry, and crime fiction from the nineteenth century to the present day, particularly the work of Patricia Highsmith. Publications include *Coleridge and Shelley: Textual Engagement* (2007).

INDEX

abjection 116
Absolon, John 7
Adams, Nehemiah 55
adornment 53–60
advertising 15–16, 37–40, 66, 70–3, 80, 131–2, 136, 145–7, 150–1
aesthetics 127
African Americans 11, 15, 53–64, 78–81, 117–37
African ethnic groups 117, 120
African hair practices 117, 120
the afterlife 27, 34
afterlives of hair 17
Age of Empire 2, 65, 116
ageing 116
Albert, Prince 8, 70, 157
Alcott, Louisa M. 40, 66, 102, 168
All the Year Round 87
alopecia 39
Altick, Richard 110
antimacassars 37, 71
anti-Semitism 167
aprons 58, 61
Atkinson's vegetable dye 42
Austen, Jane 44, 104, 146, 153–4, 158–9
Austin, Hilary Mac 130

Baker, Josephine (and Bakerfix pomade) 137
baldness 39, 70
Balfour, Arthur 20–1
Balfour, Jean 21
bandanas 80
Bangsbo Museum 9
barber shops 14–15, 62, 135
Barbers' Journal 73–4
Bardi, Abigail 22–3
Batulukisi, Niangi 117
Baudelaire, Charles 114–15
bear's grease 70, 146–7
beards 13, 45–7, 73, 75, 102, 154
beauty culture 136–7
Beethan, Margaret 75
Beethoven, Ludwig van 2

Bentley's Miscellany 92
bicycle riding 61–2
Biddle-Perry, Geraldine 10
black hair 68–9, 98, 120
black pride 129
blonde hair 161, 165
Boccaccio, Giovanni 25
Boehm, Katharina 83
Bonaparte. *See* Napoleon
bonnets 11, 54
Botume, Elizabeth 59
Braddon, Mary 85, 161–2
Bramsbury, H.J. 140
Brazil 126–7
Breton hair 92
Brewster, Billy 19
Brilliant, Ira 2
Brittian, James 123
Brontë, Charlotte 4, 22–3, 28, 104, 142
Brontë, Emily 158
Brough, Barnabas 45
Broughton, Rhoda 160
Browne, Peter 123–4
Browning, Elizabeth Barrett 4–5, 28, 103
Browning, Robert 4, 114, 163–4
Brummell, Beau 13
"Brutus" hairstyle 13
Buckridge, Steeve O. 122–4, 127, 131
Burne-Jones, Edward 4
Burroughs, Nannie H. 133–4
business ventures 76, 135
Butler, Judith 40
Byatt, A.S. 27–33
Byrd, Aryana D. 118–20, 124, 131
Byron, Lord 3

"Caesar" hairstyle 13
calico 57
Campbell, John 123–4
capitalism 168
Carlyle, Thomas 20
Cavallaro, Dani 9
Chambers's Edinburgh Journal 93–5

Champion Magazine 129
Chartist movement 154
Cheang, Sarah 68
chemises 57
Cheung, Sarah 10
chignons 68, 87, 90, 94–5, 98, 109, 132, 143, 145, 166–7
Child, W.H. 70
childlike qualities 107–9, 162
children's hair 116, 118, 121–2, 140–4, 160
Chisum, Ethelyn Taylor 130
Clark, Jessica 14–15
class distinctions 66–7, 146, 149, 152–4, 167
class marking 146, 150. *See also* status marking
class politics 139–40, 153–4
Clay, E.W. 124–5
Clay, Henry 6
cleanliness, concept of 84–5, 99, 139
Cleve's Gazette of Variety 164
Clifton, Peter 81
Coella, Silvana 27
coiling and uncoiling of hair 104
Coleridge, Samuel Taylor 4, 162–4
Collins, Wilkie 150
colonization 65
color of hair 11, 69, 161
combs 65, 80, 109
commercial products 70–1, 146–9
commodification of hair and of women 27, 40, 146, 166
consciousness of hair 37, 40, 44, 51
conspicuous consumption 75, 143
consumer culture 70
consumer goods 65, 79
Cooley, Rosa B. 61
Cornforth, Fanny 25–6
Cornhill Magazine 78
corsets 57
Corson, Richard 67
cosmetics 62–3, 78
Courbet, Gustave 4
crafts practiced within the home 75–8
Crane, Walter 4
Cranford 43–4, 47
craniology 51
creolization 127
crime linked to hair 20, 93, 96
cropped hair 139–44
Crossat, J. 8
Cross-Correspondences 20–1
Crumpsall Workhouse 141
cultural differences 68, 127

cultural products 157
cultural representations of hair 168
curling of hair 10, 15, 79

The Daily Mail 3
The Daily News 87, 90, 98
The Daily Telegraph 98
dandruff 37, 39, 70, 72
dandyism 154
dark hair 161
Darwin, Charles 2
David Copperfield 36–7, 43, 49, 51, 146–7
Davis, Jefferson 6
day caps 55
death
  associations with 9, 16–17, 76, 97
  hair continuing to grow afterwards 164–5
Debret, Jean-Baptiste 127
Dickens, Charles 21–2, 40, 43–5, 51, 73, 146
"dirt", references to 84–5
diseases linked to hair 68, 145, 163–4
DNA 28
Dombey and Son 39–40, 48
domestic servants 150–3
Douglas, Mary 84–5, 99
Douglass, Frederick 128–30
Dowell, Nellie 142
Doyle, Sir Arthur Conan 21–2
Dracula 161
drawers 57–8
dress styles 11, 54–7, 75, 122–3
Drinkall, Margaret 140
Dumas, Alexandre 129
Dunstan, Angela 166
dyeing of hair 69, 82, 147

Edwards. *See* Harlene hair products
Eicher, Joanne B. 122
"elf-locks" 22–3
Eliot, George 106–7, 160–1
Emma 44, 153–4
The Englishwoman's Domestic Magazine 166
"entanglement" 17, 85, 97
Entwistle, Joanne 9
erotic desire 112–15
The Eustace Diamonds 149
The Examiner 83, 97
exercise, taking of 37
exhibitions 70, 75, 157

false hair 85–9, 92–9, 143–5, 149–50, 166–7
  objections to the use of 94, 99

sources of 90–2, 96–9, 167
wearers of 92–3
The Family Economist 152
Far from the Madding Crowd 104–5
fashion 10–14, 42, 53–65, 68, 75, 84, 124–8, 166–7
The Favorite 45
Feldmen, Erica 15
female authors 106
femininity 75, 78, 82, 97, 99, 102–7, 110–12, 115, 154, 161, 168
fetishism 32, 101, 104–6, 114–16
Forten, Charlotte 59
Foucault, Michel 101
Fowler, Orson 49
franchising 14
Freedgood, Elaine 83
The French Hairdressers' Journal 87–8
Freud, Sigmund 101, 104
Fry, Elizabeth 96
Furlong-Clancy, Sinead 102
Fuseli, Henry 6

Galvan, Jill 21
Gardiner, James 141
Gaskell, Elizabeth 42–3, 49, 105
Gassaway, John T. 62
Gate City Millinery 62
Gilbert, Sandra 106, 166
Gillette, King Camp 75
Gilmore, James Roberts 56
The Girl's Own Paper 76–7
Gitter, Elisabeth G. 114–15, 158
Gleason's Pictorial Drawing-Room Companion 70–1
goatees 13
Goblin Market 23–6, 29, 105–6, 159
Godefroy, Alexandre-Ferdinand 15
Godey's Lady's Book 69
Goethe, Johann Wolfgang von 25–6
golden hair 68, 78, 101, 106–10, 160–4
Goodman, Ruth 144, 154
Grant, Ulysses 13
Grateau, Marcel 10, 15
Gray, Jared 78
gray hair 13, 25, 37–9, 70–2, 115, 120
Great Exhibition (1851) 2, 7–11, 45, 70, 157, 168
Great Expectations 115
Greenaway, Kate 107
Greener, Richard 129
gregarines 98

Gregory, James 154
Grennan, Simon 12, 17
Grey, Zane 107
Griebel, Helen Bradley 61
Grim, J.L. and W.C. 101
grooming 44, 99, 118, 121
Growing, Thomas S. 45–8
Gubar, Susan 106, 166
Guest, E.P. 39
Guevara, Alfredo 2

Haggard, Rider 47
hair brushes 37–9, 70, 72
hair dryers 15, 79
hair, items made from 76
Hairdressers' Journal 68, 87, 89
Hall, Gwendolyn Midlo 117
Hall, Stuart 66
hand-me-downs 57
Hardy, Thomas 22, 66, 104, 144, 149, 161, 167
Harlene hair products 16, 40–1, 70, 72
Harper, Annie 55–6
Harper, Martha Mathilda 14
Harris, Juliette 81
Harrison, Martha 121–2
Harvey, Jacky Colliss 164
Hastings, E.A. 124
hats 11, 54, 60–2
Hawksley, Lucinda 165
Hawthorne, Nathaniel 103, 107
headwraps. *See* turbans
Hedda Gabler 162
Heiniger, Abigail 165
Helsinger, Elizabeth K. 165–6
Henson, William 75
Higginbotham, Peter 140
Hobsbawm, Eric 2, 65, 78
Hodder, Ian 85–6, 97
hooks, bell 123
Houston, Sam 6
Howell, Charles Augustus 164
Hungarian folk stories 165
Hunt, Holman 37, 112–13
Hunt, Leigh 4–6
Hutton, Ronald 19

Ibsen, Henrik 162
identity construction 9, 20
India 144
individuation, sense of 153
inequality, different forms of 81

Ingraham, Joseph 123
instalment plans 63
intertextuality 28, 33
Isabella 35–7, 51

Jackson, Kennell 121
Jamaica 122, 131
James, Henry 21–2, 50
James, William 21–2
Jane Eyre 22–3, 110, 142, 161
Jesus Christ 112
jewelry 58, 76
Johnson, Pamela 81
Journal des Savons 164
Jude the Obscure 149–50

Keats, John 4, 35–6, 51
Kemble, Francis 55–6
Khailil-Bey 4
King, Edward 60
Klein, Herbert S. 120
Kosmeo hair tonic 147–8
Koudounaris, Paul 28
Koven, Seth 142

The Ladies' Gazette of Fashion 68
The Ladies' Home Journal 69, 79
The Ladies' Treasury 68, 166–7
Lady Audley's Secret 13, 48–9, 107–9, 114, 145–6, 161–3
The Lady's Magazine 55
Lamb, Lady Caroline 3
The Lancet 98
Latrobe, Benjamin Henry 121
Lawal, Babatunde 118
Leisure Hour (journal) 69
Lenihan, Jessica 112
Leslie, Emma 152
Leverson, Sarah Rachel 147
Lewis, Simon 141
Lincoln, Abraham 73
Lincoln, Amos 81
Linherr & Co. 70–1
Little Dorrit 43
Little Folks (periodical) 160
Little Women 39–40, 66, 102–3, 167–8
Llewellyn, Mark 27–8
locks of hair 104–8, 158–9
Lombroso, Cesare 20
London Female Mission 150
The London Reader 83, 87, 94, 97
London Saturday Journal 154

de Long, Anne 27, 29
Long, Emile 79
loose hair 102, 104, 159–60
loss of hair 71–2, 81
Luthi, Anne Louise 9
Lutz, Deborah 9, 17, 22
Lyttleton, Mary 20–1

McCarthy, Justin 110
macassar oil 37, 71
"Madame Rachel" 147, 149
Magazine of Domestic Economy 147
Mahawatte, Royce 10
Mallon, Isabel 69
Malone, Annie Turnbo 62, 136
Mantel, John 70
de Marbor, Baron 73
Marsh, Jan 102
Martin, Russell 2
masculinity 73, 78, 82, 114–15, 154
Max, Gabriel von 6
Medusa-based imagery 25–30, 37, 110, 161, 163
Mercer, Kobena 80, 127
Metcalf, Bingley & Co. 70
The Mill on the Floss 160, 168
Millais, John Everett 4, 6
Miller, Andrew H. 48
Miller, Daniel 17
Miller, Herbert P. 153
Miller, Janice 157, 164
Miller, Monica 126, 128
millinery 60
Mills, Clark 6
Milton, John 5–6
miniatures 76
minstrel shows 124
The Moonstone 150–2
Morrow, Willie 80
mourning and mourning broaches 16–17, 30
mulatto slaves 131
Munch, Edvard 164
mustaches 13, 45, 47, 73–4

Nana 109
Napoleon 2
Napoleon III 13
Native Americans 121
Nessler, Karl (later Charles Nestlé) 79
neuralgia 38–9
New Age (journal) 147
New Orleans 55
"new woman" image 78, 102–3, 110

New York 116, 135
    Crystal Palace Exhibition (1853) 70
New York Age 132
The Newcomes 45
newspapers and magazines 63, 69, 75, 166
Nicholas Nickleby 45
Noakes, Richard 20
North and South 49–51
nudes 4
Nunn, Joan 13

O'Connor, Feargus 154
Ofek, Galia 3, 11, 22, 24, 36–7, 40, 68, 92, 99, 102, 106–10, 143–5, 158–64
Oldstone-Moore, Christopher 73, 75, 154
Oliphant, Margaret 115, 160
Oppenheim, Janet 20
Osbourne, Garrett & Co. 68
Our Mutual Friend 44–5
Overton, Anthony 62

paganism 22, 24
Palmer, Ellen 1
Panati, Charles 79
Paris 67, 87, 144
    Exposition (1855) 9, 70
Parker's hair balsam 14
patriarchy 101
paupers 140–1
Pearline soap 151
Peel, Archibald 1
The Penny Illustrated Paper 150
Perkins, T.D. 80–1
permanent wave treatment 79
Perrin, Monsieur 79
Persuasion 146
perukes 67–8
Peterkin, Julia 61
petticoats 58
phallic symbolism 105
Philadelphia 124
phrenology 49, 51
Pickering, David 21, 24
"Pigtail" Bridget 19
Pitman, Joanna 23
Plotz, John 83
Plough's hair dressing 132, 136
Poe, Edgar Allan 4, 28, 114
pomade 37
Poor Law 140–3
Pope, Alexander 140
Poplar Workhouse 141

pornography 4, 102
postiches 79
Pre-Raphaelite art 12, 105, 110, 114, 164–5
Prichard, James 123
prison regimes 32, 96–7
private and public spheres 10, 116
products for hair care 66, 121–2, 135–6, 147.
    See also commercial products
Psomiades, Kathy 24
psychoanalysis 101
pubic hair 3–4
public sphere. *See* private and public spheres
Punch 42, 46–7, 95, 141–3, 150–1
Puritanism 103, 107

The Quarterly Review 93

racial differences 68, 123
racism 132
radicalism 154
Rapunzel-based imagery 3, 22, 26–30, 37, 101, 104
razors 75
ready-made clothing 61
red hair 108–10, 114, 137, 164
Regency period 10–11, 44
relics 28
Remond sisters 81, 135
Renoir, Pierre-Auguste 102
resistance, cultural 127
The Return of the Native 23, 61
Richmond, Nancy 114
Richmond, Vivien 150
"The Rime of the Ancient Mariner" 162–4
Rimmel, Eugene 70
ringlets 54, 62
Roach-Higgins, Mary Ellen 122
Rooks, Noliwe M. 80, 131
Rossetti, Christina 6, 23–8, 34, 105, 159, 163
Rossetti, Dante Gabriel 2–3, 23–34, 109–14, 159, 164–6
Rossetti, William 23
Rotherham Workhouse 140
Rowland, Alexander 37–9, 67–73, 155, 157
rules and conventions for the wearing of hair 102
runaway slaves 121
Ruskin, John 3–4, 107

Sagay, Esi 118
sailor hats 62
St Jacobs oil 38
salons for hair styling 14

The Saturday Review 90
saving one's own hair 39
Scott, James 126
Scott, Walter 22–3
Scott, William Bell 23
Scott, Winfield 6
Scott's electric hair brush 38–9
séances 20, 34
sensation novels 161–2
Sense and Sensibility 104, 158–9
sentimentality 76
The Servants' Magazine 150
Severa, Joan 57
sexuality and sexual desire 12, 26, 28, 101–16, 135, 159, 163–6
shaving
  before transportation to slavery 120
  as a punishment 54
  technology for 75
  in workhouses 140–2
Shaw, Lily Armstrong 130
She 47
Shelley, Mary 28, 36
Shelley, Percy 4, 28
Shelton, Elmira 4
Sheumaker, Helen 75–8, 81
Shirley 36, 104
shoes 58
Shriner, E.C. (company) 76
Siddal, Elizabeth (Lizzie) 2–3, 23, 26, 29, 110, 164–6
sideburns 13
Silas Marner 106–7
silk 67–8
Simon, Diane 120
skills needed for hairwork 78, 135
skin whiteners 63
skirts 59
slavery 17, 53–60, 64, 80, 117–28
small businesses 76
Smith, Harriet 78
Smithsonian National Museum of American History 6
Sobocinski, Florian 39
social construction of hair 48
social value of hair 155
Solomon-Godeau, Abigail 4
Southey, Robert 73
The Speaker 92–3
Speight, Alexanna 76–7
spiritualism 19–26, 32
split ends 72

Stanley, A.J.A. 39
Stanley, John 135
Stanley, Lady 65
status marking, use of hair for 139–40, 142. *See also* class marking
Stauffer, John 128
Stern, Charles 60
Stewart, George and Elizabeth 78
Stoker, Bram 6, 12, 161, 164–5
straightening of hair 62, 80, 131–7
styling of hair 11–14, 20, 54, 62, 65, 69, 78–80, 90, 102, 118–22, 127–33, 137, 139, 143, 149–50, 166
supernatural forces 20–3, 28, 32–3
Sutherland Sisters 3, 70–1
Sweden 9
symbolism 11, 160

Tandberg, Gerilyn 55, 60
Taylor, Tom 13
Tennyson, Lord 112
testimonials for products 39
Texas University 4
Thackeray, W.M. 41–2, 45, 47
Tharps, Lori L. 118–20, 124, 131
thinning hair 69
Thompson, Emma 3
Thompson, Kathleen 130
Tischleder, Babette Bärbel 93
Tomes, Robert 68–9
Tondeur, Louise 165
tools for hairwork 76
Toussaint, Pierre 135
trade
  geneal patterns of 65
  in hair 66–8, 82, 87, 143–6, 167
Trollope, Anthony 149
Trollope, Thomas Adolphus 67, 90–3
Trowbridge, Serena 24, 27
Tunisia 11
turbans 55–6, 60
The Turn of the Screw 22, 50
Twain, Mark 42

Udall, Sharyn 112
uncanny qualities of hair 164, 167–8
underclothing 57–8
Unwin and Albert (hair saloon) 144–5

vampirism 164
Vanity Fair 41–2
Varden, John 6–7

Veblen, Thorstein 75
Victoria, Queen 8–9, 70, 157, 168
Victorian culture and mores 104–7, 112
Vogue magazine 137

Waldman, Suzanne 26
Walker, C.J. 62, 80–1, 136
Walker, Juliet 81, 135
Warwick, Alexander 9
washing of hair 69, 139
Washington, Booker T. 133, 136
Waters, Sarah 27, 32
Watson, William W. 135
wedding clothes 61, 64
Weld, Charles Richard 144
"the West" 66, 81
Wharton, Edith 115–16
White, Carolyn C. 20
White, Graham 58, 121–5, 128, 132
White, Shane 121–5, 128, 132
White, Sharon 58
white hair 115–16
Whitlock, Tammy 93
Whittier, John Greenleaf 59

wigs 13, 37, 39
Wilby, Emma 19
Wilde, Oscar 13
Wilding, Alexa 25–6
Wilhelm II, Kaiser 13
Williams, Fannie Barrier 64
Wingfield, Adia 155
witchcraft 21, 24
Wollstonecraft, Mary 4
The Woodlanders 66, 144, 167
Wordsworth, William 4, 162
work clothes 61, 63
workhouses 140–2
World Fairs 7
Wuthering Heights 158
Wynter, Andrew 87

yellow hair 163–4
Yonge, Charlotte 12, 160
Yoruba culture and religion 118–19
The Young Ladies Journal 69

Zedner, Lucia 97
Zola, Émile 109